FORGOTTEN

**A SISTER'S STRUGGLE
TO SAVE TERRY ANDERSON,
AMERICA'S LONGEST-
HELD HOSTAGE**

Peggy Say

and Peter Knobler

SIMON & SCHUSTER

New York   London   Toronto   Sydney   Tokyo   Singapore

SIMON & SCHUSTER
SIMON & SCHUSTER BUILDING
ROCKEFELLER CENTER
1230 AVENUE OF THE AMERICAS
NEW YORK, NEW YORK 10020

DESIGNED BY CARLA WEISE/LEVAVI & LEVAVI
MANUFACTURED IN THE UNITED STATES OF AMERICA

10   9   8   7   6   5   4   3   2   1

Bt 22.95/12.98 · 2/91

LIBRARY OF CONGRESS CATALOGING-IN-PUBLICATION DATA

SAY, PEGGY.
    FORGOTTEN : A SISTER'S STRUGGLE TO SAVE TERRY ANDERSON,
AMERICA'S LONGEST HELD HOSTAGE / PEGGY SAY AND PETER KNOBLER.
        P.   CM.
    INCLUDES INDEX.
    1.ANDERSON, TERRY—CAPITIVITY, 1985-   2.SAY, PEGGY—RELA-
TIONS   WITH   HOSTAGES.   3.HOSTAGES—LEBANON.   4.HOSTAGES—
UNITED STATES.
I.KNOBLER, PETER.   II.TITLE.
DS87.2.A53S28   1991
956.9104'2'0922—DC20   90-23302
                                                           CIP

ISBN 0-671-70155-X

CHAPTER

1

MY KID BROTHER, TERRY ANDERSON, WAS ABOUT TO TAKE A FLYING leap and there wasn't a thing I could do about it.

It was a bright, clear, beautiful summer day and I was the adult in charge. I was twenty-one, a woman with a one-year-old daughter and my own household to run, but my mother had sent Terry to me for the summer.

I had taken Terry swimming at an old stone quarry with high walls and water that went down deeper than I cared to imagine. A little pier jutted out into it, and a sandy beach had been kicked up for us locals to lie out on. There was a swimming area roped off, and my friend and I were sitting around daring each other to dive off the diving board. It was one of those "You go first" dares: "Yeah, I'll do it. You go first."

I wasn't conservative—I mean, I had run away from home half a dozen times before I got married and left for good—but I was never the one to step out and take the lead. I didn't know how to dive and neither did she, but she climbed onto the board, said "I can't believe I'm doing this," and took a running start.

It was the worst dive I'd ever seen. Out in midair it must have occurred to her that she was in big trouble. She curled up like a dog and hit the water with a howl. She was sputtering when she dragged herself out and stumbled back to her towel.

"If you think I'm going to get out there and make a fool out of myself," I told her, "you're crazy." I was laughing so hard I almost fell off the pier.

I saw this red speck moving way across on the other side of the lake. My scrawny little fourteen-year-old brother had asked me if it was okay for him to go over and dive from the cliff and I'd told him, "No way." Next thing I knew, there's Terry.

He was a shrimp. Skinny, pasty little white legs; no chest; baggy red bathing suit. He was perched on top of this gigundus rock. I couldn't even yell at him. He was so far away that he couldn't hear me, and so ready to go that nothing I could do or say had any chance of stopping him.

He was definitely going to die. The stupid little thrill seeker was going to jump off that rock and kill himself and it would be my fault.

It was a swan dive and it seemed like it took forever.

Terry likes to be where the action is, and he was right at home in Beirut. There was a war going on, several wars, and as the Middle East chief correspondent for the Associated Press in 1982 he was in the thick of it. It was his job to get the story out, to tell the world what was happening.

Lebanon was filled with armed factions, each one with its own agenda; some who claimed to be working for Allah, others who were simply doing a job. Bombing was a fact of life, small-arms fire playing like incidental music. But this was no movie, people were dying on a daily basis, and Terry was dedicated to his job, to the story, and to the people he was covering.

One basically quiet day in Beirut there had been a cease-fire of sorts between the warring militias. People learned to enjoy these days on the rare times they occurred, to relax for a moment, to go ahead and live their lives. A Lebanese man was walking between his bakery shop and his house. He got killed by a sniper. One shot.

This was the kind of thing that really got to Terry, the randomness of the violence. Some poor guy was just trying to survive, trying to walk home, thinking it was relatively safe and, boom, here comes a sniper out of nowhere and blows his brains out. The man never had a chance. Terry wrote a story about him and got it out on the wire.

Terry had the ability to walk into a situation and make sense out of it. He probably learned a good part of it in Vietnam, where he had been a combat journalist. He'd done great on his SATs and could have gone to pretty much any college he wanted. But Terry was always one to opt for the unexpected, and he enlisted in the Marines instead. He was obviously a smart kid, even though he was trying to be a tough guy, and the Corps took one look at him and made him a Marine combat journalist. He served two tours of duty under fire in Vietnam.

Terry would walk into the Ain el Hilwewe Palestinian refugee camp on the outskirts of Sidon after Israeli sappers had blown up the houses of people who they believed were PLO terrorists. Women would be keening, young men screaming, all of them more than willing to tell him in great detail about the atrocities the Israelis were alleged to have committed. Most were hysterical, all of them had grievances to air. The bombed-out house would sit in front of him and he would stand there and try to find out what had happened.

It was one of Terry's great strengths to be able to listen and talk to a variety of people. He didn't go in and grab the first person he saw and then race off to the typewriter and file it. He had a reputation among his colleagues as a man who would judiciously sift through the stories, come up with a number of sources, and put together a powerful and balanced piece.

If you were going to be a journalist in the Middle East, you were going to have your brush-with-death stories, and Terry had his. In 1983 the coastal highway outside of Beirut was deserted because a lot of artillery was coming out of the mountains and hitting the road. Terry and AP photographer Bill Foley were about 500 yards from the safety of a guarded intersection when a mortar round landed in front of them. Before they could hit the brakes, another landed just to the rear.

Terry looked at Bill. "Should we bolt or should we stop?"

"What do you think?" Foley said. "You're the Marine."

They left the car and dove into a pile of garbage about ten yards off the road. Another round landed a little farther up. They waited. There's nothing you can do about incoming fire, Foley said later, except hope real hard that it doesn't hit you.

Finally Terry said, "Let's go for it. We're sitting ducks here. Anybody sees this white car, we're finished."

They ran back to the car, got in, and went flying back up into the southern suburbs. A couple of minutes later, just enough time for their hearts to stop racing, a mortar round fell exactly where they had been parked.

The people on the ground in the Middle East love to tell these stories. Bill Foley likes to tell about the time he, Terry, and *Time* photographer Bill Pierce were right at the edge of Tripoli, about a half-mile from one of the militias' camps. They were hiding behind some buildings because mortar fire had been hitting the four-lane blacktop highway, turning it into a slalom of potholes and craters. Terry said, "We should go down that road."

Foley looked at the chewed-up asphalt. There was no traffic. There was no movement at all. "Terry," he said, "this road is deserted for a very good reason."

But Terry was on the move. "We have to go down there and see," he said. Pierce and Foley didn't budge. "I'm going to go. You guys can stay here."

"Well, Terry, we can't let you do that."

So Pierce, Foley, and Terry set off down the road. They hugged the grass, not wanting to be on the asphalt when a round came in but having no choice but to follow the trail.

The road led to a town square and when they got there all hell broke loose. Rockets started landing in the middle of the courtyard, automatic weapons opened up all around them. They had walked into a shooting war. Doubled over, Terry with his notebooks and Foley and Pierce with their camera bags, they beat it the hell out of there and back to relative safety.

"See, Terry," Foley said as soon as he could speak, "*that's* why the road was deserted. Because anybody who pokes his nose down there is going to get shot at."

But Terry, always the journalist, said, "At least now we know that there's heavy fighting at the edge of the Baddawi camp." Foley wasn't sure that particular piece of information was worth the risk.

If there was fighting in Tripoli or in West Beirut, Terry wanted to see what was happening. He wouldn't go out for every little militia firefight, but when the U.S. Marines were taking a lot of fire in the PLO war Terry wanted to be there.

As AP chief correspondent it was his job to assign the day's stories, to decide who went where and what they were supposed to come back with. He wasn't the kind of guy who was going to sit in the office and send his reporters or his news editor, or anybody else, out to do something he wouldn't do. He liked his work.

On a normal day, Terry would wake up in the morning, listen to the BBC news broadcast, then head through two armed checkpoints to the AP office. That is, unless he had gotten a call saying there was open warfare in Tripoli or the U.S. Marine barracks in Beirut was going crazy; then he would go directly to the action.

In the office he would read transcriptions of the Lebanese radio reports. Farouk, the "old hand" who had been there forever, would tell him what the various factions' radio communiqués were saying. Terry would sometimes hold an informal meeting of the dozen reporters, editors, and staff. He would listen to their suggestions about what they thought they should be covering that day, and then he would give out the assignments.

Terry was known as a boss who would listen . . . to ideas, stories, problems. He was known as a fair guy, but you didn't want to get on the wrong side of him. He could be scary, he had a temper, and he had very definite ideas about what was acceptable and what was not. To err is human; people *would* do things that were wrong, people *would* blow it. And if it was a stupid mistake, Terry would yell at them. He was a committed journalist and he had to have exactly what he felt was needed, whether it was facts, corroboration of the facts, or exactly the right photograph to accompany a story. He could be in his office screaming "I've got to have this on time!" one minute, slam the phone down and curse the poor fool on the other end. But it would blow over soon. He was fiery but not cruel.

Cary Vaughan, Bill Foley's wife, who taught at the American University in Beirut and worked part-time at AP, remembers that Terry set the tone for the office. There was a very male way of speaking, she recalls, very self-confident—as if Terry were saying, "We know exactly what to do. We don't have to put up with sub-par writing or sloppy research. Just get out of our way and let us do our job." Some of the staff even started to pick up his speech patterns and sound like him.

From faction to faction there were bands of young Lebanese guys who had just been in battle, or would soon be in battle, all the time prepared to fight and die. They had the bravado of teenagers—many of them *were* teenagers—and they had automatic weapons. The journalists had to follow them around, talk to them and be harassed by them.

"What were you up to yesterday?"

"Oh, God, I was out covering the latest bit of mindlessness."

Terry also spent a certain amount of time contending with the requests coming out of the home office in New York.

New York once asked for an aerial view of the Bekaa Valley under fire, where Syrians and Israelis had been dogfighting all day. Eighty-three Syrian MIGs had been shot down *that day*, and anybody who knew anything about the situation at all knew that everyone was hunkered down in their shelters just trying to live through the night. New York wanted a photographer to go up in a plane and get that shot. More likely he'd get shot. Terry would sit there and get sarcastic. "Yeah, right, we're supposed to send our people to get that one. Lots of luck."

The bond that held the press corps together was the understanding that whether the home office was in New York or London, they didn't understand the situation on the ground. You were on your own.

Terry was married when he arrived in Beirut in 1982. He and his wife Mickey had a daughter, Gabrielle. But in February 1984, while Terry was out of the country on assignment, Mickey and Gabrielle were caught in a shelling. Shellings were fairly common by that time, and there was a drill for them. You went downstairs into a shelter and waited until the rockets stopped, then you went back outside and surveyed the damage.

This time, the shelling lasted twenty-four hours and Terry's wife and daughter couldn't move. There was no shelter in their building, so they were forced to sit downstairs on the ground floor for one day solid while these booming rounds landed all around them. With no shelter, if a rocket hit the building it would fall straight down on them. One shot and they would be dead.

Cary Vaughan was in a shelter only a block and a half away, but going outside to get them was out of the question. The blasts were so loud they prevented conversation. Every forty-five seconds an explosion would go off that was so near and so overwhelming that it would completely shatter her thoughts. She'd start to say, "Wow, that was a huge one," and another would pound around her and she couldn't remember what she'd been trying to say.

It finally ended and all were safe. Terry got back to Beirut, and shortly thereafter he made the decision to send Mickey and Gabrielle to Japan, where they would be much safer. It was a tough decision, but this was Terry's job and it didn't say anywhere in the Associated Press handbook that he had to risk his wife and child. Mickey and Gabrielle moved to Iwakuni, Japan, with Mickey's parents.

Anytime people are thrown together in circumstances that appear to the rational mind to be completely insane a closeness develops, and a camaraderie grew among the Western press corps in Beirut. As well as spending a lot of time on stories together, whether it was the fighting in Tripoli or in the southern suburbs, most of them lived in one or two buildings in West Beirut: the Reporters Building or the Sleit Building. Terry lived in the Sleit Building, owned and run by a man named Mustafa Sleit, which also housed correspondents from the London *Times,* UPI, ABC, NBC, and *Time* magazine. It was six stories high, with two apartments per floor, one in front and one in back. Terry's, on the third floor, had a beautiful balcony overlooking the Mediterranean.

They learned to take advantage of their free time. If things were slow one day, no open warfare or car bombings to cover, no incoming shells, the journalists would sort of take a deep breath. It was a time to catch up on office paperwork, do errands, play tennis, invite a few people to dinner.

Terry threw some good parties. He'd invite the people from work and all his other friends, and there would be music and dancing and drinking, sometimes until early early morning. And Terry would cook.

He loved to cook, and he was good at it. He was best known for his three-alarm chili. His spaghetti sauce enjoyed a healthy reputation, and Bill Foley says, "He did some interesting things with fish."

But Terry's party reputation was built on his Irish coffee. He would kick everyone out of the kitchen when he made it. His secret, so I'm told, was in the way he handled everything so gently. He used good Middle Eastern coffee, which was strong to begin with, and he would pour it very gently over a spoon into the cup. He had a delicate touch with the warm whiskey and the sugar, and he'd pour the whipped cream over a spoon as well. This was a concoction of renown. When you had an Anderson Irish coffee, it was really an event.

Once in a while, and never with men around, Terry would talk about his life. About how he loved to read. (He had hundreds of novels tucked away in a trunk at his Sleit Building apartment.) About growing up.

Terry had gotten good grades in high school. But when he graduated in 1965 and was offered scholarships to college, he decided not to go because he felt he wasn't mature enough to handle it. Instead, he joined the Marines. He was sent to Vietnam, was fortunate enough to have a commanding officer with the sense to make him a combat journalist and not an infantryman, and served two tours. He went into the Marines a hard-charging small-town Republican and came out six years later somebody quite different. For part of that time he was stationed in Japan, where in 1968 he married Mihoko (or Mickey, as we called her), a Japanese woman. He joined the Associated Press in 1974 and was on his way.

Terry thrived at AP. He worked his way up to the post of news editor and was sent to South Africa, where he grew so uncomfortable with his privileged life-style under apartheid—the house, the gardener, the driver; while none of the black people he knew there could ever hope to have half his advantages—that when he had a chance to cover the war in Beirut in 1982, he jumped at it.

Despite his sometimes hard-nosed way of appearing to the world, and despite his demands for perfection, Terry was a very sensitive human being who had interests that had nothing to do with what the press corps called covering "bang-bang." He loved to surround himself with his books, music, a few close friends, and his dog Jolie. But it was a side of himself he kept well hidden.

While Terry was running around the world as a Marine, a correspondent, a journalist, I was busy raising two kids, getting divorced, moving around. I never did know Terry all that well. He was sort of a nonentity in our family when he was younger. Quiet, well behaved, he managed to carve a place for himself that nobody much noticed. It seemed almost deliberate, as if he wanted to stay removed from the chaos around him. Our house heard a lot of screaming and every time there was a conflict you could bet Terry would be out in the car with a book.

It seems like I was always taking care of my family. My parents, Glenn and Lily Anderson, had what could politely be called a troubled marriage. Alcohol played a large part in their lives and our home, and I was the one who was supposed to pick up the pieces.

I was the oldest daughter. My brother Glenn Richard Jr. was eleven months older than I am. Then came Bruce, who was five years younger, and Terry, seven years younger. When I was fifteen the twins were born, Jack and Judy. By that time my father was driving trucks, and when he was home he was mostly sleeping. My mother was out of the house all day working. It was pretty much up to me to care for the twins. Mostly it didn't seem like work. I doted on them; they were somebody to love me back.

This was thirty-four years ago in a small town in western New York called Albion, near Batavia. There were no such things as disposable diapers or canned formula, or if there were, I had never heard of them. Plus, I was a fifteen-year-old high school girl and there were more than a few other things I would rather have been doing. But I would wake up early every morning, feed the twins breakfast—and if you've never been around twins, you have no idea what kind of a trial that is—and then go off to work.

Finances were tight in our family; we were lower middle class, and had to have money coming in. The Campus Restaurant was right across from the high school and I worked there for an hour and a half each day before school started, then went to class, came back and worked during the lunch hour and maybe a couple of hours after school. Then I would have to go home and cook for the family, take care of the twins until they went to sleep, and do my homework before falling into bed.

My parents were very particular about my work habits. On weekends they would get home at two or three in the morning and I would get hauled out of bed if I had left something undone. In the 1950s, when I was a teenager, cleaning the house was still women's work and my brothers were not expected to help. If, God forbid, I had not gotten something right, I had to get out and do it over.

But, particular as they were, there was only sporadic supervision. My father would go from one extreme to another. Either you were grounded for the rest of your life for a minor infraction or he would ignore it altogether. My mother always hated that. I remember her telling me, "You're worse than another woman in my house," because Dad would let me do anything. I didn't see it that way; Dad let me do anything mainly because, I had the feeling, he didn't care what I did.

My older brother, Glenn Richard, got most of the attention, but not in the way he wanted it. When he was fifteen, Rich contracted Hodgkin's disease. They found a tumor the size of a grapefruit in his chest.

Everybody thought Rich was going to die. He was taken to Roswell Hospital in Buffalo and they performed miracles. At first they told us Rich only had perhaps a month to live, but, with nothing to lose, the doctors tried a new experimental treatment . . . and Rich recovered. With Rich on the brink of death, any problems I had were seen around our house as pretty minor.

Despite my concern over Rich's condition, I wanted a little piece of the attention my parents were showering on him. As hard as I tried, I couldn't seem to strike the chord of affectionate response I so desperately needed.

I ran away from home half a dozen times. When I was about fifteen a girlfriend and I took off. We packed a couple of bottles of vitamin pills and three pairs of shoes each, and thought that would do it. Now, we lived in a very small town where everybody knew everybody else, and when my mom found me missing she went and alerted the local police. They picked up me and my friend and these vitamins, and hauled us by the nape of our necks into the restaurant my mother was running, in full view of a lively Saturday-night crowd.

As I grew older, the trips grew longer. I was never a person who confronted people; I would just get to the point where I couldn't take it anymore and leave. One time I went to my aunt's in Ohio. I was always very quiet about everything I did. I would just pack my things, leave a note (''I'm gone. I'll be back''), get on a bus and go. Sometimes it was days, sometimes weeks; as far as I was concerned I was never gone long enough. But I would always get to missing the twins and go home.

I stayed away one whole summer. I went to the home of a girlfriend in Rochester, New York, who had a very nice, conventional family. I was in heaven there. They had dinner all together at the same time every night, and she didn't have to cook it. They talked without shouting. My friend's father owned a jewelry store, and the whole family was very good to me. So it was hard for her father to tell me that he had finally contacted the authorities. It was even more difficult for him to let me know that my mother didn't really care if I came home or not. They wanted to keep me, but legally they couldn't. Her father cried when they came to take me home. So did I.

Every time I ran away I would come back again and stick it out as long as I could. Part of me wanted to stay in school—I was doing very well in school and I really enjoyed it—but the other part found it just impossible to cope with the situation at home. I was very intent on going to college, but after the twins were born I came to the realization that, financially, it was not possible. That, and the fact that it just wasn't something my parents encouraged.

So I wasn't going to college. I wasn't going to see the world. I wasn't going anywhere but in front of the stove and behind the counter. There weren't a whole lot of options for young women who wanted to get away from home. A career was out of the question. It seemed like the only real option was to get married.

I met my first husband at a pizza parlor. He was twenty-three and had recently been discharged from the Air Force. I was seventeen. After a brief courtship we drove down to South Carolina and came back husband and wife.

I'd had a steady boyfriend all through high school, his name was Joe. My mother hated him and tried her best to make me stop seeing him. Joe and I had hoped to get married, but in senior year he went and joined the Marines.

For the first several months he kept up a barrage of letters, and then all of a sudden they stopped. I wrote to him and said that if I didn't hear from him I'd have to assume we were through. I never got another letter, and not long after that, I got married.

About two or three months later, I was cleaning my mother's house when I found a stack of letters Joe had sent me. He *had* written! But my mother hadn't given them to me, she had hidden them. By then it was too late; as much as I wanted to, I didn't think it was fair to my new husband to undo our marriage and go back with Joe. When I asked my mother about the letters she said, ''Yeah, isn't it funny the way life turns out sometimes?''

I dropped out of high school and my new husband re-upped in the Air Force. I moved with him when he was stationed first in South Carolina and then at Fort Dix, New Jersey. I had my first child, my daughter Melody, when I was twenty; my second, Edward, when I was twenty-two.

It's amazing what you'll do when you don't know any better. There was never any question but that I had to work, so I waitressed in some dives I shouldn't have even been allowed in.

I was always tired. I would work all night and then stay with my kids in the daytime while my husband was at the base, and then cook him dinner and try to catch some sleep before it was time for me to go to work that night. There were times when I would have paid a million dollars just to be able to put my head down and go to sleep for five minutes.

After seven years of marriage I got a divorce from the father of my kids and moved back to Albion. Where else did I know, where else could I go?

I waited tables for years and then got into cooking and tending bar, generally a combination of both. Like many women of the time, about the only skill I had was cooking. On almost the first job I got on my return to New York, the guy that owned the place didn't like to cook, and I didn't like to tend bar, so we matched up perfectly. It was then that I really learned how to prepare food.

My family kept calling. Whenever something went wrong, my mother would call and tell me to come home and solve it. And I would do it. I would pack up and drag my two kids over, do what had to be done to set things right, and drive back home. Once I had accomplished the chore of the day, my mother would find an excuse to get rid of me until the next crisis. She'd yell at me, "Get out of my sight, I can't stand you!"

Several years later, my folks moved to Batavia. I was visiting when my mother was having one of her feuds with the woman next door. They'd had an argument and weren't speaking. My daughter, Melody, was old enough to babysit by that time and the neighbor had asked her if she would come over. I told Melody, Fine, if you want to babysit, go ahead.

Well, my mother got very offended. I knew this neighborhood disagreement would blow over, but while it was going on she demanded complete family loyalty. Melody went next door and I was sitting at the dinner table trying to ignore my mother's almost physical seething. All of a sudden she jumped up and started screaming at me.

"I hate you! I hate you! I hate the way you are!"

My place was always made very clear to me. When Terry was coming home from abroad, or Rich telephoned to say he was coming in from wherever he was, my mother would call me up and tell me to come clean the house and get everything ready "for the boys." One time she sent me shopping for an anniversary gift for my brother and his wife, *and it was my birthday!* I got no present, but they did.

Once while Terry was home on leave from Japan, a couple of guys I went to high school with asked me to open a restaurant with them. They had the money but they needed someone to come in and set up the kitchen, hire the help, create the menu, and be head cook. I did all of that for them. I didn't have a piece of the place, but it was a good experience for me because from the day we opened the door the restaurant was a major success.

Mom and Dad, Terry, and my sister and other brothers all came to the restaurant for dinner, and the whole crew was sitting around congratulating me on how I had become this great success. The place was packed, the customers were raving about the food; the business seemed to be booming. My family was beaming and congratulating me on what they perceived to be the culmination of my career. It was as if they had decided that I was as far up the ladder as I would ever climb.

I was hurt and bewildered. I was still young and I had other dreams. Although I had wanted to real badly, I had never gone to college. There were things I wanted to do that the rest of my family didn't know anything about.

"What makes you think this is what I want to do with my life?" I told them. "Run a restaurant? You don't know me, you don't know anything about me." I had this strange sense of observing everyone from a distance. Although we were a family we really did not know one another's hearts or goals.

Not long after, my mother wrote me a letter going on and on about Terry and how successful he was and how proud we should all be of him. (My mother was a great one for writing letters, even if we were in the same town.) In reply I wrote, in all honesty, "I don't even know Terry. I don't know him as a person. He's my brother, and I love him because of that, but I've never spent any time with him. I have no idea what he stands for. I don't know if I even like him."

"How dare you!" my mother wrote back. "How dare you!" To her, this was blasphemy. This was Terry, the family celebrity, my brother. I had to like him. My mother never understood that I was neither condemning nor praising Terry. I was stating a simple fact; I didn't know him well enough to make a judgment.

In 1975, when we knew my mother was dying, I tried to sit down with her and say, "I don't understand. I *never* understood. Out of all your kids, you used me the most and liked me the least. I need to understand why."

She was mystified, totally baffled by what I was telling her. "I didn't mean it," she protested. "I didn't mean to do anything to you." But it was done, and she died before I could really straighten it out. It was only years later, after I figured out that it wasn't my fault, that I began to heal.

I moved around a lot, but the family kept in touch. In 1966, at the age of twenty-five, I had gone back and gotten my high school equivalency diploma, and in 1978 I met and married a wonderful man, David Say. We moved to Florida, where he worked as a contractor.

The early years of our marriage were a difficult time for us. I was cooking in a restaurant from three in the afternoon until ten at night, six days a week; David was working days, so it didn't leave us a lot of time to spend together. Plus, with my mother having died, my father was living with us, and privacy was at a premium. David always showed the patience of a saint as he listened to hour after hour of Dad's ramblings. The more Dad drank, the saintlier my mother became, and the more perfect their marriage.

Terry would pop in and out of my life. Mostly out. He and my dad were very close. All of his life, as far as Terry was concerned Dad could do no wrong. To Dad, Terry was the star of the family.

Terry invited my father to come visit him in Lebanon. Dad had visited him in Japan when he was stationed there, and they had formed an even stronger bond because of it. My brother liked to give excitement and variety to his father's life, and Dad lived for it.

Things were quiet in Beirut, and Terry felt it would be safe. Dad was going to stay with him for six weeks. David and I were saying under our breath, "Thank you, thank you. We can have a little bit of privacy!" Dad went off to Lebanon and we began to relax.

A couple of days after my father got in, the shelling started. He was staying at Terry's apartment with Mickey and Gabrielle, but the rounds were a little too close for comfort so Terry took them out of his place and installed them in a suite at the Commodore Hotel. The Commodore was across the street from the Associated Press office; Terry could see it from his window. The hotel was traditionally a safe haven, off-limits to the fighting that went on around it.

But that season all bets were off. Terry could see the shells landing closer and closer to the side of the building that their rooms were on, so he quickly had Dad and Mickey and Gabrielle moved to the other side.

The mortar fire came in from the opposite direction. Mortar rounds are scary; they can take out a tank in one shot or collapse a small apartment building. They're not something you want on your vacation.

Dad's room was the only one that sustained a direct hit. The shells blew out the wall. A big hole appeared at the exact spot where my father had just been standing. Then the snipers started firing. Plaster dust filled the room so thick that he could hardly breathe, but Dad suffered from severe emphysema and, despite small-arms fire everywhere, he careened to the shattered wall and hung his head out to gasp some fresh air. "If the snipers got me, they got me," he explained later. "But I was surely going to die if I didn't get some air in my lungs."

The shelling stopped and my father lived to tell the tale. But less than a week into his six-week trip he was back at my house in Florida.

That adventure was the highlight of my dad's life. From then on, at the slightest opportunity he'd chime right in with, "When I was in Beirut . . ." His son Terry had provided him with the most excitement he'd ever had.

With my mother gone, I was the oldest woman in the family and my home became the center for family occasions and holidays, which were always iffy propositions. There seemed to be three generations of Anderson kids: when we were young it was me and Rich, then Bruce and Terry, and then the twins Jack and Judy. As we grew older, Terry joined us older folks and Bruce spent more time with the twins. Bruce is now what is politely called estranged from the family. I continue to pray to God that He create a miracle for Bruce, but, if that miracle is not forthcoming, that Bruce be kept where he is and where he belongs: behind bars.

When the rest of us met there was always a lot of banter. We older ones were all pretty verbal and when we got together it would be puns and cutting remarks and a real thrust at the jugular.

At some point, finally, the difference between fun and cruelty became apparent to me. I wanted to stop the bloodletting but I could never convince my older brother Rich. Nothing was sacred to him, and he had a streak of real meanness when he was drinking. I told him as much, but he wouldn't cut it out.

Something else was bothering me as well. Terry was home on leave at the time and I tried to explain. I was tired of being the mother to this bunch. Mom was dead and I couldn't and wouldn't take her place. "I'm your sister," I told Terry and Rich both. "I should be able to come to *you* when *I* have a problem."

I was tired of being used. Terry, of course, was rarely on the scene, but Rich and Jack lived nearby. "I have never been to any one of your houses for dinner," I said. "Everything is always at my house."

"Well," they said, "you're a professional cook. We can't cook like you can."

"Hey, look, even if it's only hamburgers, it's the difference between me having to cook and not having to."

Terry said, "Oh, come on now, you know you love it."

"Terry, watch my lips: I *don't* love it. I'm tired of being the mother here."

I don't think anything would have come of it if Rich hadn't chosen that evening to get schnockered.

I don't remember exactly what it was that caused it, but I came home from a meeting and found Rich totally bombed. David was still at work, but my dad and my three brothers were at the kitchen table celebrating life or some other auspicious event. For years Rich and I had barely spoken because I could not tolerate him when he was drunk, and I must have made some smart remark because all of a sudden Rich was snarling, "I hate you! I hate you!" I had seen that look before, on my mother's face. It shocked me and I burst into tears.

No one in the family had ever seen me cry. Jack looked stricken, Dad seemed stunned. Terry wrestled Rich out the door.

At the time, Terry was a drinker in the Anderson family tradition. He was also quite a wine connoisseur, he had toured the French vineyards and knew his stuff, yet he would drink Ripple if that's what you had in the house. He was not a snob and eased comfortably into whatever situation he found himself in. I really admired that.

The temptation on the part of the men was to try to keep up with him, and in the three days since he had arrived home on leave in spring 1979, everyone had given it his best shot. This night my husband, father, and brother Rich had gone to bed early, they didn't even want to see another bottle. So it was just Terry and me sitting around my little living room. He had his wine, I had my pot of coffee, and we just started talking.

First we had to figure out who we were. By family reputation I was always the oddball, the outcast; they just didn't think I was a conventional person. I mean, what did Terry know about me? Only that I had run away from home all the time, and had been married and divorced and couldn't seem to fit in anywhere. I was the family hippie. He didn't know if I was a crazy person, and I didn't know him at all. We had grown up in different worlds.

Terry had had to invent himself. Unlike my other brothers, who blamed every terrible thing that happened to them on how they had been raised, Terry was able to function in a family that was basically malfunctioning. He didn't learn how to run in sophisticated circles from what he was taught at home; he'd gotten out and done it for himself.

Now we were sitting in the dead Florida quiet, catching up.

I've always got a lot of questions to ask. I'm interested in how and why people choose certain paths in their lives, especially people I'm close to. Terry had been all over the world. My kid brother.

I asked him how he felt about what he was doing. He started talking about his life and his work, one and the same to him. The words flowed easily, it was late at night and no one but me was listening. Terry was caught up in the spirit of his job; he had the great ability to influence people by what he wrote, and he took that responsibility seriously.

As Terry began to talk about himself, I tried to explain myself to him. ''Regardless of what you believe spiritually, or in religion,'' I said, ''I really believe that you have a responsibility to make your life matter. That doesn't mean just going to work and coming home and being a conspicuous consumer. You have to try to do what you can to improve the *quality* of life.''

Terry agreed and I began to sense a kindred spirit. I liked his commitment to his work, his moral standards. Journalism wasn't just a job to him, he had some very definite ideas about what he would and would not do in that role. He told me he would never do a story just for sensationalism; there would be none of this going up to a disaster victim and asking, ''How do you feel?''

He was also kind of flushed with success. He had already served as vice president of the Foreign Press Association, a huge organization. He was meeting a lot of important people and functioning at an extremely high level. And at thirty-two he was still a young man. I think he had gone a lot farther than he ever expected to go, and he was thriving on it.

Best of all, though, was when he told me that if he could have any job in the world he still wouldn't change professions. He was one of those rare people who actually loved what he was doing. I was still desperately searching.

I wasn't jealous, exactly. Envious, definitely. At the time I was working as a cook at a country-western place a mile down the road, and though I knew I didn't have any reasonable expectations of getting out and doing it, I felt that there was more to me than slaving over a hot stove. The values Terry was putting into his stories I was working hard to instill in my two kids. Terry and I found we had a lot more in common than we had thought. We liked each other. From that evening on, we grew close.

I felt really good about finally getting to know Terry, finding out that I actually did like my little brother. His life was so different from mine—globe-hopping, hobnobbing with people I could only read about in the paper—and he had so much confidence where I had so little. It was good to know that he could come from our background and make something worthwhile of his life. It gave me hope. I was proud of what he had accomplished, and I was happy that through it all he had been a good and thoughtful man.

There was so much that I hadn't done. I had wanted to be a journalist but had only gotten a high school equivalency diploma. And here I was working, cooking for strangers. If I left, there'd be another person at the Garland stove preparing the meat loaf and no one would know or care.

I had to make some changes.

Daytona Beach Community College was within driving distance, and in 1983 I decided to get my feet wet and enroll in summer school. I took a psychology course and figured, with all those whiz kids around, and at forty-two my being an older student, I would get left in their dust.

I'll never forget the first day; our assignment was to read the opening eighty-two pages of our psychology text. I thought, "I'll never get through this. If this is college, it's over my head." I struggled through the course and got a B, with which I was very happy.

From then on it seemed to get easier. In fact, I got all A's, except for a B in algebra, which I'm hopeless at.

I was going for a two-year associate degree in social work. I had wanted to take mental health, but by the time I enrolled the program was filled up.

I knew from the first social work class that this was what I wanted to do. I was the one who was always prepared, always raising my hand and talking. My teachers appreciated my dedication, but to me it was completely natural; I had waited so long for this opportunity, I wasn't going to waste a minute of it.

For my first-semester internship, I had gotten involved with the local Literacy Council and spent two nights a week teaching migrant workers to read and write English. One of the ACLU workers from Miami called the area of Florida where we were living "the Bermuda Triangle of civil rights."

My husband David was, at the time, working as the general foreman at a fernery. His boss was one of the first to bring illegal aliens up to Florida. Now I was organizing his workers. David said to me, "You know, it's quite conceivable that I could lose my job here." Plus, we were living in a house that belonged to his boss. "But," he told me supportively, "you do what you feel you have to do."

So I did. I kept coming in contact with children who, because they were illegal aliens, couldn't get medical care, couldn't get proper schooling. I thought that was wrong, and I felt that the people who brought them in had a moral obligation to provide social services for them. Most growers didn't share my opinion. Another social worker and I joined forces and decided that we would gather some like-minded folks and try to get some action.

Well, it seemed the national Farm Workers Union had been waiting for somebody to start something like this, and within weeks, when we began to get a little publicity, the organization started to snowball.

A radical Irish priest from Miami heard about our coalition and asked if he could come out and address our next meeting. I was astonished. What had I started? We got an attorney and he pressured a judge into coming and explaining to our meeting why he had let off some redneck who had killed a young Mexican. We were really stirring things up and getting things done.

Of course, I was eating it up. Who ever thought anyone would listen to us, we were such a small group?

My last semester I had to quit work because I was taking so many classes. I went to everything I could get to. If there was a seminar, I had to take it. So all of a sudden our income dropped; there was David's flat wage coming in, nothing extra. We were poor as church mice, but I was happier than I'd ever been. I was making a difference and I was thriving on it.

That summer, 1984, Terry came home on leave again. I was happy to see him, but I had a busy schedule. School, social work, organizational work. I was running from meeting to rally and I said, "Terry, I'm real sorry that I can't spend the time with you that I'd like to."

"I'll help you out," he said. "Let me type your term paper for you. That way we can get some time to go fishing." He did a crummy job, and I ultimately had to type the whole thing over, but I appreciated the effort. It allowed me to hit the ground running the next morning.

That December my father had moved into a trailer that David's boss had provided. But just a few days after he moved in, Dad's emphysema kicked up and he went into the hospital. The doctors wouldn't give us a clear reading on his condition, just that it was serious. Terry was back in Beirut, and when he'd heard about Dad he said, "Look, I've got leave coming, I'm coming home."

I said, "I don't know how Dad is going to feel about that, Terry. He'll look up and see you standing there and he'll think he's at the gate with St. Peter."

Dad was having so much difficulty breathing that the doctors had to put a tube down his throat, which he hated. Once it was in, though, he began to depend on it and after a while the doctors could not wean him off it. My dad was in pretty touchy condition.

But when he found out that Terry was coming in, that's all it took. I had never seen such willpower. I sat in the hospital room with him and he would take out the tube and count—one, two, three, four, breathe. One, two, three, four, breathe. When Terry came home Dad was sitting up in bed just as normal as could be. He had virtually willed himself off that machine.

Terry had told me over the phone that he was getting a divorce. The fact that this had been coming for several years didn't make the final steps any easier. It was extremely emotional and depressing to end a marriage of almost twenty years, and Terry's pain was evident when he told me of his decision.

Although Terry's divorce was not yet final he had brought home his new fiancée, a Lebanese woman named Madeleine. Madeleine was pregnant. They planned to be married as soon as possible and were eagerly awaiting the final divorce decree.

Terry had turned cocky, arrogant, kind of cold. Sitting around the house one evening, Terry was telling stories about this one young kid, a militiaman, chasing him down the street with an AK-47, spraying windows and cars with machine-gun fire, people diving for cover. The way Terry told it, it was quite a hoot. I was petrified, horrified, but to Terry that kind of scene had become commonplace. Even admirable. It was the most excitement to be had by a journalist. I did not like what Lebanon had done to my brother.

I seriously considered telling him so, but I was having these terrible premonitions about Terry being kidnapped. The last thing I wanted was to have a big fight with him just as he was going back to Beirut.

Once he got back to Lebanon, Terry would call on Sundays, just to chat, and I began trying to get him home. He was telling me the latest of his adventure stories when I broke in. "Terry, the joke is over. It's time to get out of there. Something is going to happen to you."

Terry couldn't be bothered. I was an outsider, I wasn't part of the Beirut fraternity, I wasn't on the ground.

"You don't understand," he told me. "They don't kidnap journalists. It would be counterproductive. These people need me; I tell their story to the world. That's my job and they know it."

"Terry. . ."

"You don't understand."

Maybe I didn't. I was no Middle Eastern expert. I had a hard enough time finding Lebanon on the map. All I knew was that I was having terrible premonitions. It may sound a little strange, and I'm certainly no psychic, but all that week I had worried. I would get home from school and tell David, "I'm afraid to turn on the television. I'm afraid I'm going to see where Terry has been kidnapped."

"Peggy," my brother had said over the phone, "stop it. They don't kidnap journalists."

Less than a week later, three men armed with automatic weapons wrestled Terry Anderson out of a car as he was returning from a tennis game with an AP photographer, Don Mell. They forced him into a green Mercedes and turned their weapons toward the photographer. "At that moment Terry's and my eyes met," says Mell. "His look said, 'Do something.' Mine said, 'I can't.'"

We had one of those cheapie phones in the bedroom. One of those "The first thousand people who send in two dollars get this wonderful modern telephone." You could barely hear on it. When that phone rang at four o'clock on Saturday morning, March 16, 1985, it was almost a relief. The shoe had finally fallen.

David picked it up and without knowing who was on the line I ran to the dining room phone so I could hear clearly.

Nate Polowetsky was the Associated Press foreign editor in New York. He said, "Terry has been kidnapped. He was taken out of his car by three armed men. At this point we don't have any more details. We don't know who has taken him and we don't know why. We will let you know as soon as we hear anything further."

I was standing in my nightshirt in my dining room in Florida at four o'clock in the morning. I didn't know what to say.

"Thank you very much."

CHAPTER

2

WHENEVER A CRISIS OCCURS, DAVID AND I PUT THE POT OF COFFEE ON first, then we try to figure out what to do.

I remember thinking it would be over with very quickly. Terry's whole staff had been kidnapped just shortly before that. They had been released within twenty-four hours, and Terry had told me stories about these goofy kidnappings that went on all the time. To the seasoned veterans on the ground in Beirut, most of it was a big joke. I could almost hear Terry calling me back and saying, "You'll never guess what happened to me." So I was worried—nobody likes getting kidnapped—but I thought it was short-term.

Dad was in his trailer. I didn't know whether to wake him up and tell him or let him sleep. I didn't want to leave the phone; they could call back at any minute and tell me the whole thing had been resolved.

David and I are both the same; when something happens, or we are upset, we get very quiet. Neither of us knew what to say, so we just sat there. It was that still, eerie time of night when nothing is moving. Four in the morning. I didn't know whether to call my family or to wait until it was time for them to get up. The rest of our world was asleep and we were up drinking coffee.

We sat there in silence, our minds reeling, for about an hour. The sun was coming up, things began moving outside. I called my brother Rich and asked him to get my brother Jack, who lived near him in Ocala, and go down to Dad's trailer. I didn't want to tell my father by telephone that Terry had been kidnapped, and I didn't want to leave my house because I just knew that they were going to call back and say, "He's out."

Rich and Jack woke up my father. When Dad came to the door he said he *knew* something had happened. He thought Terry had been killed. He had worried about Terry getting accidentally caught up in a car bombing. They all came over to my house. We called my sister Judy in New York and some of my aunts, to tell them what had happened.

We didn't know anything about Lebanon or who would take my brother or why they would want to. I had asked Terry several times when I'd seen him to plot out what the situation was, what he was covering, and he had tried to explain that there were about 50,000 different groups and who each one of them was, but it was all so confusing that I had just turned it off. Now we had no idea what had happened other than the bare fact that Terry had been kidnapped. We didn't know what to do except wait for him to be released.

The phone started ringing. The media started calling and I didn't know what to say. I asked my dad, "What do you think we should do? Should we talk to them?"

"Yeah, we need to talk to them. Terry is a journalist, he would want us to talk to them."

At about eight o'clock the cars started pulling up in my yard. First one car with a reporter, then a television van, then more vans and cars and cameras than had been pointed at me or anyone I knew in our entire lives. They just started pulling up like some electronic wagon train and after a while I just stayed out there and welcomed them one by one.

Right off the bat Rich and Jack and David didn't want any part of the media. They faded very quickly into the background, which left Dad and me. We just started talking about Terry.

The first interview I did, I thought the young woman was just talking to me. It was almost a casual chat, she and I sitting on the couch in my living room talking about my brother. It wasn't until she said, "Okay, that's it, thank you very much," that I realized I had just been interviewed. And painlessly, as it turned out.

In retrospect I think I was very dumb, talking about Terry's Marine background and other details of his life. The Marine barracks had been car-bombed eighteen months earlier by one of the Lebanese groups and it could easily have been the one that kidnapped Terry. Now they knew he had been a Marine, and if that was the fact that could decide his fate, I might have just killed him.

But we didn't think that way. I was in my living room, they were in Beirut. The concept that the captors might hear what I was saying never crossed my mind.

It was all very confusing. After talking to the fifteenth journalist and drinking my twentieth cup of coffee I couldn't keep track of what I had said to whom. Not that it mattered. We were all swept up in this spin cycle of the news, and once they had drained us they all went home.

My ego as far as being on television was concerned left me right away. I remember seeing my dad and me on the news that night and being horrified. We were sitting in my living room watching one broadcast after another and we looked worse from one channel to the next. I said to him, "You look like a bulldog and I look like your puppy."

Judy's daughter Rachel saw a report on TV saying that Terry had been kidnapped. As she was being tucked into bed that night she asked her mom, "How many men with three arms took Uncle Terry?"

"What do you mean, dear?"

"Well, on TV it said that Uncle Terry was kidnapped by three-armed men."

NBC called. They wanted me to be on the *Today* show the next morning. I thought it was tacky, kind of like the "How do you feel?" stories that Terry had said he'd never do. Plus, I was terrified of flying. I had flown only once in my life and I was not about to get on an airplane with this crushing anxiety all around me and jump on over to their nearest studio.

My dad had no such reservations, so I touted the trip off on him. I was just as happy to get him out of my hair and keep him busy. And I knew he would love to be on national TV.

A private plane picked Dad up at Daytona Beach and took him to Miami, where they hooked him by remote to New York. He had a fine old time, and when he got back he was going on and on about this gorgeous woman limousine chauffeur with her skirt split up to her thigh. Typically Dad, he had fallen in lust with this Italian charmer. I reminded him that he was sixty-seven years old and asked just when he was going to hang it up with women.

"The day they bury me," he said.

But as fast as the notepads and cameras had arrived, they disappeared. We woke up the next morning and it was as if the whole thing had never happened. We were literally yesterday's news. The phone wasn't ringing, we weren't getting any new information. Nothing. Except that Terry was a hostage.

We were sitting in our kitchen, same as the day before, drinking coffee, completely stunned. David had to go to work and life was supposed to carry on. It was like when someone close to you dies; you think everyone should be caught up in your grief, and they're not. What's happened here? Doesn't anybody understand that my brother has been kidnapped!

It occurred to me, sitting there in the anxious quiet, that for all my involvement, for all my activism, I had not made a real friend in Florida. There was nobody to call to help me through this. I had made casual friends and some valued relationships, but there was nobody I felt I could dump this situation on who would remotely understand. I found it difficult to understand myself.

It was just David and me. I didn't leave the house for four or five days. Just sat there waiting for something to happen.

Terry's best friend in Beirut, Robert Fisk of the London *Times,* called when the kidnapping first took place and said, "Peggy, this will be over within twenty-four hours." The day Terry was taken, Fisk had had thousands of posters of Terry printed with the legend HAVE YOU SEEN THIS MAN? and a telephone number to contact. He had then driven all the way from Beirut almost to Damascus, Syria, stopping to distribute them at every single checkpoint. This was very brave and very dangerous; he was a major British journalist, much as Terry was a major American journalist. If they wanted Terry, they could just as easily be lying in wait for him.

But Fisk felt that the kidnappers might try to transport my brother in or under a car, and if the checkpoint guards were vigilant they might be able to recapture him. "Keep a watch," he told them. "Check the trunks." Fisk offered a reward for Terry's return.

Fisk called the next day and said, "It may take three to five days." But on his next call he said, "Maybe we've got a real problem here."

AP got a call. The captors had finally taken credit for the kidnapping. It was the Islamic Jihad. I didn't know much about the Middle East, but I did know that name. They were the ones said to be responsible for the bombing of the Marine Corps barracks. All of a sudden this little incident was beginning to take on gigantic proportions. I started to get panicky. These people had killed 241 Marines, now they were going to kill my brother.

My father moved in with us, and in the middle of my panic attacks I was doing my best to control him and my brother Rich. They were very outspoken. Early on I knew that our credibility was important—I had seen enough strange birds on television to know that you had to be rational to be taken seriously—and when Dad and Rich had a few belts, God only knows what they would say.

The State Department had assigned a Mr. Jones to contact us. He would call each day and say, "This is Mr. Jones from the State Department. We just want you to know that we are doing everything we can to resolve the situation as quickly as possible. Thank you very much." I appreciated the fact that our government was taking an interest.

About the fifth day after Terry was taken, I withdrew from college. I was only a month away from graduation and my diploma but I knew I could not go to classes or study while Terry was in captivity; there was no way I could concentrate, no way I could justify doing anything but working to get my brother back. I left my dad at the house while I went to the campus to do the paperwork. He would be alone with the phone and I told him, "Please, if anybody calls, just try to watch what you say."

So I got back from school and my father was in fine fettle. "Well, I guess I told that Mr. Jones guy!" he roared.

"What happened?"

"Well, he called and he wanted to talk to you and I told him that you weren't home and that I was Terry's father and I could take the message. And he said to me, 'I knew Terry had a brother, Glenn Richard Anderson Jr. What is your name?' I told him, 'Well, you stupid son of a bitch, if my son is Glenn Anderson Jr. what the hell do you *think* my name is!' "

I called Mr. Jones and apologized.

A week after Terry was taken, we got a call from the State Department saying they wanted to send a representative to visit us. He would be coming from Miami, would we be available to meet with him? Well, I had great faith in our government, and I was more than pleased that it would be actively involved in the process. Yes, of course, I would be happy to meet with him.

I talked with Rich the day before their representative was to arrive and he said, "I'll handle this. I'm going to cook up a big pot of spaghetti and we'll talk to this guy. I'll be in charge."

I was so relieved. I had hoped this crisis would bring out the best in my big brother, because it was wreaking havoc with me. I was completely out of it. I had this terrible sense that if I enjoyed anything, I would be betraying Terry. If he had to suffer, then, by God, I was going to suffer with him. I wouldn't eat, I wasn't sleeping, I stopped making love to David. I was totally housebound. I guess I was in shock. If I were called upon to do anything, I just knew I would collapse. Now Rich had taken on the responsibility. He was going to be the older brother, the point man. I was so grateful.

Rich came over the day the agent was to appear, brought all the makings for the spaghetti sauce and began to prepare it. He was drinking Kool-Aid, not a bottle of alcohol in sight. So why was he acting so increasingly weird? He wasn't drinking but somehow, it was finally occurring to me as the afternoon wore on, he was smashed.

Rich's girlfriend kept disappearing. Rich was sending her out to the car, where he had a bottle to keep the bite in the Kool-Aid. The sauce kept simmering and so did I.

My father was drinking openly, and by early evening when our visitor walked in the door he had two angry drunks to contend with. He seemed like a nice person, not intense, and he said he was there to do what he could. Unfortunately, it turned out that he was not very involved in the case. He was only there to get samples of Terry's handwriting, not to give us information. He was trying to be pleasant, but Rich and my father jumped on him.

"What are you doing about my brother?" Rich snarled. My father joined in and between them they began to savage this guy.

My father wore out first and went to bed early. Rich and I sat with the government representative and it became clear that if I wanted to know something I was going to have to ask it myself. Rich was mean and hostile, and this man who was on our side could not get a word in edgewise. There was a chance that he knew something we didn't, but every time I tried to interject a rational question Rich would shoot me this real dirty look like, "Who do you think you are?"

Finally Rich exhausted himself and went home. There was an embarrassed silence when he left. The State Department representative had quit smoking a few months earlier, but by the time Rich left he had smoked a full pack.

I apologized for my family's behavior, but mostly I was at a loss for anything constructive I could do for Terry. I was completely empty. I just sat in my chair in my living room and found it almost too difficult to move.

"What should I do?" I asked the man.

"It's not my place to advise you," he told me, "but if I were you, I would make as much noise as possible."

"Really?"

"Really. The State Department's official position is to tell you not to go to Washington, to keep a low profile. But you get your behind up there. Go see everyone you can see. Make them look you in the eye, so that every time they think of Terry Anderson they'll see your face."

I didn't want to do this. I wasn't up to this at all. But what choice did I have? My father and brother couldn't handle the pressure, so they pressed Terry's torch into my hands. I had no choice but to carry on.

Five days after Terry was abducted, three CBS newsmen were shot and killed in Beirut.

Former hostage Jerry Levin called from his retreat in the Virgin Islands offering his help, and a few days later I got a phone call from the sister of Father Martin Jenco, the Catholic Relief Services priest who had been kidnapped in Beirut in January of that year. She and the wife and son of the Presbyterian missionary Rev. Benjamin Weir, who had been kidnapped almost a year earlier, were going to hold a news conference in the Chicago suburb of Joliet, Illinois, and they invited me to come with them. I didn't know what I could do to help. I didn't know what to do, and I didn't have anyone to help me.

David and I had decided to go back to New York State. At least there I had some sense of where I came from, some place for Terry to come home to. We had just renovated our Florida home, bought all new furniture. It didn't matter. Everything became meaningless. Even my social work degree, which had been my life. I had just been named "Outstanding Student in the Program" and had been looking forward to graduating with honors, my moment in the sun. It all faded. So we decided to sell everything to the Mexican farm workers. We packed up what was left and drove back to New York.

My sister Judy called, wanting to help. I had just hung up on Rich, who had been screaming at me. "Judy," I told her, "I can't cope."

Judy was my kid sister. She had always looked up to me. She wanted to be just like me, which I did my best to discourage. "I've had my problems, God knows," I said, "and I don't want you to make the mistakes I did."

I told her about the press conference in Chicago. "Let's go together. I want you to be equal with me in this. I don't want to tell you what to do. If they talk to us together you're going to have as good a grasp of the situation as I do, so we can work together."

Judy was always a tiny little girl and I envied her for it. Dad called her "Princess." People always wanted to take care of her. With me it was "You're a big girl, fend for yourself." But Judy is stronger than she looks, and I believed, when pushed to the wall she could do what she had to. She agreed to come to Chicago.

I had never been to a press conference before. I had seen the results on television, those little sound bites where you heard about five seconds of someone and got more of a sense of them from how they looked than what they said.

The one in Chicago was horrendous. I was overwhelmed by the pushing and the crush and the almost complete insincerity of the people who were supposed to be covering and interpreting the news.

I thought they were all barbarians. Being in social work, where part of your education is learning to communicate and listen and feed a conversation, I was unnerved and stunned when a reporter asked me a question, stuck a microphone in my face, and while I was speaking turned around to talk to one of her technicians. I found it grossly offensive. Don't ask me questions if you don't care about my answers. I was talking to these people about an emotional topic—my brother's life—and they were treating it like the Chicago Cubs were trading for a shortstop.

Judy had it worse. The minute the TV camera's red light went on, she lost her voice. Completely panicked. She couldn't cope with it at all. In the middle of the turmoil she pulled me aside and said, "I cannot do this. I *can't* do it." Much as I wanted and needed help, I didn't push her.

The Jencos and the Weirs were very public in trying to encourage, petition, pressure the government into negotiating with the captors for the hostages' release. They wanted me to join them. With the benefit of their experience, I could avoid making the same mistakes they had made, and jump in one step ahead. They urged me to go to Washington.

But I wasn't secure enough in understanding who had taken Terry, and why, and what could actually be done about it. I didn't want to go to Washington and get involved in a situation where I didn't know what I was talking about. I knew that if I spoke on camera without really understanding the situation, I'd make a fool of myself, and I didn't want to do that to me or to Terry.

Also, in my brief dealings with them, the State Department had made it very clear that they preferred me to stay out of the newspapers, say nothing at all, and leave the situation to be handled by the professionals in the U.S. government.

One of my main concerns was getting Terry's fiancée, Madeleine, out of Beirut. Pregnant as she was, she didn't want to leave, but I knew that Terry wanted his baby born in the United States. Finally we convinced her, and by Easter she had arrived in New York. We took her back to David's mother's house in Batavia, where we were staying.

The New York Associated Press kept calling. They didn't know me, I didn't know them. I had been very anxious early on: Please, God, do not let me embarrass Terry with the Associated Press. As far as money was concerned, I could be starving to death and would never ask anyone for a dime, and I certainly would not ask for help from the AP.

Nate Polowetsky was our initial contact with the AP. I liked him, but several times he casually suggested, "Why don't you fly out and we'll do lunch." Now, I'm a small-town girl, I don't fly to New York City to do lunch. Besides, we couldn't afford it. Finally, they decided to fly Madeleine and me to New York at their expense to meet with the staff.

We met with Nate Polowetsky, Carolyn Turolla, and Wick Temple, who were on the AP staff at the time. Not a lot was accomplished. In retrospect I don't know what the purpose was, except to get a look at Madeleine and me. I do remember being absolutely outraged, even though I was not paying, at the cost of a cheeseburger. Fourteen dollars! And it was not a good cheeseburger!

I had been telling them about what the Jencos and Weirs had said about the importance of going to Washington. I had decided to go, but I had no idea what I was supposed to do once I got there, or who I was supposed to see. I had visions of myself trudging around with my little suitcase, knocking on doors, saying, "Will you help my brother?"

The Associated Press, of course, had a lot more clout than I knew. They decided to arrange and pay for a three-day Washington blitz by Madeleine, Judy, and me.

We were met, chaperoned, and pointed in all the right directions by an AP representative. Here was this pregnant Arab and these two small-town upstate New York women, and he didn't know what to do with us. We didn't know what was going to happen or what we could even ask for. Although Madeleine was more experienced in travel and politics, Judy and I were so far over our heads we were almost giddy.

Our AP guide had arranged our itinerary. The first meeting we had was with a representative of the State Department. It was a blur. I was shuffled past maybe half a dozen different people at what they called "desks": the Middle Eastern desk, the Counter-Terrorism desk. I was told their names and their functions, but it all eluded me.

From there we were steered to the proper embassies: the Algerian, the Syrian, and the Lebanese.

"What do they have to do with Terry?" I asked.

"Everything," we were told.

We were coached for each meeting. "You've only got one line and you stick to it: Your brother is a hostage and you want him out. How can they help you, what advice can they give you?"

That's pretty much what I said. I tried to be very direct and simple. "My name is Peggy Say and my brother is a hostage. I would truly appreciate anything you can do to secure his release. He is a journalist, he is not on either side of the conflict in Lebanon. He was just over there covering the news. He's my brother, he is very important to me. Can you be of any assistance? Who else do you think I should talk to?"

When I thought of going to Washington, I thought of my congressman. That's the first thing everyone always says to do: Go see your congressman. I went and saw mine.

I hadn't been the most devoted participant in the democratic process. I was busy with other things, like raising a family, working, trying bit by bit to get an education. I felt society started falling apart when mothers left their children and went out and got jobs. I was not interested in politics, I was not an educated voter. I wasn't a voter at all. But when Terry got captured I had to rethink all that.

My congressman was a Republican named Fred Eckert. I was this little housewife come to Washington to see him on behalf of my brother. I was ushered into Eckert's office and seated in front of his desk.

"How may I help you?" he asked.

"Well, my name is Peggy Say. You're my congressman, you're Terry Anderson's congressman, and we would like you to make every effort to pressure the administration to negotiate for the release of my brother and the other hostages."

I could almost see Eckert's back go straight. He cut me right off.

"I'm not going to do that," he intoned. "I'm going to do what Mr. Reagan tells me, not you. I'm a Republican and I'm going to do what my President tells me do to."

"Excuse me, Mr. Congressman, I'm just one woman from Batavia," I said. "What you're saying to me is, if the people who elected you give you a mandate to pressure this administration, you're not going to do it?"

He gave me a hard stare. "I am going to do exactly what Ronald Reagan tells me to do."

That was essentially the end of our meeting. As I was leaving the building I thought, "Welcome to the wonderful world of politics."

Father Jenco's family was in town, as well as the nephew of Peter Kilburn, another of the hostages, and the Weirs. We met with the Algerian ambassador to the United States, Mohammed Sahnoun.

Ambassador Sahnoun was a fine-boned man with dark, wavy hair. He moved and spoke with the careful air of a diplomat. We hit it off from the start.

Sahnoun didn't beat around the bush. If I asked him a question, I got an answer. I found that extremely valuable, and a refreshing change from my dealings with American officials. He was extremely knowledgeable about the politics and personalities involved in the situation. He also gave me information that the State Department was surely privy to but had told me to my face they didn't have.

But what impressed me most about the man was that he never, as a prelude to passing along information or in the middle of a privileged conversation, told me, "You must keep this in complete confidence." He assumed I was trustworthy, that I understood the absolute need for discretion, and, since Terry's life might at some time depend on it, that I was as good as my word. I left his office with the real sense that I had an ally.

We saw the Algerians, the Germans, the Japanese, the Syrians. I'd never met anyone from any of those countries before. I had a hard enough time keeping them straight on a map. I was absorbing everything as fast as I could, but my head was buzzing.

Then there was Washington, D.C., to deal with, starting with our hotel. My sister Judy was blown away by the size of the suite and the fact that it had a television in the bathroom. She had brought along a hair dryer for the trip and was fascinated to find there was already one there. One morning I heard yelping in the bathroom. I ran in and found Judy doing a hot little two-step, trying to get over to the electric outlet. She had turned the hotel hair dryer backward and it was sucking her hair right up into it.

I was addicted to *Dallas,* had to watch every episode. Our second night at the hotel, Madeleine, Judy, and I had eaten dinner in our room and when I went to push the room-service cart into the hallway so the TV wouldn't be blocked, I caught my hand in the doorjamb and cut it. It was only a scratch, but I'm a bleeder and I couldn't get the flow to stop. Nothing could budge me from the television, so I soaked a washcloth in cold water and held it in place. The gusher still didn't stop, so Judy called down to the front desk for a Band-Aid. "My sister cut herself," she told them. "Could you have someone come up here with a Band-Aid, please, so she doesn't get blood all over?"

I was sitting on the bed, holding my hand, totally intent on my program, when there was a knock on the door. Madeleine had been in the bathroom when I hurt myself and I had forgotten to tell her about it. She opened the door and in walked this guy with a walkie-talkie.

There was a medevac team in the hallway—a gurney and three medics.

"Where's the emergency? We have a call here that's a medical emergency."

"Uh." I was a little at a loss. "I asked for a Band-Aid."

Madeleine is standing with her hand on the doorknob, dumbfounded. The guy's intercom is crackling with static, he's looking at me, I'm looking at the bloody washcloth and almost dying of embarrassment.

They made me sign a lot of forms promising not to hold the hotel liable. I made them promise not to tell anybody. Judy was rolling on the floor with laughter.

The AP had hired a chauffeured limousine for our entire three-day stay. All three of us were in the back seat heading back to the airport at the end of our trip when something suddenly occurred to me and I whispered to Madeleine and Judy, "We're probably supposed to tip this guy. And we're not talking five bucks here. He's been with us for three days. What are we supposed to do?"

I tapped the driver on the shoulder.

"Excuse me. We have a little problem here." He kind of cocked an ear as he drove. "You may have gathered that we are not from the city, and, you know . . . are we supposed to tip you?"

He chuckled. "Well, a tip is a gratuity. You only give a tip for good service."

"We've had excellent service," we told him; neither Judy nor I had been in a limo before and it had been a rare experience. "But we don't know how much to tip you."

"Well, I can't tell you that. My fee is forty-five dollars an hour."

We just about groaned out loud. We started going through our pocketbooks. Together we came up with twenty dollars. I handed it over the transom and said, "I know this is not nearly enough but, what can I tell you, it's all we have." We got out of our limousine at the airport, totally humiliated.

CHAPTER

3

WHEN WE LEFT WASHINGTON I THOUGHT I WAS FINISHED, THAT I
had done the thing that everybody had told me to do and now the
government and the professionals would bring Terry home.

When nothing happened, I started getting antsy. I knew I couldn't
keep quiet.

Then I met Jesse Jackson.

Terry had been on the plane when Jesse brought back the downed
American airman whose release he had reportedly negotiated with
Syria, so there was a human as well as political connection. Terry had
told Jesse's story, now I wanted Jesse to tell Terry's.

The Jencos had contacted Jesse and he had returned to his home
in Chicago and done a fund-raiser for them. They suggested I try to
get him to add Terry's name to his list. I got a phone call from the
Jackson office saying that he would be appearing at a high school in
New York City at a ceremony marking the tenth anniversary of the
end of the Vietnam War, and that this would be a perfect platform

from which to appeal for the release of the hostages. He wanted me there.

Judy and I decided to attend that rally. Now mind you, we didn't have a dime; Judy's church, Bethany Center Baptist in Batavia, gave us enough money to fly cut-rate People Express down to New York. A local Batavia reporter named Sharon Larson came with us. We were trudging around with our satchels because we didn't have enough money to stay overnight. We took one taxi, had a muffin and coffee, and that about busted our budget for the day.

We got to the high school and it was like Hippie Heaven. Long hair, wild clothes, lots of blacks and Orientals. We were about the only white faces there. I wasn't used to this at all.

I got a program and sat down to read it, and among the sponsors were the Communist Party USA and the Socialist Workers Party. It turned out that this event was a celebration of the tenth anniversary of the "Vietnam Victory over American Intervention."

We were definitely not used to this.

It was a long program, with folk songs from Nicaragua and speeches and chanting. My sister slipped me a note saying, "Get me out of here!" But we hung in there.

Jesse did get up and speak in our behalf. He wasn't very well prepared. He had to read from a list who the hostages were, and the photo opportunity afterward was a bit awkward. When we finally escaped I said to Judy, "I'm not going to do this again." But Jesse was lending his name and considerable prestige to our cause, and once we got away from there I appreciated his efforts.

The next time I saw Jesse was a few weeks later in Washington, D.C. He met with the hostage families and was going to attend a State Department meeting with us and act in our behalf in pressuring the government to get our men home. The captors had just released three communiqués: one to "World Opinion," one to the families, and one to Jesse Jackson. On the way to the meeting I had stopped off at the AP to get a literal translation of these messages, which had originally been written in Arabic.

When we reached the State Department building there was press all over and Jesse was in his element.

"The captors appealed to me!" he announced. "The captors called me by name!"

"Jesse." I tugged at his sleeve and fought the commotion to get his attention. "Jesse, you need to see the name they called you by."

I handed him the translation. It read: "To the American Reverend who is out of breath for power in the United States. To Jesse Jackson who revealed his political ignorance in the problems of the Middle East area, through the message he directed to the Shia sect. . . ." He stuffed it in his pocket and continued to hold court, and that was all we heard about that.

I sat next to Jesse in the meeting at the State Department. We were facing National Security Adviser Robert "Bud" McFarlane and Jesse was saying, "We want to go to Iran and see the Ayatollah."

I almost choked. I whispered, "Jesse, I don't think I want to do that," but he went right on. As far as he was concerned, it seemed, we were going to resolve this problem then and there.

But first, some questions needed to be answered. Jesse and the government officials agreed that we needed to reconvene. "Well, we'll be back here next week," he told them. "We want this meeting."

I had barely scrounged enough money to get to Washington; our church had sponsored a car wash to raise money for the trip. David and I, our families, church members, and friends had participated, and it had been just one more humiliation that we had to endure. We had raised several hundred dollars, but doing that again in seven days was impossible. "Jesse," I said, "I can't come back next week."

"Can you come back if I give you a ticket?" he asked.

"Well," I admitted, "yes."

Two days later his office wired me a round-trip plane ticket to Washington.

A short while later, some involved local citizens, the Genesee Country Mall merchants, decided to sponsor a Terry Anderson Day in Batavia. There would be speeches and a church service to drum up support for Terry's release. We didn't know what else to do except keep making loud noises.

My brother Rich called about three days before the event and said,

"Peg, why don't you give Jesse a call and see if he'll come." This wasn't help, it was torment. There was a needle in there for me.

"Rich," I told him, "Jesse Jackson is not going to come to Batavia."

"What the hell," he said, "give him a call. What've you got to lose?"

He was right about that. So I called and his office put me in touch with Jesse. "How many people do you expect to be there?" he wanted to know.

"To tell you the truth," I said, "I don't have any idea. I assume several hundred."

"Okay. Why not."

The organizers were thrilled when I passed on the good news to them. They could not believe that Jesse Jackson was coming to their town. Even though we were pressed for time to advertise Jesse's appearance, the news spread through town like a flash fire. This was a huge honor for a town the size of Batavia, and we were all touched by Jesse's willingness to come.

My sister-in-law Penny and I were sitting in my living room the day before the rally when I got a call from a woman in Jesse's office. She wanted to know who was going to pay the $1,200 that it was going to cost to have Jesse come to Batavia.

I just started laughing. "Lady, Jesse just had to buy me a ticket to Washington. How in the world do you think I'm going to pay twelve hundred dollars?"

"Well," she said, "maybe the people who are organizing the event would have it."

"I assure you, there is nobody here who has twelve hundred dollars." We both got kind of quiet. "How about if I just tell the press that Jesse cancelled because we couldn't afford him."

"No, no," she said quickly. "That's all right. If Jesse said he'll be there, he'll be there."

I don't know that Jesse was aware of this call; it may just have been his office being overzealous. I prefer to think of it that way. I told Penny, "Let's keep this between you and me. I've already had so many illusions destroyed, I don't want to do this to these people. Everyone is so thrilled about it, let's just let them think that Jesse is doing this out of the goodness of his heart.'' Which he did, although I don't know whether he actually planned it that way.

The major rally was going to be held at the Batavia mall, followed by a fund-raiser. Now, I was raised never to talk about funds. It wasn't something you talked about to other people, particularly when you were in need. When Bethany Baptist Church told me they were going to start a Terry Anderson Fund to help with our expenses in the fight to bring Terry home, I told them several times, ''No, I just can't do this. I can't ask people for money.''

But it got to the point that there was nothing left. I did not have a job; my entire day, every day, was taken up with trying to get Terry home. I called everyone I could, I wrote letters, I tried to keep his name in the news. If I didn't look after Terry, who would? There was nothing else that mattered to me.

But I opened up my phone bill one day and that was it, there was nothing to pay it with. Finally I went to the church and told them okay, if they still wanted to organize a Terry Anderson Fund I would be embarrassed but grateful. This rally was going to be the kickoff.

I wanted to treat Jesse right. I called the local judge, Larry Shultz, and asked would he want to go and pick up Jesse Jackson at the airport.

Certainly.

I called the church and asked our minister, Tom Vickers, ''Tom, would you mind having a guest preacher this Sunday?''

He said, ''Well, who?''

''Jesse Jackson.''

It just about blew his mind.

''But,'' I told him, ''let's keep this private. No press.'' I didn't want to seem like I was flogging this one celebrity I had met. So we arranged for one local station, the one that had filmed and aired our appeals for Terry, to tape the sermon and share it with the others.

Jesse got off the plane at the Rochester airport and came walking down the corridor alone. There were no crowds, no press. I was no organizer, plus I was a little embarrassed at having to ask for his help in the first place, so I didn't tell anybody when he was coming. He looked so crestfallen, striding through the airport, nodding at everyone who caught his eye, waving. Anytime you see Jesse on television, there's a crowd around him; yet here in the airport he seemed all the larger for being alone.

We got to the church, and there was no press there either. By this time Jesse was getting uneasy. It was one thing to be alone in an airport, it was quite another to come to a rally and have no one show up.

But in small-town New York word travels fast, and when Jesse rose and took his place in the pulpit the church was packed. He didn't disappoint them. He was mesmerizing. I had heard snippets of Jesse's speeches, mostly on television, and he'd always had a persuasive way with words. But in person he was magnificent. Here was a black Southern Baptist preacher talking to white Northern Baptists, many of whom doubted he really had anything to say to them, and he was moving them like crazy. I had never heard anyone talk like that.

When we walked into the mall through the back entrance and nobody was around I thought, "Oh, no." Footsteps echoed, things you'd never noticed before became very vivid. Then we crossed into the main concourse and it was packed, and Jesse lit up like a light bulb.

There were banners and flags and a PA system. Maybe in a city this would have looked rinky-dink, but to us it was really big-time.

Part of the program was going to be an appeal for funds by our minister, but when he came over to Jesse and me and said, "I'm going to make the appeal now," Jesse said, "Sit down, Tom. I'll take care of this."

Jesse used all of his charm and persuasion on that crowd. He told them how important our work was, how Terry was a hometown boy who needed the help of his home town. He preached the gospel of Terry, and the crowd was with him. Then he asked for more than their attention.

"Who's the first one here with a hundred dollars to give to the cause?" he began. "Who's the first one with a hundred dollars to bring Terry Anderson home?"

If a hole had opened in the earth I would have gladly dropped into it. I was thinking, "Oh geez, Jesse, this is Batavia, New York. Who's got a hundred dollars to donate?"

One woman, bless her heart, actually did. She donated one hundred dollars. Jesse was beginning to be very impressive.

And when you start at a hundred, anything less seems like small potatoes. So when he got down to "Who's the first with a twenty-dollar bill?" a stream of people came forward.

I was amazed. I could never in my wildest dreams have asked for that much from any one of my neighbors. Yet now the aisles were full of people with cash—some approaching, maybe, just to get near Jesse—and he told me, "Peggy, come up here and take their money." I might have been inwardly cringing at the idea, but I stood beside him and accepted it.

The pitch went on for about twenty minutes. By the end he was down to "Bring your nickels and dimes." It was so humiliating, but in twenty minutes he had raised two thousand dollars and that money enabled me to keep on working day and night for Terry. When he left that night, Jesse had really done a bang-up job.

I hated having to ask for that money. It was so totally, absolutely alien to me to ask for outside help. I had always been on my own. I had to learn that I needed people.

Not only financially. Projects grew beyond my ability to handle them alone, and when I finally did ask for help I got to know a lot of wonderful people. One woman kept writing me notes and calling me for about a year, offering to pitch in. I would write back and say, "Thank you for your kind offer and if I ever need you, I'll call you." But I had no intention of ever actually asking her to do anything. I was going to do everything by myself. It had been my experience that, whether you asked for it or not, help was simply not there. When I finally broke down and did write back that, yes, her help would be appreciated, she turned out to be a totally dedicated and valuable worker who developed from a sort of pen-pal correspondent into a friend.

Her name was Anne Zickl and she just about took over the mail. After a while her family joked that they hadn't seen the dining room table in a year and a half, it was piled so high with postcards and letters in support of Terry Anderson.

Several years before, I had had a conversation about religion with a man whose ideas and opinions I truly respected. He asked me, "Do you ever pray for help?"

"No."

"Why not?"

"Well, I figure I got myself into it, it's up to me to get myself out. Nobody takes responsibility for what I do."

He began trying to explain to me the concept of God the Father, and I was having a hard time with it. "When you were a teenager," he said, "and you did something wrong and you got in over your head, couldn't you go to your father?"

"Yeah, lots of luck, Charlie."

It was a whole new way of looking at things, the idea that you could actually pray for help and expect that somebody was going to be there to help you out of this. I had never thought of it that way.

I wouldn't ask for anything and I rarely had much. David and I didn't have money in the bank. We didn't even have credit cards; he had been divorced and kissed everything but his wife good-bye. We were used to working hard all our lives and, like most Americans, we were getting by.

When the television networks realized I was an active advocate for Terry's freedom, they started to extend me invitations.

When you travel for the networks, to participate in one of their broadcasts, they will pay for your hotel room but you have to submit an expense account, for which they will reimburse you. Now in those days if I traveled with fifty dollars I was doing good. I didn't know what expenses were, I didn't know what taxis cost. Before I went on a trip I would call up my sister-in-law and my best friend's daughter and they would bring clothes over and I would select an outfit.

My first time in New York City I was booked into a beautiful hotel. When I arrived I was asked for a credit card. I thought it was for identification, so I pulled out the only one I owned; I was very proud of my gold card from the Fingerhut corporation, a catalog company that allows you to take about a thousand weeks to pay for each purchase. The desk clerk was not impressed and told me that this card would simply not do. "We need a *major* credit card," he told me.

"I don't have one."

"Well, then we need a two-hundred-dollar deposit."

"I don't have two hundred dollars." This would happen to me time after time and I was always humiliated. They always let me stay but I usually had the feeling that when I left they were going to check my luggage for towels and silverware.

That same trip, returning from doing an interview, I noticed that there was a flashing red light on my telephone. I had no idea what it meant. I pushed and prodded it and nothing happened. Finally I called the hotel operator and asked her what it was for.

"The light means you have messages," she told me.

"Oh, I see." I thanked her and hung up.

The light was still on, it wouldn't turn off and it wouldn't talk to me. It didn't respond to pushing, and I was completely baffled. I called the operator again and told her I couldn't get the red light to give me my messages. She tried unsuccessfully to suppress a giggle as she explained to me that the light was a signal and that she, the operator, was holding my messages, which she then passed on. Between the credit card and the red light, I was almost too embarrassed to leave my room.

True to his word, Jesse Jackson gave me the ticket to Washington. But I had nowhere to stay. I had called the Jencos and they told me there was a Catholic retreat house which would put me up for twenty dollars a night. When tour groups came in they served meals in the dining hall, which was also included in the price. The amenities, they told me, were not outstanding. But for twenty bucks, hey . . .

They gave me the name of the nun who was in charge and I called her to make arrangements. It turned out there weren't going to be any groups staying at the retreat, so there would be no dinner, but I was welcome to sleep there. Someone would be in the building to let me in.

So I met with Jesse and the State Department people, and despite the big build-up nothing much happened. I spent the rest of the day tottering around Washington, going from office to office on my high heels. I have a bunion, and my feet kill me when I go on trips. It was a series of How Bad Do My Feet Hurt stories before I learned what kind of shoes to wear.

So I had my little suitcase and I stopped at the AP office. Of course, I didn't know anybody there very well. I was very independent, I didn't want anything from anybody, thank you very much. They asked, "Can we get you a hotel room?" and I said, no, it's taken care of, thank you.

By the end of the day my feet were so swollen and hurting so badly that I could barely take another step. I was near tears. I hadn't eaten all day and I got it into my head that I wanted a cup of coffee *in a cup.* I didn't want Styrofoam, I didn't want paper, *I wanted a cup.* In my agitated state of mind, a good solid porcelain cup was a symbol of home and reality. I needed to wrap my hands around something familiar.

Nowhere. There was a Roy Rogers, there was a Wendy's, I went into three places and none of them had anything resembling porcelain. It was locked into my mind: I want coffee in a real cup and I'm not taking anything less!

I couldn't walk another step. My feet had had it. I figured I would get a cab, go to the retreat house, and get my coffee in their sanctuary.

I caught a cab. The retreat, it turned out, was a little hard to find. The cabdriver got lost, he was driving around and around, he was going to pay phones to call people who might know how to get there. Finally he got me to the place—it was back in a cul-de-sac somewhere—dropped me off, and charged me twenty-five dollars. I found out later it was ordinarily a $2.40 fare, but the guy said twenty-five dollars and I paid it. It was just about all the money I had on me.

The retreat was dark. There was not a light on. The cabdriver had dumped me and was gone. I looked around and found I was in the middle of a neighborhood that was obviously not one of the best. I knocked on the door.

Nobody answered. I knocked again. Nobody. I knocked and knocked and knocked.

I didn't know a soul in Washington. If there had been a telephone nearby I wouldn't have known who to call, but I didn't have that problem because there was no phone in sight. I took off my shoes and wandered around the building, tapping on windows, beginning to blubber, near hysteria. I sat down on the front step and just started to lose it.

A woman opened the door.

"I thought I heard somebody out here. It suddenly occurred to me, you must be locked out."

I looked up. She didn't know me from Adam but she could see I was in bad shape.

"What can I do to help you?" she asked.

"I want a cup of coffee," I whimpered, "I want something to eat and there's nobody anywhere . . ."

She took me in and calmed me down. It turned out there was a restaurant a couple of blocks away that served coffee in real cups, and she took me there and I finally pulled myself together.

I spent the night at the retreat. If you've never taken a shower and dried yourself with brown paper towels right out of the dispenser, you've never lived. Right then and there I determined, by God, I would never go through anything like that again.

Madeleine had her baby on June 7. A girl. She named her Sulome. Terry now had a daughter he had never seen.

Because I had been on television, I started getting some phone calls that were more than just strangers being helpful; they were more than just strange. Mostly it was people claiming that they could go to the Middle East and come back with Terry, and wanting to get their expenses paid. At first I wanted to believe anyone who told me he had a way to get Terry home.

The Associated Press had been contacted by people claiming to have Terry. Their representative, the callers said, was in Cyprus, he was flying all over the Middle East, we had to meet them in Athens, we had to do this, we had to do that. Finally the AP called to say they had severed the connection with these people because it was not a productive one; nothing seemed to come from them. However, I was warned, I might get a call.

So the next day I was making cookies for vacation Bible school and Madeleine and David's sister were sitting around joking that if these people called me asking for $50,000 I'd have to tell them, "I'll just have to go on the streets because I don't have it."

The phone rang and I answered it.

The woman on the phone had a Middle Eastern accent. "We have your brother. He is all right, not to worry, he's going to be all right. We will get back to you with our instructions."

I think I said "Fine." I don't know for sure. I didn't know what to do.

These people called several times during the following weeks, often at odd hours. Normally I would have dismissed them all as the terrorist equivalent of encyclopedia salesmen, but there was the one chance in a million that they really did have Terry, and then what would I say to him? "Terry, I could have gotten you out but I didn't believe it when they called"?

The calls became so commonplace that early one morning David answered the phone and woke me. "Honey, it's for you. It's the terrorists again."

Their demands changed with every contact. Their final demand was for $50,000, break-dance records, and Levi's blue jeans. I was to drop the stuff off in Athens and then go to Damascus and pick up my brother.

I was always careful not to offend these people, or anybody else who called; you just didn't know what their connections really were. I finally told them, "I believe you, of course, but I don't have fifty thousand dollars. And the people who do have fifty thousand to give me are adamant about needing proof that you actually have my brother. They'll give me the money when you give me that proof."

That was the end of the phone calls.

Our chief contact at the State Department was a man named Bob Oakley. He was the head of the Office of Counter-Terrorism. Periodically, he arranged meetings between the State Department and the hostage families.

Just to get into the Counter-Terrorism office, you'd be faced with a reinforced steel door with a lock on the outside that someone with the proper code would have to punch numbers into. A security camera looked each of us over as we entered.

Inside, there were computer screens at the desks, and when the file drawers were open they always had a removable sign on them reminding everyone that this was an Open Secured File. Looking around as we marched to the conference room, we found we were in a virtual bunker, the inner sanctum of the war against terrorism.

The press was trying to get me to say I was mad at the State Department for their lack of action and that was why I had turned to Jesse Jackson, but I was adamant that my seeking help from him was *in addition to* what the State Department was doing. At one meeting the families were angry and griping about the State Department not doing enough to get our guys home, and I said, "Excuse me, but that doesn't go for me. I know you are doing everything you can." Bob Oakley told me, "You are the most rational family member we have ever dealt with."

They were stroking me like crazy and I was cozying right up. I just knew that I had a better grasp of the situation than anyone else in the hostage families.

Bob Oakley was a nice man. He was informed, concerned, and willing to help. I considered him almost a friend, someone who would give me information that I needed, someone I could rely on for hope. He was my source for news of Terry, he was my government at work.

Oakley was not cut from the normal State Department cloth. He had a little bit of a mountain twang to his voice, as if he came from West Virginia, and he was a plain-spoken, sincere person. He did not play games with me, did not make me think he was giving me something he wasn't. He was guarded, but he seemed actually to care.

That kind of sentiment couldn't have done him a world of good in his chosen profession. I've been told there were published reports that Bob Oakley had been considered for a particular State Department assignment and it was decided that, no, he wasn't the right person for the job because he couldn't lie as well as the other candidates. Not so good for his career but very pleasant and fortunate for me and the hostage families.

I met with Oakley many times. At one point he handed me a piece of paper with a name on it. "You will find a lot in common with this woman," he said. Her name was Penne Laingen, and her husband Bruce had been the chargé d'affaires at the American embassy in Iran when it was seized. She did indeed turn out to be a great help and comfort. Penne and Bruce have been loyal supporters of our cause and provide both advice and humor when things get bleak. I am proud to call them friends.

We knew that Terry had been kidnapped by Islamic Jihad, specifically by a man named Imad Mughniyah, a member of a Shiite fundamentalist group called the Hezbollah. The Islamic Jihad had, in return for the release of the American hostages, demanded the release of seventeen Arab prisoners being held in Kuwait. The State Department, and anyone even vaguely familiar with the situation over there, knew that the only prisoner the Hezbollah was really interested in was Mughniyah's brother-in-law, who had been sentenced to death for terrorism but had had his sentence commuted to life in prison. Mughniyah wanted his brother-in-law, I wanted my brother.

The solution seemed obvious. "Why can't you talk to Kuwait," I asked Oakley, "and see if they are willing to deal?"

"Oh, Peggy," he said as he leaned back in his chair, "we couldn't possibly do that. We don't interfere in the internal politics of another country."

"Excuse me?" I had a hard time with that one. "My tax dollars are financing rebels in Nicaragua and you are going to sit there and tell me that we don't interfere in the internal politics of another country?"

Oakley just shrugged his shoulders, as if to say, "It's my job, I have to tell you that." He seemed embarrassed.

Then came the TWA hijacking.

TWA flight No. 847 was going from Cairo to Rome with 153 passengers, including 104 Americans, when it was hijacked by two Lebanese Shiites. First they landed in Athens, then spent the next two days shuttling between Algiers and Beirut. At first President Reagan took a hard line, saying there would be no concessions, no negotiations, no linkage between the passengers on TWA flight No. 847 and any prisoners held anywhere in the world.

On the second day, after releasing nineteen passengers in Beirut and twenty-one in Algiers, the hijackers beat and then killed a U.S. Navy diver named Robert Stethem. That day the Greek government released the hijackers' accomplice, who had been captured on the ground, and the hijackers released the Greeks on board.

Within the first two days, behind the scenes, the U.S. government almost cut a deal in which the Red Cross would supervise a swap of the remaining American passengers for some three hundred Shiites held by Israel. But the hijackers got worried that the U.S. was planning a military assault on the plane and quickly flew back to Beirut.

After a week on board the airliner, the Americans, forty men—the women had been released earlier—had been taken off the Boeing 727 and hidden in strongholds and safe houses inside Lebanon. It took seventeen days of intensive negotiations, with the Syrians playing a large role, before they were released.

In the United States the crisis caused a media frenzy. Prime-time television showed the gunmen peering out the pilot's window, they showed Robert Stethem's body when it hit the tarmac. It was front-page news from day one.

The hijacking was a terrible tragedy, but I began to feel that some good would emerge from it. The same people who had hijacked TWA had kidnapped Terry, the demands were the same. There was no way, to my thinking, that the U.S. wasn't going to make a deal for all of them; they couldn't ignore the seven men already taken hostage.

On the third or fourth day of the crisis I got a call from the State Department. Our liaison there was a woman named Jackie Ratner, whose job it was to keep the families of the American hostages informed of what was going on, to meet with us, hear our ideas and concerns, and presumably pass them along further up the ladder. I liked her. Ms. Ratner said to me, "You are not to try to connect Terry and the others with the TWA passengers. They are not connected, and if you try to put them all together you will complicate the situation and prolong the captivity of the TWA passengers."

I couldn't think of much more to say than "Thank you very much." I was always thanking everybody.

This was beginning to look to me like betrayal. I thought, "This is not right. They can't seriously mean to do this."

I was glued to the tube, watching all three networks and monitoring

CNN very carefully. I had never instigated an interview but I called CNN in Atlanta, introduced myself and said, "Excuse me, but you keep talking about forty hostages. You need to understand that there are forty-seven, and seven of them have been there for a very long time." They responded by inviting me to Washington to be on their broadcast. To hell with the State Department.

I knew these forty guys were coming home. Everybody knew it. The U.S. would not let forty American citizens sit in Lebanon forever; the American people would not allow it, not with that plane on the runway and all those cameras running. It might take a few days, but this thing was so public, was such a hot news item, they were definitely coming home. Terry had been in captivity for three months already and, the more I thought about it, nothing I had seen or heard made me believe there was any progress toward getting him out. I began to get panic-stricken that they were going to leave Terry and the others behind.

I went to Washington to be on CNN and didn't get home for four days. I went to New York and didn't get back for another four. A lot of it is still a blur to me, because I was operating on sheer willpower. I was doing sixteen to twenty hours of interviews a day, everything from *Meet the Press* and *Face the Nation* to Larry King and Phil Donahue. I was on every morning show several times. I was doing local radio and television, even Brazilian TV. Everybody who asked me, I did.

It wasn't a lot of political debate. Mostly I was pleading. I was very intense. I knew I had two minutes to make my case for Terry Anderson—on some shows, only sixty seconds—and I had to do it clearly and right on the button. I couldn't afford to mess up; my brother's life was at stake.

Sometime that week I was sitting in the green room of the *Today* show watching Vice President Bush on TV saying the administration refused to rule out retaliation against the hijackers and all terrorists once the TWA passengers were home. I sat there thinking, "This is another case where Terry's life is expendable. What are they doing to us! Are they daring the captors to keep the hostages for protection? I can't believe he's saying this." If they go in and bomb the terrorists, then Terry is a dead man; either the guards will kill him or we will.''

On the air, Jane Pauley asked me, ''What did you think of what you just saw?''

I didn't stop to think. I just said, ''We bandy about the word 'terrorist,' and the true meaning is 'One who inspires terror in the hearts of others.' Well, George Bush certainly did just that to seven families when he refused to rule out retaliation.''

I was going to have to learn to be more careful. ''Peggy Say Calls George Bush a Terrorist on National TV,'' screamed the headlines.

I received excellent advice from Terry's friends through all of this. Right at the beginning, at one of the first major press conferences I attended, with everyone shouting questions and snapping at one another, a friend pulled me aside and said, ''Don't let them rile you. Think before you answer. Don't let them push you. Think about what you are saying and maintain your credibility. And more than anything else, don't be shrill.''

Afterward, when the questions were over and I had a chance to breathe, a reporter said to me, ''You know, the press really likes you, Peggy, because you answer every question as if you'd never heard it before.''

I said, ''That's because I can't remember what they asked me five minutes ago. I *am* answering them fresh.''

After a while I developed some moxie. You do something long enough, you stop being intimidated by it. I learned how to answer questions briefly and to the point. I learned what not to say, when not to offend. I started to catch on.

I was so intense I didn't think about, Here I am talking to Lesley Stahl, here I am talking to Larry King. I was so focused on getting my message across that none of that was real to me. I walked in and out of those rooms like I was delivering a package, which was a plea for my brother's life. I didn't have time to stop for a sandwich and a chat, and I was certain that these people wouldn't want to sit and chew the fat with the likes of me.

The only time I was really terrified was before some of the other hostage family members and I went on *Donahue*. I had always been an admirer of Phil Donahue and I was kind of star-struck. By this time I had lost many of my illusions about the brilliance and honor of the people I'd seen on television, and I said to myself, "Please let him be what I think he is."

He was. He was very kind and gentle. Before we went on he told us, "This is an hour-long show, but when you take out time for commercials and for talking with the audience, each of you will only have about three minutes, tops, to say what you have to say. It'll be over so fast you won't even realize that you've done it." He was absolutely right.

A young reporter from Rochester came with me to Washington to cover my odyssey. One day I was out doing a couple of shows and when I came back he told me that there were over a hundred requests for interviews under my door. On the third day he left me a note: "I'm sorry, I can't take it." And this guy was twenty-three years old.

I remember waking up somewhere to do a morning show and thinking, "I cannot get out of this bed and make my body work." And then I thought about Terry and I forgot my exhaustion and jumped into the shower.

Once, I had been going all day and knew I had to do a show that night, but for the life of me I couldn't remember what it was, just that a limousine was coming to pick me up. I had to ask the driver, "What am I doing?" He said, "The Larry King show."

We got there and there was a general in the green room reading a newspaper. He had a chestful of ribbons and I said, "Excuse me, but are you doing the Larry King show?" He said yes. "Well, my name is Peggy Say and I'm the sister of Terry Anderson. Are we supposed to be on opposite sides here?" He said, "No, honey, I'm on your side."

After the show the general turned to me and said, "Someday this hostage situation is going to rise up and haunt Ronald Reagan."

The TWA crisis was the most traumatic time for the hostage families because all the attention that the passengers got could have been given to Terry and the others months and years before. We had a good group then. Ben Weir's son John was with us, and he had been raised in Beirut. I loved to do shows with him because whenever there was a question about Middle Eastern politics, John knew all the answers. We had Ben's wife, Carol, who was a powerful speaker, and family members of other hostages, which gave us a large and well-rounded lobbyist group. Jerry Levin, who had been a correspondent in Beirut and had been kidnapped and escaped, was also with us, and he had a brilliant mind. All of us hit Washington and New York and we were available to everybody.

The morning we were getting ready to do the Donahue show we were backstage when Jerry brought in the *New York Times*. There on page one, for the first time, Secretary of State George Shultz admitted that there were forty-seven hostages, not forty, and that we wanted all of them back.

This was vindication. The media had caused this turnaround. *Our* taking our case to the media had caused it. We had won a commitment from the media and the government that these would never be the forgotten seven again.

Nineteen days into the hijacking, at one in the morning, I got a phone call from the State Department. I had committed to go to Washington the next day to be on a CBS morning show because, from all reports, it looked as though the situation was going to be resolved. The TWA hostages were supposed to get out the next day. In exchange for their freedom the Israelis had agreed—of course with U.S. blessings, though we've never admitted it—to release three hundred Shiite political prisoners. Israel never publicly admitted this either, but that's what happened. They negotiated, we negotiated, the people came out. There ended up being a delay of twenty-four hours before the passengers were released, but the next day was the target.

Our State Department liaison, Jackie Ratner, said, "Peggy, we have reason to believe that when the hostages reach Damascus, Terry and the others will be with them."

Every time something significant happened, we would all analyze what we thought *really* was happening. This time we came to the conclusion that the State Department would not call me at one in the morning merely to pass on a rumor. They must've had solid information.

We knew the hostages were not in Beirut but were probably in the Bekaa Valley. The way the State Department worded their message we figured that the entourage of TWA passengers and their captors was supposed to drive through the Bekaa into Damascus and they would pick up Terry and the others on the way.

Terry's friends in Beirut were monitoring the situation closely. One of them called me that same night. He said, "Peggy, you've been screwed."

"What are you talking about?"

"Reagan made a deal and he left out the seven."

I refused to believe it. "No," I told him, "you are wrong. Reagan was in Chicago two days ago and he told the Jenco family that they are coming out. I just got a call from the State Department telling me that they are coming out. You are way off base."

"Peggy, I am telling you. Reagan could not wait for the seven. They are not coming out."

It would have prolonged the TWA situation—probably for several days—to include the seven hostages. What this journalist on the ground in Beirut was saying was that Reagan wanted the cameras turned off the TWA hijacking *immediately*. The President didn't want to see that plane on the tarmac anymore, didn't want to be embarrassed one moment longer. The situation had begun to be compared to Jimmy Carter's Iranian hostage crisis. Reagan had forty men he could bring home that day. It would make a big splash and he would look like a hero. He said Reagan was prepared to sacrifice the safety and future of the other seven just to get the crisis over with *now* and get the press off his back. He wouldn't wait that extra few days.

I totally rejected it. Ronald Reagan was our President. He wouldn't lie to the Jenco family. He wouldn't let my brother rot just to get the cameras turned off.

We stayed up all night, kind of giddy that it was finally over with. I went to Washington with no sleep, running mostly on adrenaline. I did the CBS show and had a lot of other interview requests, but I said, "No, I'm staying in my hotel room so I can see my brother when he reaches Damascus."

A press conference had been arranged in Damascus for the released hostages. About five minutes before it was scheduled to begin, I got another call from Jackie Ratner.

"We've got a head count. Terry and the others are not there."

I was shattered. I thought, "Terry's friend was right. We've been had. I can't believe my own government did this to me."

But I had faith that the media would keep on them, would make the government produce the forty-seven hostages they had committed to produce.

The press conference was a madhouse. The men were glad to be free. I felt good for them, it had been a terrible seventeen days. But it had been 106 days for Terry. And counting.

When the press conference was over, I started flicking the dial, watching the news reports. Everywhere I looked they were saying, "Take your yellow ribbons down, folks, the crisis is over. The hostages are free."

Within twenty-four hours we were yesterday's news again. We were right back where we started. Nobody wanted to hear about the seven men who were still over there. People had been hostaged to death.

I sat in my hotel room and cried all day. Jack Kirby of CBS, who were paying for the room since I had appeared on their show, called right after the press conference and I was just sobbing. He said, "Is there anything I can do to help?" I was too destroyed to tell him to remember my brother. He said, "Look, you stay in that room just as long as you need to, you do what you have to do and CBS will foot the bill." I will never forget his kindness.

I did stay for three days trying to generate some continuing interest, but nobody wanted to hear it. I contacted political people, journalists, everyone I could think of, but it was all over. I finally went home, exhausted and confused.

What were we going to do? I talked with the other families and for a couple of weeks we were all in a daze. We couldn't think, we couldn't act. We all just kind of sat there.

I'll never forget a telephone interview with a radio station in Tampa. The producer had hooked me up and asked if I wanted to listen to the show before I went on. I said yes. The host introduced the upcoming topics. "In the first portion of the show we will be discussing Florida seals. In the second portion we will be discussing fleas—if you were a dog, you'd care. And in the third we will be talking to Peggy Say, the sister of Terry Anderson." When the producer came back on the line I said to him, "That just gives you an indication of how quickly we have fallen. A week ago it was Phil Donahue and Larry King, *Face the Nation* and *Meet the Press*. This week I have third billing to fleas and seals."

CHAPTER

4

WE REGATHERED OUR FORCES. WE HAD TO. WHAT ELSE COULD WE
do? Within a month we were pushing hard in Washington for what we
called a Day on the Hill.

All of the hostage families came in and we held a major press
conference, followed by a panel discussion. The room was packed,
standing room only, and I was so gratified. We had invited congressmen, senators, State Department people, the media. We wanted to
know what was being done to get our fellows home. It was every bit
that simple. We wanted some answers.

I had been chosen as moderator of the panel discussion. I was so
flustered and apprehensive about having to run this show that I was
concentrating on my written remarks more than on what was happening around me. As the room filled and I recognized some major political figures being seated, I became even more nervous.

As the program started, each of the political dignitaries said a few
words about the hostage situation. I was only half-listening to most of

them but as one man spoke the words gradually began to penetrate. This guy went on a tirade, berating the "madmen and barbarians" who had kidnapped the hostages. I was horrified, and before he had finished his last sentence I was at the microphone trying to put as much distance as possible between the hostage families and those remarks.

I told the audience that this was an opportunity for the families to appeal to, not alienate the captors, and that it wasn't in anybody's best interest to stand up on national television and call them names.

I sat down shaking. Didn't this guy get it? The captors could kill the hostages any time, any day, on a whim.

"Who was that idiot?" I asked hostage David Jacobsen's son Eric, seated beside me.

"That was Congressman Robert Dornan. He and Congressman Mervyn Dymally organized this event."

This was going to be a tough day. Dornan was a strong supporter, but he'll always be "Bullet Bob" to me.

I was doing my best not to be intimidated. Politicians were a new breed for me; I'd really only seen them on television, where they all sound very studious and dignified. Hearing them talk like regular people surprised me.

Bob Oakley and other State Department representatives were sitting in a row, and they took a lot of heat. They were in charge not only of getting the hostages home but also of us, our briefings, our information. And they weren't doing us much good. Congressmen Claude Pepper and Norman Mineta had taken an interest in our cause, and Mineta turned to Oakley and said, "Bob, do you think these people are mushrooms, that you can keep them in the dark and feed them shit? Help them out."

Pepper added, "Come on, Bob, give them their people back."

Oakley said to me, "Peggy, we don't have them. If we had them we would give them back. The bad guys have them. Try to keep that in mind."

I didn't have to do a lot of moderating. The discussion took on a life of its own. The meeting went on for several hours.

We were pressing for a meeting with President Reagan, but Reagan was refusing. I had just read *All Fall Down,* a book by Gary Sick about the Iranian hostage crisis in which President Carter laments ever having met the hostage families; they personalized the situation for him and he could not forget it. I was convinced that President Reagan was not meeting with us because he knew that these hostages were going to die and he didn't want to know any of us, to face us, to confront our pain.

At the press conference I was asked about the prospects of our actually meeting with the President, about why it was so important. What I wanted to say was that I wanted to meet Mr. Reagan face to face because I wanted him to have to look at me and have to take that image—a *real* person with *real* loss and *real* pain—to bed with him every night. What I ended up saying was, "I want Reagan to sleep with my face."

You could hear the titters in the press room. It was one of those things where, okay, it's done, it's said, I've put my foot in it. I got a lot of razzing from the other hostage families. As embarrassing as it was, all I could do was laugh with the rest of them.

Our next stop on the Day on the Hill was a closed-door meeting with the House Foreign Affairs Committee. This was the first time I got a full dose of rough-edged politics.

The families had compiled a list of requests we were submitting to the government which we thought would be constructive steps toward bringing the hostages home. One of these requests was that the United States ask our ally Israel to stop shelling the Bekaa Valley. The hostages were believed to be held in the Bekaa and we thought that a limited cease-fire would be taken as a positive sign by the captors.

Well, Congressman Tom Lantos of California just about peeled us alive. He was scathing, furious. He just screamed at us for about five minutes straight, then stood up and stormed out of the room.

There was a stunned silence. We had come before this committee of Congress with all good intentions, with serious needs and concerns.

"Excuse me," I said finally, "but I want to make sure that I understand what Mr. Lantos just said to us." Congressmen Lee Hamilton and Dante Fascell sat in front of me, looking as stunned as I was. "If I'm not mistaken," I said, "what he said to us was that six million

Jews died in the Holocaust, so what the hell are we griping about seven lousy Americans for.''

Lantos's aide leaned into his microphone and said, ''I think you are doing the congressman a great disservice.''

''Well, I'm sorry,'' I told him, ''but I think the congressman just did us a great disservice. He practically accused us of being anti-Semitic, and that has nothing to do with the issue here. And,'' I said, ''he wasn't even gentleman enough to stay and let us defend ourselves.''

We were just innocent hostage families with no power at all, trying to get our fathers and brothers and husbands home, trying to find some way to get our government to move. I couldn't believe this man had attacked us.

Dante Fascell gave us hell in a much more restrained sort of way. He said, ''Look, if you think that this government has not already spoken to Kuwait, you're crazy. You can count on it.'' He spent several minutes telling us sternly, but with obvious concern, that the American government doesn't just sit back and allow its citizens to be kidnapped without making every attempt to get them back.

When he had finished I leaned into the mike and said, ''Mr. Fascell, I have the feeling that we have just had our butt chewed and I want you to know that I appreciated it very much. You are the first person who's talked honestly to us in this whole city.''

He just started laughing. Later he dropped me a note signed ''Dante.'' I felt I had made a friend.

But that's all any of us wanted. This was our government, and we wanted to feel protected. Talk to us. Tell us what in God's name is going on here; tell us that you are going to do something about it.

When the meeting was over I broke down in tears. I had promised myself I wouldn't, but I did. It was the first time anybody had yelled at me in public, and I was very intimidated by congressmen and senators. This was the big time.

My family thought I was getting far too much attention. The media no longer called to speak to Dad or Rich or Judy, they wanted to talk to me.

Dad had this habit of leaning up against a doorjamb and scratching his back like a bear. He'd just lean there and slowly twist like he was alone in the forest. I was exhausted one evening, having just finished cleaning the house, and was sitting in my chair watching CNN and worrying about having to fly to the United Nations the next day to meet the Secretary General, Javier Pérez de Cuéllar. My father came in behind me, began his scratching and said, "Well, I read in the paper today where Terry Anderson's sister is doing everything she can to get his release. I'm sure your brother Rich would enjoy reading that."

Mind you, I had never raised my voice to my father or mother. I had listened to my brothers Rich and Bruce shout back at our parents many times, but I could never get up enough nerve to do it. But this just hit me. I jumped out of the chair and whirled around at him and started screaming.

"What the hell do you want from me! You people want me to travel, you want me to go everywhere, do everything to get Terry home, and then I come home and I have to listen to grief from you? You think this is a picnic, you get your fat butt up to the U.N. You make that trip and see how much damn fun this is."

My father looked ashen, like he'd picked on the wrong guy in a bar. "Okay, I will," he blurted.

I didn't go. He and Madeleine and the baby made the trip, and by the end of the travel and meetings and waiting and speaking, he was exhausted, dragging his sagging behind around like a flabby field hand at the end of a harvest. He got back to Batavia, collapsed in an armchair, and told me, "I cannot do this anymore."

Rich was even more angry. He was the older brother, and he thought I was stealing his thunder. He would call me up, drunk, and tell me all the terrible things I was doing.

Rich was convinced I was on some kind of a big star trip. Finally, when he gave me a particularly hard time, I told him, "Okay, you get your butt to Washington, you're going on this trip with me. You're going to see what I have to do."

"Fine." Anything I could do, he could do. That was Rich.

He met me in Washington for a huge press conference with Jesse Jackson. It was one of those bizarre times when the press was more interested in what I had to say than in Jesse. The press conference was held at an airport, and when Jesse got off his plane and headed toward the microphones he found that most of them were pointed at me. I was surprised; he was shocked. Gracious, but shocked.

So there we were, Jesse Jackson on one side of me, Rich on the other, the press out in front of us, and, as always, smelling blood. They started shouting at us and shoving microphones in our faces, and Rich just kind of evaporated. I'd never actually seen somebody sidle before, but Rich did a little get-me-out-of-here two-step and faded into the scenery.

We spent the rest of the day shuttling between embassies, me talking, Rich not talking. By the end of the day he was dead on his feet. He hit the pillow with his clothes on.

The next morning he told me, "I could not do what you do. There is no way that I could do it. I want you to know from here on in, you have my support, and I will see to it that you have the support of the rest of the family."

From that point on, Rich and I became closer and closer. I was trying not to bring the Terry Anderson hostage situation into my own household; I didn't want to be so totally preoccupied that I deprived David and my children of the attention they needed. So Rich was the one I would talk to. We talked on the phone every day.

I was concerned about his drinking. For some reason he began having trouble holding down his liquor. He would drink and get sick. That was a first. He didn't mind the throwing up so much, it was the fact that he couldn't drink like he used to that was bothering him.

I told him, "Rich, I want you to do something. Every time you reach for a drink, just picture Terry's face and decide which is more important to you, helping your brother or drinking that drink."

It only partly worked.

I was in Nashville, having been invited to speak to the national convention of the RTND, the Radio and Television News Directors, when the hotel room phone rang. David picked it up, spoke to someone, and turned to me. "A hostage has been released."

"It's Ben Weir. I know it's Ben Weir, I can feel it in my bones."

On September 9, 1985, the captors released Rev. Benjamin Weir. I had closely observed Carol Weir, Ben's wife, during the six months since Terry had been kidnapped. Ben had been taken sixteen months before, and Carol was on the ragged edge, ready to lose it. In fact, I had been praying that if only one hostage could be released, let it be Ben Weir, because otherwise, I felt, Carol was not going to make it.

But Ben didn't show up for several days. Carol Weir called the networks but they wouldn't believe her. I got a call from someone at NBC who said, "Peggy, we just had this strange call from someone who says she is Carol Weir. She says that Reverend Weir is out. Do you know anything about this?"

"I believe Ben is out," I told them. "I don't know where he is or what has happened to him, but all my instincts tell me that Ben is out there."

Carol had never had an easy time with the press, she was not comfortable with them, so it did seem out of character that she would call them herself, especially without telling the other families first.

But she had. Carol had found out that Reagan was planning to announce her husband's freedom at a big press conference, at which the President would take full credit for masterminding the release. After sixteen months of sitting through all of his talk and nonaction, she couldn't let Reagan get away with it. She called all the networks, trying to take the wind out of Reagan's sails, but nobody believed her.

Ben Weir had a strange trip out. The U.S. military kept him under wraps for a couple of days in Virginia Beach, Virginia, having his brains picked. We didn't even know he was out for sure until he was already on U.S. soil. Bam, he was in Virginia Beach, on his way to Washington, D.C.

One of his first acts in Washington was to hold a news conference at the National Presbyterian Church. It was a free-for-all. It was our first hostage release and we didn't know what to expect.

The return of a hostage is a newshound's ritual. The crush of people is overwhelming, the cameramen are all vying for the best angles, the correspondents for the best quotes. The newly released captive is the latest hot commodity. For those of us with a personal interest in the situation there is a combination of envy, rage, and comfort: envy, that another family has their loved one home; rage at all of these strangers trying to get a piece of a person they hadn't shown the slightest interest in freeing even one day before; and comfort, because if all these people are so hot after this hostage, then surely they must still care about mine.

People handle their feelings in different ways. Through all of his captivity to this point I could not think about Terry in a concrete way at all, because if I did I would get incredibly upset. I could relate to his situation on an intellectual level, but if I started feeling for him I was a goner. Madeleine and I had a problem about that because she wanted to talk about Terry and I didn't. I finally had to say to her, "Madeleine, I cannot do it. You are going to have to find somebody else to talk to about him because I can't think about what's happening to him and still function."

The only concrete information I had up to that time came from Jerry Levin, who had been taken and held by the same people who kidnapped Terry. We gave interviews together often, and whenever Jerry would start to describe the conditions under which he had lived I would lose it. It became almost Pavlovian; he would talk and I would cry. Jerry felt bad about what it did to me, but he felt—and he was right—that the details of captivity needed to be made public. Isolation, chains, blindfolds, despair; it was just too horrible to think about.

The first question they asked Ben Weir was, "Have you seen the other hostages?" He answered, "I left them only two days ago."

I was so relieved. This was the first person I had heard who had seen and touched and talked to Terry since he dropped off the face of the earth the previous March, and he was saying that Terry was all right. It was as if someone had shot me full of tranquilizers. I hardly heard anything anyone said from then on.

When the Weirs left the stage, the press turned their attention to us. Usually I was intense, trying to keep on my toes, to make sure every point got brought home. But this time I was almost in a daze.

My brother Rich noticed. He took me aside and told me, "You're not handling the press very well."

"Who cares," I said. "Terry is okay. I can think about him now because I know that he's okay."

After the press conference Rev. Weir had scheduled a private time for the families, and we finally were able to find out how my brother and the others were living, how they were doing. We met for an hour and a half at the Methodist Center, right across from the Supreme Court.

It was like going to church. I was transported by Rev. Weir's inner strength and spirituality. His serene confidence, his compassionate understanding and sense of purpose, held me in awe.

They had all lived together, Ben Weir told us, and the conditions were not good. Five of them—Terry, Ben, Father Martin Jenco, David Jacobsen, and Tom Sutherland—were held in one eight-by-ten-foot basement room. They were in chains and they were blindfolded, but they had each other.

Terry had been totally traumatized when he was brought in. For several days he just sobbed. Everything that he'd believed in—his faith in the power and safety of the press, in the Lebanese, in God—had failed him. The prisoners were told they could not talk to each other, that if they made the slightest noise they would be shot. Terry was chained to a cot, and when he shifted his body to try to get comfortable the metal would creak and he would curse the bed, terrified the guards were going to kill him.

But even terrified, Terry was defiant. The guards would interrogate him, trying to get him to name the other newsmen who lived in his building, and all Terry would say was "Fuck you." Terry had remained a Marine and a hard-ass.

Ben Weir understood Arabic, and he said that by the time of his release the captors had come to a grudging respect for Terry. In fact, until he was told differently, Ben thought Terry had orchestrated his release.

The head captor was a man called Hajj. As the hostages understood it, "Hajj" was a Muslin title of respect given to those who had made the pilgrimage to Mecca. They were told that in the case of their head captor it was in honorary title; he had never made the trip.

Terry had asked to meet with him. The jailers were the hostages' day-to-day keepers, but Hajj was clearly the man in charge, and he would come around only once in a while. Terry requested a meeting with Hajj and asked Ben to be the interpreter.

Terry presented Hajj with this scenario: Release one hostage and be a hero.

The release of a hostage, Terry told Hajj, would focus world attention on the Shiite cause. It would allow them to be humanitarians where their enemies were barbarians. Terry said that he himself would be the best candidate for release because, being a newsman, he had the greatest access to the media. Plus, he said, they still had four other hostages to use in trade for the Kuwaiti captives.

Hajj said he would take the idea under consideration. Terry thought he was on his way home.

A short time later Hajj came back and told the hostages, "One of you is going to be released." Terry had convinced him. "You are to vote on whoever leaves," Hajj said, "but you are to leave Terry Anderson and Tom Sutherland out of the voting."

Father Jenco and Rev. Weir prayed on it. All the hostages discussed it. There was a lot of heat on the subject. When Hajj returned and asked for their decision they told him, "We have decided that we want Terry Anderson to be the man who is released."

Hajj was not moved. "Because you cannot follow orders," he said, "we will tell you who will be released. It is Pastor Benjamin Weir."

Ben Weir said that when Hajj told them Terry would not be going, Terry went nuts. When his fellow prisoners selected him, Terry had allowed himself to believe he was going to be freed, and now he was not. He lost control, began to shake, pounded his head against the basement's stone wall. Father Jenco walked over to him, put his arm around his shoulders, and said something softly into his ear. Terry calmed down immediately. He just had to accept that the man released was not going to be him.

So here was Ben Weir, only days out of being chained to a bed in a basement in Lebanon, sitting in a church in Washington, D.C., and we were just devouring every little anecdote we could squeeze out of this poor guy. The other families were there too—the Jencos, the Jacobsens—and they were doing the same thing. These stories were food, they were sustenance. Our concentration was unbelievable; we didn't want to miss a syllable, a breath.

Ben had brought out letters for the other hostage families from their loved ones, who were desperate to get firsthand news. I hadn't received anything, and when I asked Ben why he seemed totally bewildered. He explained that he hadn't known but assumed that Madeleine had remained in Beirut to work for Terry's release. He had given our letter to a trusted Lebanese friend to hand-carry to the AP office there. Ben's eyes glistened with tears when I told him that the letter had never been delivered.

After the meeting we adjourned to a restaurant in Georgetown. We were a large, noisy, diverse group, probably thirty in all. Our tension had lifted, we had gotten our questions in, and we began to get giddy. It was the sense of freedom; Ben Weir was free, next it could be Father Jenco, or David, or Terry.

We got a phone call: we could have a meeting with Vice President Bush.

Astonishingly, my brother Rich took charge. He was the liaison with the White House on this one. He told them, "Well, we are going to have a discussion, 'cause we don't know if we want a meeting with Vice President Bush."

The man on the other end of the line was next to sputtering. "What are you saying? You don't want to see the Vice President?"

Fact was, we weren't sure we did. In that room there were many different opinions. Some people felt that by foisting us off on the Vice President, who clearly didn't carry a lot of weight, the White House was just trying to get us off Reagan.

At the same time, we knew how important it was that we maintain our image with the press, and if we rejected such a high-level meeting—whether we expected anything good to come from it or not—it might be seen as sour grapes. I mean, how could we refuse to see the Vice President?

This went on for hours, and we couldn't agree on anything. Phone calls went back and forth to the White House. People were getting impatient.

Finally we called and said okay, with conditions. We said, "We will attend the meeting with Vice President Bush with the stipulation that this is *in addition to,* not in place of, a meeting with President Reagan." The White House agreed, and we all trooped in.

I was about to meet the Vice President of the United States and what I was most worried about was my clothes.

Before this trip to Washington I had gone shopping at the local Zayre's. We had been pushing for a meeting with Mr. Reagan and, who could tell, it just might happen. Money was certainly an issue with me; I was trying to buy an outfit and I had all of twenty dollars to do it with. Still, I wanted something new for the occasion, not something borrowed.

So I was looking and looking and couldn't find anything, when finally a salesgirl came up to me and said, "Can I help you?"

"Well, I'm looking for a simple dark suit," I told her. "I've got twenty dollars to spend."

"What's the occasion?" she asked.

"I'm going to meet with the President."

That stopped her. "Excuse me?" She backed away from me like I must be demented.

I finally found a suit, but as the time for the Bush meeting grew closer I was still dressed in slacks and a sweater. With all the discussing and arguing over tactics, it was too late to go back to the hotel and change. Everybody was saying, "Oh, Peggy, it's fine, it's fine." But I felt very underdressed for the occasion. When was I ever going to meet the Vice President of the United States again, and how could I explain how I looked?

(Frugal me, later I went and returned the suit.)

In front of the White House a reporter asked me, "How are you going to feel about meeting Bush after you called him a terrorist on national television?"

I said, "I'm going to be embarrassed, how do you think I'm going to feel? It's easy to call somebody names when you're not face to face with him."

There were about twenty of us when we walked into the Roosevelt Room, which is the West Wing conference room right across the hall from the Oval Office. President Reagan had had the room decorated in Teddy Roosevelt style, with Rough Riders sculpture and various artifacts of T.R., whom he admired greatly.

We got the whole treatment: Secret Service men all around us,

National Security Adviser Bud McFarlane, Anti-Terrorism chief Bob Oakley, various members of the State Department and other unidentified branches of the government packing the place.

Vice President Bush entered with a flourish. Carol, John, and Ben Weir were closest to him, with the rest of us fanned out in rows of chairs to the Vice President's left. I was two or three rows away. The room was close and we were ringed by government security people with their walkie-talkies crackling.

Pictures were taken. In the one of me shaking hands with Mr. Bush, Rich is in the background with a big grin on his face because he didn't know what the man was going to say to me. Bush didn't say anything then. He sat down on a straight-backed chair. It was all very formal, as if we were supposed to be quiet in the face of this impressive array of authority.

But it didn't work. We were fit to be tied. Number one, we hadn't gotten our meeting with Reagan. He had time to spent with Little League baseball teams but he couldn't meet with the families of American men who were being held in chains by murderous terrorists. Number two, we were listening to Rev. Ben Weir saying, "Those terrorists are going to kill the hostages!"

Rev. Weir didn't know what had prompted his captors to release him. He had said as much to the press. All he knew was that Terry Anderson had suggested a prisoner release in return for publicity about the Shiites' position, and he felt he had to come through.

As we told him of unfulfilled promises and our real displeasure at the government's lack of action, the Vice President seemed to sink lower and lower into his chair. Eric Jacobsen said to me later, "I wanted to slap him one and tell him, 'Sit up straight, you're the Vice President of the United States!' "

Rev. Weir repeated heatedly, "If you don't do something, the hostages are going to die!"

The Vice President gathered himself and retorted sharply, "I don't care *what* you think. I'm telling you that we are responsible for you sitting in that chair today."

Ben, who is such a soft-spoken, kindly man, was bewildered and quite taken aback. He was sure it was thanks to Terry he had gotten out. But he was only a couple of days out of confinement, and this was the Vice President of the United States he was talking to. You could see him blink; well, gee, maybe they did do something.

Of course, no one in that room would tell us any details of what it was they were supposed to have done.

My brother Rich, who had no trouble being belligerent, was getting pretty peeved and I was trying to keep him calm. But he was right to be angry. I turned to Mr. Bush and accused him of not caring about the hostages.

"How can you accuse me of not caring," he shot back at me. "I am a Christian man."

"Excuse me, Mr. Vice President," I said curtly, "but where I come from, you don't tell people you're a Christian, you *show* them. And I will tell you where you didn't have a very Christian attitude.

"First, when we got death threats, when the terrorists said they were going to hang my brother, the State Department told me not to make it public. And I didn't. All we wanted was a picture of you with the families that we could have sent to Beirut to show the captors that we were doing what they told us to do, which was to pressure our government. You wouldn't even pose for a picture with us.

"Second, your State Department told me that my brother was coming out with the TWA people, and I was by myself in a hotel room when one of your peons picked up the phone to tell me that my brother was not coming out. The Christian thing for you to do would have been to pick up that phone yourself."

"Well," he said lamely, "maybe we have made mistakes." He gave us platitudes and hand gestures. "Doing everything we can. Promise you we're working on this. Working behind the scenes."

"If you had not made major mistakes you wouldn't today be facing an angry mob," I told him, "and that's exactly what you've got on your hands."

It was an awful meeting. They offered us nothing, and we had no power to make them move.

The press was waiting outside, and we had to put a pretty face on it. You can't go out on the White House lawn and bitch and cry; we'd just had a meeting with the second highest man in the United States government, what more did we want?

An odd thing happened. As angry as I was, I had just met the Vice

President. I'm an average American, I guess, and I wanted to believe him so badly that I came out and thought, "He promised me they would do everything they could. Silly me, I must have misunderstood this whole thing; they really are doing something, I must just have missed it."

But my brother Rich got off the best line of the day. They stuck a camera in his face and asked him, "How did it go? How do you feel?" He said, "Well, I've been stroked but I'm not purring."

CHAPTER

5

I BEGAN TO GO TO WASHINGTON, D.C., ON A FAIRLY REGULAR BASIS, which was hard for me because I am deathly afraid of flying. I get the shakes, I can hardly breathe, I'm a total wreck. I'd rather face a lion than get on a plane, but there was nothing I could do about it; if I wanted Terry home I had to talk to the people in charge, and the people in charge were in Washington.

By this time I had made many friends, and they were always on top of things. They went out of their way to learn exactly who the people were in that city who I should see. For instance, if I was scheduled to do a network show and had twenty-four hours in the capital they would do the legwork and make telephone calls and set up appointments with as many people as I could possibly talk to. If there was a visiting dignitary from a country that even breathed in the direction of Iran or Lebanon, they would call and arrange a meeting for me.

Nobody ever refused to see me. Some were more agreeable than others, but everyone did respond. I would simply make my case: ''This is my brother who is in captivity. I know that you don't have anything to do with this, but is there any way you can help me, what advice do you have for me?''

On one of my earliest trips I met with the Syrian ambassador to the United States, Rafic Jouejati. Syria's role in the hostage situation has always been very much undefined. Are they or are they not responsible for the hostage-taking? Do they or do they not have influence with the captors? Do they know where the hostages are? It has never been clear.

I was trying very hard to establish a relationship with Ambassador Jouejati, but when I first met him the ambassador had been quite formal. He had sat with me in the embassy anteroom and offered me a tiny cup of Arab coffee, which will grow hair on your chest. He had been proper without holding out much hope.

But when I began to get calls from the people claiming to hold Terry and who wanted $50,000 and a stack of Levi's in return for him, I thought, ''This is a good excuse to get in and see Jouejati. Maybe he'll tell me something.''

I was hoping that Syria did indeed have influence, that they might even be responsible. At least then I would be talking to the right people. I called and said, ''Mr. Ambassador, I am coming to Washington and I was wondering if you would see me. I have just been in contact with a group that claims to hold Terry.''

''Oh, yes, come see me,'' the ambassador said quickly. ''Can you be at my office tomorrow?'' He seemed quite excited. I didn't mention that the deal was falling apart.

When I arrived at the embassy he ushered me immediately into his office, his inner sanctum. This time he offered me a *large* cup of coffee. I must be on to something, I thought.

Ambassador Jouejati was excited. He started speaking to me quickly, asking me what had happened, what did I know? It occurred to me, this man desperately wants these people to be the kidnappers. I said to him, ''Mr. Ambassador, I was forced to conclude that these people are not truly connected.''

He was disappointed. He told me, ''If you ever are contacted again, you tell them that Syria will give them anything within reason to get those hostages out of there.''

This was good news; here was a country that wanted to help release my brother and the rest of the men in captivity. But the bad news was that, contrary to suspicion, Syria obviously did not have influence over the kidnappers, otherwise they would not be asking me for my contacts. So now we had an ally but no leads.

The State Department's advice to us had been to totally rule out Iran. We didn't know at the time—though the State Department clearly did—that the whole situation was controlled out of Iran. We didn't know the groups or their connections or alliances; we didn't know anything. The State Department told us that Iran was unapproachable, that we were not to approach them in any way. We did as we were told.

The State Department explained that they would like the Syrians to be the people the U.S. dealt with in the Middle East because they felt that Syria's President Hafez Assad was probably the most rational character on the horizon and they surely did not want to have to deal with Ayatollah Khomeini.

I would go to Washington and see whatever politicians agreed to see me. I would visit the Middle Eastern embassies—the Lebanese embassy, the Algerian, the Syrian—and plead my case. They were always very open, it's just that nobody could help me. But I kept at it. I figured I would keep going back until someday somebody would come up with an answer.

The Associated Press had generously agreed to underwrite some of my expenses. They paid my hotel and travel and telephone bills. Every time I made a trip they would give me expense money, which I used very judiciously. I did not want to be extravagant with the AP's money; I did not want to in any way embarrass Terry.

A local television company, Genesse County Cablevision, had produced a half-hour special called *Visions of Hope*. They had interviewed family members, friends of Terry's, Jesse Jackson, and others, and told the story of Terry and the other hostages. The program was beautifully done and at the end they ran a request for donations to the Terry Anderson Fund. Beautifully done or not, it was still a public appeal for money and very hard for me to do.

Copies of the tape were made available to anyone asking for one, and a copy was sent to the Associated Press in New York. The program generated many generous donations and I think it may have had something to do with AP's eventual funding of my trips; they may have felt that it really didn't help their image for Terry's family to have to go begging.

I began to write to world figures. I wrote to Sheik Mohammed Hussein Fadlallah, the spiritual leader of the Shiite sect that kidnapped my brother, asking him to intercede on humanitarian grounds. I wrote to General Mustafa Tlass, the Syrian minister of defense.

My sister Judy said to me one day, "You write to people like you actually think that they're going to read what you write."

I said, "Judy, what have I got to lose?"

That fall, Madeleine decided to move to England to be near her sister. I fully understood the need to be near family during times of crisis, so we reluctantly kissed Sulome good-bye.

Someone phoned a Western news agency in Beirut and announced that the hostages had been executed, that their bodies could be found in a burned-out cola factory in West Beirut. Of course, everybody panicked. Within hours of that statement, a packet of letters was thrown at the feet of a guard in front of the AP's Beirut office.

8 Nov 85

My Dearest Madeleine, & all my family,

Once again, our captors are allowing us to write to you, as well as to the President & others in hopes that perhaps we & you can persuade someone to break this deadlock. . . .

Madeleine, my love, my heart, I saw our daughter on TV the other night & I cried for joy. I only saw her for 2 or 3 seconds, enough to notice your black hair & beautiful, bright eyes. But I can't describe how it felt to end months of not knowing. . . .

Keeping occupied is our main problem. It's the only way to keep away the depression. I miss you terribly. I didn't think it was possible to hurt this much. . . .

I have been seeing bits & pieces of news about Peg & Judy & Dad &

their efforts to get someone to do something—it's about the only encouragement we get. I love you all for it. . . . I would like to see us all together again at least once—Dad, Rich, Peg, Bruce, Jack & Judy & all the grandkids we could gather. Such joy that would be! . . .

Reagan says he will not negotiate with terrorists. Where does that leave us? . . . Our captors say they've done their best to settle this peacefully, but the U.S. simply says nothing—publicly or privately. However distasteful it might be, Reagan must negotiate if he cares at all about our well-being.

We finally got word that Reagan would meet with us in late November.

It looked like it was intended to be simply a photo opportunity. The President would breeze in, tell everybody how sorry he was, and breeze out again. And that would be the end of that.

But I felt it was important that the government understand that we had a lot of credible people in and behind these families. We settled on Paul Jacobsen, the son of hostage David Jacobsen, to be our spokesperson at this meeting. We wrote down a list of what we wanted the government to do for the hostages, and we brought the President a yellow ribbon.

I knew I had only a couple of minutes with Mr. Reagan and I had to make a believer out of him. I didn't want him to walk away from me not knowing who Terry Anderson is: he's a person I want you to think about. He's not just a hostage, he's not an issue, he's a human being and he's chained to an iron cot, blindfolded, in a basement in Lebanon twenty-four hours a day.

We got the full treatment again. The Roosevelt Room, the ring of government personnel, the security detail with their walkie-talkies. We were served coffee in beautiful little china cups. It was all very impressive, very scripted.

Reagan came in, shook everybody's hand, and then sat down at the table directly across from me. (I was ready to sit down at the end but all the family members said, "Oh, no, you're the one who wants him to sleep with your face. You're sitting right in front of him.") He started talking. "I want you to know that I really care about these hostages. We are doing everything in our power to get your loved ones home. We are working behind the scenes for their release. Please believe me.''

Then he made some remark about Nancy waiting in the car and got up to go. It had been no more than four minutes since he made his entrance. I had to bite my lip to keep from blurting out that my brother had been waiting in a basement in Beirut for a very long time.

''Uh, excuse us, Mr. President,'' I said. Chairs scraped, there was a moment of confusion and a small bubble of commotion. ''We have waited a long time for this meeting. Would you please listen to what we have to say?'' The President seemed surprised. He sat back down in his seat as Paul Jacobsen read our list of requests and suggestions.

But Reagan wasn't listening. He had been primed, he knew exactly who I was: I was the troublemaker right across from him, and he was going all out with the eye contact, trying to appeal to me silently in spite of the fact that Paul was talking.

He knew he needed to get through to me and the way he did it was through his eyes. Without speaking he showed a real sense of compassion. I expected the tears to roll any minute.

I felt so sorry for him. I felt, ''Oh, how badly I have misjudged this man.''

I looked into his eyes and I believed him. This man, I told myself, really does care.

And I wanted to believe him. I wanted to believe that my country and my President were caring and honorable and would be there for me when I needed them.

On the other hand, the man was an actor. This had always been his strong point. He was emoting so much he almost dissolved in tears. And for all his assurances, we still didn't have the foggiest notion of what he meant by ''quiet diplomacy'' and ''working behind the scenes.'' We were supposed to take that on faith.

I bought it hook, line, and sinker. Again. I didn't want another disappointment.

Our yellow ribbon did go up on the White House door.

I took a lot of criticism from people who were adamantly anti-Reagan when I said, ''My feeling is that this man is sincere, he cares, he is going to do everything he can.'' I just wanted to believe it so badly.

When Reagan left, the meeting was turned over to Bud McFarlane and his staff. The families were briefed, allowed to ask questions and given answers for well over an hour. I didn't know it at the time, but I was told later that this unusual largesse was a deliberate attempt by the people who were running the show to miss the evening news. The whole White House press corps was waiting outside for us, but by the time we could speak to them their deadlines had passed. I still had a lot to learn about how the system worked.

Bud McFarlane was an impressive man. I had seen him previously at the meeting with the Vice President and he had been an extremely stern-looking character, but at this meeting he was patient, informative, and compassionate. There were a lot of family members present, and most of them were naïve as to the international politics of the situation. That was okay; they didn't have to understand the Middle East, they only wanted their loved ones out of there, and they wanted to know what anybody was doing about it. Mr. McFarlane didn't talk down to these people; he very patiently explained everything.

He told us the government was involved in several "initiatives." He couldn't tell us the details, he said, because that might compromise their success. But he did say that the government was pursuing all kinds of different avenues with many different countries, trying to bring diplomatic pressure, trying to encourage other countries to offer enticements which the U.S. government could not. Our government's policy was non-negotiation—"We do not negotiate with terrorist nations" was almost a password, a State Department mantra—but they were not above encouraging our allies to meet some of the captors' demands. It seemed like double-talk to me—I mean, who's kidding who; our allies got most of their supplies from us, and whatever they were giving away was at our request—but the government employees around the table seemed to take it extremely seriously.

During the meeting there were questions which needed more specific clarification. Several times Mr. McFarlane turned to his right and said, "Ollie, do you want to explain this?"

Lieutenant Colonel Oliver North would talk us through the details.

Mr. North was dressed in a dark suit, dark tie. He didn't get up and make a major speech or anything. He didn't run the meeting. But I did notice the government men around the table deferring to him.

Now, this was a meeting that included a dozen or so civilians, and I understood that with so large a group we would not be given confidential information because there was too great a possibility of its leaking out. On occasion that sort of thing did happen. But Ollie North seemed to be in command of the facts, and I thought he was more open with us than he probably should have been. I think he, and all of the men at that table, were trying to convince us that, yes, they really were making every effort to get our fellows home. I took note of his name. Here was a guy who was involved, here was a guy who seemed accessible. He wasn't a vice president or a national security adviser; he was a hack, just like the rest of us, except he had his hands in everything.

At the end of the session, a niece of one of the hostages found herself standing beside the National Security Adviser. She had heard a lot that day and was trying to absorb it all. "Excuse me, Mr. McFarlane," she asked meekly, "do you work for Mr. North?"

The holidays are very important to me. I try to gather my family—it's always at my house because I love to cook for them on these occasions—but it means a lot of cooking and cleaning and preparation. Christmas of 1985 was no different.

Reporters kept calling up and wanting to come to the house and document our Christmas Without Terry. They'd all ask, "It's the holiday season and your brother is a hostage in a strange part of the world. Aren't you depressed?" And I'd think to myself, "Well, hell, I wasn't before you started asking me." But I was always courteous on the outside.

I had learned by then that the media was truly a two-edged sword. I desperately needed them to keep the hostage issue alive, and knew I couldn't simply deal with them when it pleased me to do so. I tried very hard to work with the media in what I felt was an ethical way: no exclusives, no gross invasions of my privacy. And I expected reasonable behavior in return. Most of the time our relationship worked smoothly, but sometimes the situation rubbed my nerves raw.

We had received Christmas cards from Mr. and Mrs. Reagan, Mr. and Mrs. Bush, and Mr. and Mrs. George Shultz. The day before

Christmas eve, as I was mopping the floor, a special delivery letter arrived from President Reagan. It had the presidential seal on the envelope, my name all nicely typed, the kind of envelope you slit very carefully and keep for a memento. I got up and wiped my hands before I touched it. The letter read:

Dear Friends:

In this holy season when families everywhere draw close in a spirit of joy and celebration, I know your burden of waiting and hoping must be terribly hard to bear. Please be assured that we continue, in every way we can, to lift that burden from your hearts and gain the release of all those held hostage in Lebanon. Because millions of your fellow countrymen share your burden, I have ordered that the lights of the National Christmas Tree be dimmed on Christmas Eve as a sign of our prayerful solidarity with those who are not with their loved ones at Christmas.

Nancy and I join with millions of other Americans who pray that God will soften the hearts of those who hold Terry Anderson and that he and the others will be released safely and soon. You have my solemn vow that we will not rest until all the members of our American family now being held hostage are returned home to their loved ones. May God bless and sustain you.

Sincerely,
Ronald Reagan

I called my brother Rich and read it to him and burst into tears. After a year of trying to get the barest of acknowledgments out of him, it really touched me that the President would think to dim the White House lights in tribute to the hostages. It told me that we existed, that Terry would not be forgotten.

But right afterward I got mad at myself. How could I let such an easy gesture touch me? Wake up! Terry didn't need gestures, he needed action. He was blindfolded in a dungeon, and once the lights came back up he would be not one moment closer to seeing freedom. Dim the White House lights? Blink and you miss it.

*   *   *

The days around New Year's David and I spent remodeling a small house my daughter Melody and her husband Randy had bought. We had promised to do the work and were going to surprise them by completing major renovations while they were on vacation in Detroit. David was doing the carpentry and electrical work while I was taping and plastering sheetrock. Terry Waite, whom we had only recently heard about, was intensely involved in the hostage negotiations, so we were in a time of expectancy and simply trying to keep busy while waiting for the process to be played out.

On January 2, a Wednesday, Dad called to say he was going into a hospital in Deland, Florida, for a checkup. He hadn't been feeling very well, which was not all that unusual, but he wanted to make sure he was reasonably okay.

On Saturday, about midmorning, Dad called again. I could feel something was very wrong as soon as he said hello. His voice cracked and he blurted it out: "I've got cancer."

I was stunned. I hadn't been worried at all about this checkup, and if I had worried, it would have been about his emphysema, a problem he'd had for a long time. I could feel and taste his fear, even over a thousand miles of long-distance.

"Do you want to come home?" I knew he would. What is it about most of us that we want to go home when troubles come?

He said yes.

I told Dad that David and I would come for him as soon as we could, and that everything would be all right. When David got home for lunch he agreed immediately that we needed to go and get my father. We would fly down, and David would drive Dad's car and belongings north while Dad and I flew back to Batavia.

Such a pathetic lot his belongings were. It was so sad to see all the worldly goods Dad had accumulated in a lifetime loaded into the Mercury Marquis that was his pride and joy. It was his first new car and it was a symbol to him of success.

Dad's doctor in Florida told us he suspected the cancer was widespread, but I refused to consider it. I was anxious to get my father to the cancer hospital in Buffalo, Roswell Memorial Park, that had worked a miracle for my brother Rich thirty years before. I was counting on them to do the same for Dad. So was he.

I was very shaky on the trip home, both from fear of flying and from worry that something would happen to Dad before I could get him to the hospital. David would be another day driving Dad's car, and without him I was a wreck. I am absolutely a waste during a medical crisis; my mind shuts off and my body's instinct to bolt takes over. Dad looked and felt very bad, but we managed to get through the night and left for Roswell early the next morning. My best friend, Marsha Barton, who has always been there when I needed her, rode with us.

We got Dad admitted, both of us greatly relieved that he was finally in more competent hands than mine. Rich had decided at the last moment to ride back with David, and by the time Marsha and I made the hour's drive back to Batavia they had arrived. Rich wanted to hear what the doctors had to say firsthand, and Dad was very pleased that he had come.

David and I tried to persuade Rich to admit himself for a checkup while he was there, but he outright refused. He didn't look well, had constant coughing spasms and a lot of chest pain, which he attributed to his three-pack-a-day smoking habit. He finally promised us that he would see a doctor as soon as he returned to Florida.

I stayed at home for the next two days, and with Marsha's help tried to customize the house for Dad's homecoming. Although we didn't expect him to be bedridden, we knew he would have some special needs. Dad had always had back problems, so David had borrowed a hospital bed from the local Red Cross so he would sleep more comfortably.

David, Rich, and my sister Judy took turns visiting Dad, a two-hour round trip, and on the following Saturday, Judy drove Rich to the airport for his flight to Florida. They were still in the testing process at Roswell so there was no definitive diagnosis when he left, but Rich needed to return to his job.

Dad seemed in reasonably good spirits, and we all took turns visiting him over the weekend. Longtime friends and buddies from his truck-driving days also came by, and Dad was in his glory entertaining his audience. The following Tuesday, after being told that the test results were in, David, Marsha, and I went back to Roswell.

The grim-faced team of specialists told us that Dad's time was "borrowed." The cancer had rioted through his body and there were few parts that were untouched. His liver, chest, stomach, lungs, and even his neck had been invaded. "We still have a few tricks up our sleeve," one doctor promised. That's what I heard: the miracle still seemed possible.

Dad had become increasingly disgruntled after the weekend and complained he was being treated in less than his usual royal manner. Dad's previous hospitalizations had always turned into mutual admiration societies between him and the staff, and he always made a determined effort to charm and romance his nurses. It was not like him to be such a grump.

It was not Roswell's policy to provide in-room telephones for the patients, even though the rooms were equipped with jacks. Having a telephone was a vital link to the outside world, especially given Terry's situation, and so I called a congressman, leaned on some political allies and got a phone installed next to Dad's bed. The day after his phone went in, though, they decided to move Dad to another room and left the phone behind.

That evening Dad called in a truly rabid mood. The hospital provided portable telephones in the corridors for patients and visitors, and Dad had wheeled the one from outside his door into his room and informed me that he was "holding it hostage" until they returned his own.

He also recited a list of what he perceived to be moral abuse from the doctors and staff. He had been kept waiting "for hours" in a wheelchair until an orderly finally came to wheel him down for more testing. While waiting outside his room he saw one of his doctors passing by and stopped him to ask just when they were going to come for him. Dad said the doctor snapped, "Don't bother me, I've got problems of my own."

He wanted out, and he expected me to make the arrangements. I said I'd do my best. I hung up the telephone, put my head in my hands, and thought, "Oh, no, what am I going to do now?" It seemed like that's all I'd been saying for months.

I called our family doctor in Batavia, Dr. Rathor, and explained the situation to him. He recommended that I try Dr. Phelan, a local and well-respected oncologist, and see if he would be willing to take over Dad's case. Dr. Phelan consented and I called Roswell to tell them I was removing Dad from their care. There was a lot of media attention over Dad's condition, and many journalists and television reporters were calling the hospital for updates. I sensed Roswell's reluctance to engender any negative publicity.

When I got to Dad's room early the next morning and told him that the arrangements had been made, that he was going to St. Jerome's under Dr. Phelan's care, he seemed somewhat surprised. "You want it," I told him, "you got it."

As I was waiting outside Dad's room while he got dressed, I noticed two sober-looking men in business suits striding purposefully in my direction. "State Department types," I thought.

"Mrs. Say," one of them inquired politely, "could we talk to you?" He motioned me to accompany them to the nearby family visiting room.

They introduced themselves as the hospital administrator and his assistant. They wanted to be sure that I understood I would be taking Dad out of Roswell against his doctors' wishes and would be required to sign an affidavit to that effect. I told them I understood the legal ramifications, but it was Dad's wish to transfer and I would honor it. I also told them that I felt there was nothing further they could do for Dad, and the more I thought about it the more uncomfortable I was with the intimation from the doctor who promised "something else up his sleeve." Had Dad been younger and less ill, experimentation would be acceptable, but I didn't feel he should be subjected to it at his age and in his condition.

Their major concern turned out to be publicity, and I assured them that I believed Roswell to be an excellent hospital and would not say otherwise. With that out of the way, and after telling them who would be taking over Dad's case, the discussion became far more cordial. Dr. Phelan was on the staff at Roswell. I did not have to sign a "Discharged Against Medical Advice" form.

I bundled Dad up and took him directly to St. Jerome's, and his state of mind brightened almost immediately. I was very relieved that he was then within five minutes of our home and the family could visit him much more often.

The next week involved more testing, but Dad seemed much improved. My son Ed had come home from Texas to see him, and although we were all very concerned, we felt that Dad would pull through yet another crisis. At the end of the week Dr. Phelan told us Dad could come home and be treated on an outpatient basis. He also told us that Dad was dying, but I wasn't listening.

I was in an upbeat frame of mind during the next week as Dad continued to do well and my daughter announced that David and I would become grandparents the following September. This was wonderful.

Dad was so funny sometimes. Always very independent, he hated it when I had to dole out his medication to him. I tried to be unobtrusive about it, but there were so many pills that I was afraid he couldn't keep them straight. He tried, though, and one day when I came back from an errand, he was sitting at the dining room table with the pill bottles in front of him, looking disgusted.

"Well, if that isn't one of the stupidest damn things I ever did!" he snorted. He had taken a sleeping pill by mistake and it was only two o'clock in the afternoon. I laughed. "It seems to me you'd best go in and get in bed." He wasn't amused.

The next week, Dr. Phelan readmitted Dad to the hospital for chemotherapy treatments. He told us the treatments would, at best, give Dad a little more time. Very little. I explained to him how well Dad was doing and he described that period as "the lull before the storm." "He will start deteriorating very rapidly," Dr. Phelan told us gently. "He has, at the most, only days to live."

"Yes, David, I *heard* what Dr. Phelan said, but it just can't be true! People don't die like that. They just don't."

My family was trying to make me accept the imminence of Dad's death, and I was rejecting it. I also rejected vehemently the suggestion that I was trying to *deny* the possibility that Dad would die. I mean, I knew that someday, probably soon, he would die, but not just yet. Not before Terry came home.

My mother had died eleven years before, but she did it in an acceptable way; she went in for bypass surgery and died on the operating table. It was a terrible shock, especially since she was only fifty-six years old, but death during surgery happens. I think most of us are somewhat prepared for that possibility every time someone we love is whisked away to the operating room. I know that every time I've had to undergo anesthesia, I've gone to sleep firmly convinced I would never wake up. At least not in this life.

People aren't walking around and taking showers and eating and joking and then suddenly dead, I told them. At least not from cancer. They get sicker and sicker and pretty soon you put them in the hospital and they slip into a coma and eventually they die.

Dad was home again and seemed comfortable, although his appetite was poor. I was tempting him with homemade soups and desserts. He ate only a few bites at each meal, but still he seemed okay. I was getting really upset at my family's attitude and was particularly put out when Rich decided he should come back to New York.

I was generally put out with Rich anyway. I had finally caved in to his demand that I tell Dad he was going to die. Rich and I had argued by phone for weeks. He insisted that Dad had a right to know what his prognosis was, and kept insisting that I tell him. Rich described his own feelings of betrayal when he learned, only many years later, that his doctors had told the family he had only months to live after his operation for cancer when he was a teenager. That they were wrong didn't lessen Rich's conviction that he should have been told at the time.

I didn't want to do it, not only because I didn't know how I could, but I didn't believe it myself. I finally screwed up the courage and determination to tell Dad what the doctor *said* was going to happen. It took several trips in and out of his room and a couple of false starts before it finally came out. I still hate that I had to do it.

"I don't know any other way to say this, Dad, but just to say it right out. Dr. Phelan says that you don't have very long to live."

Rich had promised me that Dad knew the truth somewhere inside him, but it sure didn't seem so to me. Dad's face turned very pale and he asked in a shaky voice, "How long do I have?"

"They say just a few days."

He seemed in a state of shock and we both sat in silence until it became unbearable. We reached for each other finally and both started crying. He gained control very quickly, though, and started in a very businesslike manner to tell me some of the things that needed taking care of before he was ready to go.

Always first on any list of my Dad's "things to do today" was to reach out to his lady friends. It was February 12 and he asked me to go down to the drugstore and pick him up a couple, "No, better make that six or seven . . . oh, hell, get a dozen Valentine cards. Nice ones."

The next day Dr. Phelan put Dad back in the hospital and told us to be prepared; Dad would probably not be coming back home again.

On February 14, the day before my birthday, Rich and David said they wanted to take me out for dinner. I didn't realize it, but they were sure that Dad would die within hours and there would be no birthday celebration for me. I reluctantly agreed, and my sister-in-law Penny said she would be happy to stay with Dad while we were gone.

After a subdued and hurried dinner I insisted that David and Rich drop me off at the hospital, where I intended to spend the night. I guess I was beginning to accept the idea that Dad was not going to make it this time. I began to picture the scene. I would be sitting quietly at Dad's bedside, holding his hand, and he would begin to mumble. Gradually, I'd understand.

"What's that, Dad? . . . I love you too . . . Yes, I know . . . I'm your special favorite . . . always have been? Yes, I know . . . Shhhh, it's all right, I'm here . . . Shhhh, it's okay . . ." He would give my hand a final squeeze, I would feel his overwhelming love for me . . . and then he would slip quietly away.

It's too hard for me. I've asked Penny to write what she saw and felt as she shared that time with Dad and me:

"If you had ever met my father-in-law you would have liked him. He was short and stocky, with brown eyes and close-cropped gray hair (no trace left of the color that in his younger years gave him his nickname, 'Red'). His face was lined and seamed and pouched, showing every minute of his sixty-odd years and giving proof to what Peggy always says: 'The older any Anderson gets, the more they look like bulldogs.'

"He was intelligent, witty and charming, liked by men and women both, but especially by women.

"When I arrived at the hospital on Friday the 14th, I could see that Dad was much worse. The family members present didn't really want to leave, but I convinced them they needed a break. I tried to sit unobtrusively in a corner of the room so that Dad wouldn't feel a need to interact with me. Soon, however, his pain and distress began to scrape my nerves raw until I wanted to scream — or cry. His pain was a huge, suffocating, almost physical presence in the room, until finally I ran into the corridor, grabbed a nurse, and asked if please wasn't it time for Dad's medication. The nurse came in right away and set up an intravenous drip and Dad sank into a restless sleep. I was exhausted after only one hour. I couldn't understand how the others had survived a whole day of this.

"At that moment, an old girlfriend of Dad's appeared in the doorway. I tried to fend her off but she was determined that Dad needed to see her. Short of ejecting her bodily I felt helpless. She began to call Dad's name, dragging him back to consciousness. One of my clearest memories is of Dad's sweet smile and effort to respond.

"The woman left triumphantly, sure that she had done the right thing. Of course, now Dad was awake, his pain was back in overwhelming power, and the next pain-killing shot was two hours away.

"When Peggy returned around 9:30 she planned to spend the night alone with Dad while everyone else rested up for the ordeal they thought lay ahead. As she looked at her father I saw her face pale and I quickly offered to stay with her. She hugged me and said she had hoped I'd stay but hadn't wanted to ask. After watching Dad for a few moments she ran out into the hall to cry, but only for a few moments. When she came back in she seemed angry at herself. Dashing tears from her face with her palms, she told me, 'That's not what he needs from me now!'

"The night moved with agonizing slowness as Dad twisted and turned and muttered and fought. We began to consider that he might even die that night, but we couldn't believe it would happen so fast. Why, just yesterday he had told me one of his dumb jokes and propositioned a nurse. We held his hands and talked to him and prayed for God to ease his suffering. Every once in a while, when we could no longer bear to see him struggle, one or the other of us would run from the room.

"Finally we could no longer deny the nearness of death. We were about to call the other family members when Dad grabbed the bed rails, jerked himself up and shouted, 'Come on! Come on!'

"His heels drummed frantically on the mattress and his body strained to reach something invisible to me. Peggy shouted at me, 'Get a nurse, Dad is dying!'

"I ran down the hospital corridor and raced back trailing behind two nurses. Before we reached the room Dad had pulled himself up, roaring from pain, raging into Peggy's face until she thought her own heart would burst as he hurled himself into death. We heard Peggy cry out, 'No. No. Don't leave me!'

"When we ran into the room it was over. The nurses examined Dad and shook their heads. Peggy lay across her father's chest, sobbing hysterically. I put my arms around her and tried to draw her away but one of the nurses stopped me. She said that Peggy needed to grieve. When I looked up, I saw that both of the nurses were crying."

CHAPTER

6

Terry had been a hostage for almost a year and nothing was happening. Contact with the State Department was sporadic. There's only so much of "We're doing everything we can . . . We're working behind the scenes . . . We have not forgotten you" that a person can take before you want to see a little action. They were not negotiating with terrorists and we were not seeing the men come home.

We decided to organize a candlelight prayer vigil in front of the White House to commemorate the one-year anniversary of Terry's kidnapping.

No one in the families had any experience in organizing demonstrations. We knew we were supposed to contact the press, but we didn't know exactly how. Drawing crowds wasn't something we were good at, we were housewives and firemen, teachers and hospital technicians. But we had to do something. We contacted some people who had organized rallies before, and they got us started. John Stein and his organization, Nova, stepped in to help.

On March 16, 1986—a year to the day after Terry was taken

hostage—a small band of family members holding candles began to march in a little circle in front of the White House lawn. It was pitiful. It was colder than all get out and none of us was dressed warmly. Rich was huddled up against a statue there in Lafayette Park just shivering, his teeth chattering.

The vigil was supposed to start at seven at night, and at 6:45 there were Paul, Eric, and Diana Jacobsen, Rich, David, and me—that was it. We were waiting for the crowds to arrive and nobody was showing up, and here comes the press. We were six little icicles and we started to panic. "What are we going to say? This is so embarrassing. They're coming to film this vigil and nobody is here!"

We were stomping around trying to get warm, semi-hysterical, and everybody started laughing. Eric, whose sense of humor tended toward the bizarre anyway, said, "Let's take seven pigeons and wire them to the fence, and tell the media we will let them go when the seven hostages are freed."

Finally some of the people who were organizing the rally started showing up. We were supposed to have an audio system, and all they brought was a bullhorn, which sent us all into renewed fits of laughter. Luckily, the media brought an audio system and we borrowed theirs, so real disaster was averted.

Hardly anybody showed up for our vigil except the organizers and the families, and not all of them. We saw some people gathering in another part of the park to protest American involvement in Nicaragua. We kind of joined forces; if we gave them our candles when we were done, they said, they would join us and increase our numbers. It was a deal. At least on the news it looked as though we had attracted a crowd.

The next day we met with the State Department again. It was a huge meeting and we were in a foul mood. Eric Jacobsen turned to the National Security Adviser and said, "So, what's new, Mr. McFarlane?" and it went downhill from there.

McFarlane said, "We believe it would be a good idea if you wanted to contact Ayatollah Khomeini in Iran."

"Excuse me?" I said a little incredulously. "Last November you told us to stay away from the Iranians. What has happened to change that?"

They seemed quite perturbed, as if they were offended that I remembered what they had said four months before, that they might actually be held accountable.

They talked around it. They didn't give us a real answer, just limp generalities. "Well, things change, you know. Maybe the Ayatollah does have some influence here. We personally don't want to deal with him but we are always looking for suggestions." Essentially, it was a "Hey, go for it."

There was nothing new. They did mention Libya a couple of times in passing, but there was absolutely nothing going on, they told us; they didn't negotiate with terrorists, they didn't have any information that they hadn't already given us; there was nothing we could do. Hostage Peter Kilburn's niece asked Ollie North, "What are you doing about my uncle?" North looked her straight in the eye and said evenly, "You don't even want to know."

The place went wacko. People started pounding on the table. It was practically a screaming match.

They had brought in a man named Charlie Allen, who was sitting right next to me. (I found out much later, going through a chart titled "Bush Task Force," that Charlie Allen was a CIA intelligence analyst.) At one point there was a lull in the shouting and I turned to Mr. McFarlane and Bob Oakley and said, "By the way, fellas, today is Father Jenco's 444th day in captivity. Have any of you jotted off a telegram to Jimmy Carter to tell him now you know how it feels?" (The Iranian hostage crisis, the one that did in the Carter presidency, lasted 444 days.) Charlie Allen chuckled, but I got this dead fish-face silence from across the table.

The TV and newspaper people, as always, were waiting for us when the meeting was through. Eric Jacobsen and I had evolved into the families' spokespeople and we huddled before we met the press. "What are we going to say? This has been awful."

For some reason we decided to pretend everything was all right. Maybe we were worried that they would stop whatever meager efforts they actually were making. Maybe we just were beaten down. We were casting about for a strategy that would work. Confronting them hadn't done us any good; maybe they'd respond if we covered for them.

We didn't castigate the State Department, we didn't stroke them. It killed both of us but we stood up there and told the press, "Oh, everything went fine."

It takes me some time to digest information. In the beginning David was always after me to tell him what had happened at meetings, and I would say just give me a day to put it all in order. It's hard enough to remember everything that goes on, without figuring out what it all means. But I was disturbed at the mention of Libya.

It sounded to me, from the tone of the State Department people at the meeting and from what I had been reading in the papers, that Libya was about to take a beating. "The handwriting is on the wall," I told David. For the first time I could see the government consciously manipulating the public. Everywhere you looked, there was some government official saying that Libya was the bad guy. I didn't have any concrete evidence—I couldn't look them in the eye and pin it on them—but I knew they were up to something. I also knew that if they bombed Libya some hostage was going to die, and I knew that the State Department knew it too. I went home in a frenzy.

The State Department had become a big shoulder shrug. We needed some action. We needed someone who would actually take the situation in his hands and move it forward. There was only one man I had met in government who seemed to have the willingness, the zeal, and the capacity to get my brother home. I called Colonel North.

All of these stories about Oliver North working out of the basement of the White House are nonsense. Ollie had a brand-new office in the Old Executive Building, and when I arrived they were just finishing it.

The first thing you noticed was that, here, security was most definitely an issue. Ollie had a coded punch-key lock on his suite of offices. You walked through the door and sitting at a very busy desk was Fawn Hall with two computer screens lit up at the same time. Fawn had three cigarettes going at once, half-full coffee cups all over the place. The office automation system was grinding out documents. There was a frantic, pressure-cooker atmosphere—you could feel it just standing there—and she was a manic, driven helper. She also seemed to have no idea how beautiful a woman she was.

Colonel North was in his office when I arrived and I stood in front of Fawn's desk trying to read the documents with bright, inch-wide red lines slashing from top corner to bottom, marked "Top Secret," that dared me to look at them upside down. There was literature on Central America; something along the lines of the latest State Department Report on the Growing Subversion of Central America by the Communist Menace.

Ollie's office was to the left of Fawn's desk, and when he came and welcomed me inside we sat down at a small conference table and began to talk.

My mission was to find out what was going on, and to make my case that something *should* be going on. I immediately went into my spiel: Terry Anderson is my brother, he's been in captivity for an entire year, he has lived in chains, blindfolded, in one filthy room with four other men. He is given fifteen minutes each day to go to the bathroom, otherwise he has to hold it for another twenty-four hours. On the rare times he is transported he is nailed in a coffin or bound to the underside of a truck.

North knew all that. His information was probably better than mine. What exactly did I want him to do?

Get Terry out.

Very quickly, Ollie impressed me as a can-do guy. He had the reputation in Washington of being the only four-star lieutenant colonel. He was able to convey to his immediate listener the idea that he was an extremely important person who was the President's right hand. He never told me exactly what he had in mind, or how he was going to get it done, but he nonetheless—by what he would talk about, and by his body language and the whole way he carried himself—conveyed the message that this was an Action Marine. And I knew a Marine quite well. In fact, I had the feeling that Ollie got Terry firmly in his sights because Terry was a former Marine. This meant a lot to Ollie.

Meanwhile I began looking around the room. Sitting in the left-hand corner of his credenza, like some sort of trophy, was a Soviet-style military helmet with a big red star on it. You've seen the posters of famine-plagued Africans that say, "For $2.50 a day you can feed this hungry child"? Well, on Ollie's wall there was a poster of an armed but scruffy-looking Latin American soldier, and underneath the picture it said, "For $2.50 a day you can feed this contra."

Ollie gave me a tour of his new office. "See that gold stuff around the window?" he said with pleasure. "*Nobody* can beam into this office. They can't tap me with satellites because that's the stuff that keeps them from doing it." He was, he explained, protected from eavesdropping by detection of vibration by windowpane.

He pointed to the blank wall in front of us. There was a little eye in the middle of it. He told me, "I've got the security system shut off with you in here, but when I throw the switch, if there's a sudden movement"—he faked two jabs at my face—"that light will set off an alarm in the outside office. Watch." He jabbed twice more and a red light went on. He loved his motion detector and all his toys. He took kind of a gee-whiz fascination with the gadgetry of security, and he liked to brag about it. I had the feeling this stuff would be no fun for him unless he could show it off.

I didn't know whether to respect Ollie North or to be scared to death because this was the man who was trying to get my brother home. I could easily see him just sitting at his desk playing with one of those guns that turns into a knife that turns into an umbrella.

My brother Rich hadn't looked too good at my father's funeral. We made him promise to go to a doctor when he got back home to Florida, and he did. They told him it was stress, then it was his arteries, then his heart. They scheduled him for double-bypass surgery. I flew down to Florida to be with him.

Rich didn't think he was going to survive. He was convinced he was going to die on the table. I was operating on the assumption that God would not let this happen.

Rich had been working very hard since our earlier confrontations and was a source of great emotional support for me. He was always coming up with new ideas and suggestions, and helped me to sort out options and ideas for the future. Although we were closer than I ever dreamed possible, he was deeply saddened that Terry would only remember the Rich he had known before his abduction.

"I was a drunk," Rich said, "and Terry won't know that I was here for you and for him, or how hard I worked for his release."

I assured Rich that Terry would know because I would tell him.

Rich did almost die on the table. He had begged the hospital to send for his records at Roswell. He told them, "I've had major heart surgery, I've got ribs wired, you've got to have those records." They never sent for them, and when they opened him up it was all scar tissue. It was a mess. But I watched him wake up from the operation and I could see it on his face the moment he regained consciousness: "My God, I'm still alive!"

Four days later, April 14, 1986, the United States bombed Libya. Reagan said the bombing was in retaliation for a terrorist attack on a West Berlin disco, and to serve as a warning to future terrorists.

I couldn't believe my government. How could they be so heartless as to jeopardize the hostages' lives? The State Department knew that Peter Kilburn, a librarian at the American University of Beirut, was in the hands of thugs led by the notedly bloodthirsty terrorist Abu Nidal. Kilburn was not held with the rest of the hostages, and his captors had demonstrated that they were motivated as much by political concerns as by greed. Although Terry's captors were more interested in nationalism, Islam, and their leader's brother-in-law, there was nothing to stop them from killing him on the spot.

Libya chose another path. Muammar Qaddafi bought four hostages with cash. He purchased them from their captors and took his vengeance. First a videotape was released that the Libyans said showed British freelance journalist Alec Collett, hanging; its authenticity is still in question. There was no doubt about the others. Several days later the bodies of Peter Kilburn plus two other British journalists, Leigh Douglas and Philip Padfield, were dumped out of a car. Kilburn was shot through the head.

I knew the Kilburns. I knew Alec's wife, an American woman, Elaine Collett. In fact, I had the terrible experience of telling her about the tape. When the tape was first played there was a mix-up and they thought the hanged man was Peter Kilburn. When he was identified as Alec Collett, no one from the State Department had thought to call her. I called to console Elaine and found that she had not heard the news. It was a very bad time.

I was frantic. Their deaths were tragic and horrible. And one of those men could have been Terry.

The country's mood was euphoric. We have a way of celebrating displays of military muscle; they seem to make the whole nation feel powerful. We had sent a squadron of F-111 fighter planes into that military colossus, Libya, and squashed it. We'd showed the bad guys. Nobody wanted to know that we'd just lost four human beings. Whenever I gave an interview, though, I talked about it. I was terrified that, in all this celebration, people would forget that there were still hostages sitting in a basement out there, waiting to be freed.

I flew to Washington to try to make the media understand, and the government pay attention to, the grave danger being piled upon the hostages. Bud McFarlane had within the past month left the office of National Security Adviser and set up his own shop. He was a hired gun—because of his experience and knowledge he was in demand as a consultant—and he wanted to continue to be a player. I think he might have pictured himself as the Henry Kissinger of the Middle East situation.

On one of my visits to Washington I called Mr. McFarlane and asked if I could meet with him. It never ceased to amaze me that people would invariably say, "Come over."

We discussed, as I always discussed with everyone I met in Washington, what I could or should be doing to get Terry freed. Contacting the Iranians came up. Mr. McFarlane felt this was the most fruitful way to get Terry home. The government wouldn't involve itself—apparently the most fruitful way to get Terry home was not something they were interested in pursuing—but I could.

So eleven days after Rich's surgery, and four days after the bombing of Libya, I was in Bud McFarlane's office collaborating on a letter to Iran.

We had letters hand-delivered to the ambassadors from Japan, West Germany, Switzerland, and Syria, asking them to relay our message to the Iranian government in Tehran:

My name is Peggy Say. I am the sister of Terry Anderson. . . . I know the Iranian government deplores the kidnapping of innocent victims as much as I do. Thus, when I met privately with Robert McFarlane, former National Security Adviser to President Reagan, on April 21, he suggested that I request a meeting with Iranian government officials to ask their help in gaining the release of my brother.

I ask your permission to visit Tehran to meet with Ayatollah Khomeini . . . and others. . . . If you will allow me to visit Tehran, I will bring with me the good wishes of the American people and I will come in the hope that our meeting could help improve the future relationship between Iran and the United States. Thank you and may God be with you.

That was a hard week. On April 21 I wrote the letter to the Ayatollah, trying to get my brother released from captivity. On the twenty-sixth, we buried my father. (We had held off interment, hoping that somehow Terry would arrive home in time to join in the service.) On the twenty-ninth, I went to Peter Kilburn's funeral.

As I watched Peter's coffin being carried into the chapel, the emotion almost overcame me. I sorrowed not only for his family but for mine. I knew that Terry had gotten lucky; but for mere chance that could have been his coffin leading the procession.

Except for a very brief play on the news, Peter's death seemed to have occurred in a void; Americans were still too caught up in celebrating our "victory" over Libya to notice the price we had paid. Muammar Qaddafi, the obvious target, was still alive, and it was innocent Libyan and American families who were the real victims of the raid. Despite overt denial and the fact that it was in violation of our own laws, we had obviously intended to assassinate Qaddafi. Nobody seemed inclined to take our government to task over this criminal act or suffer any guilt over the loss of innocent lives.

Also around this time Jack Anderson (absolutely no relation) came out with a column saying that an understanding had been reached and the hostages would be coming home. Anderson said he had had a meeting with President Reagan, who had filled him in on details of a deal in the works.

I blew my top. I thought, who is Jack Anderson to have access to information that I don't have? I'm Terry's sister and I've been dying for information for more than a year.

I called the families' liaison at the State Department and really let him have it. He said, "I'm not fully aware of the details, but, yes, Jack Anderson did have a private meeting with the President, at which time he was given some details concerning the hostages."

So they *were* holding out on us.

I was furious. "How interested do you think Jack Anderson would be in the Peter Kilburn deal?" I asked him.

"Peggy, you wouldn't."

He knew what I was talking about. The State Department used to send me photocopies of various newspaper articles that they thought might interest me, mostly concerning Terry. One day I turned one of these copies over and saw penciled notations on the back. It was somebody's notes on the Peter Kilburn case! They were deal points. According to these notes we knew where Kilburn was and who had him, and the captors wanted money. It was going to be a cash-for-hostage ransom. It was that simple. So much for not negotiating with terrorists. What was even more disturbing was that the exchange was within two days of being made—and then Reagan bombed Libya and Peter Kilburn was killed.

Looking at the handwritten notes I thought, "They are going to go nuts when they find out what they've sent me."

I called up the State Department person who sent me the clippings and said, "Are you missing anything?"

"You know," he said blankly, "I have no idea what you are talking about."

"Oh? Well, let me read you something." I began to list the Kilburn balance sheet.

"*Oh, my God!* How did you get that?"

I told him.

"Please, please send it back."

I did, but not before I went down to the drugstore and made some photocopies of my own.

So when our liaison said, "Peggy, you wouldn't," I was disgusted with myself. I wanted to show the world that all these pious pronouncements our government was making were a pile of manure, but I couldn't bring myself to do it.

"You're right," I told him. "I probably wouldn't, because I'm still enough of a patriot. But don't ever let me read in the paper again information that I don't have firsthand. This is my brother."

*   *   *

They had taken some tissue during my brother Rich's surgery and ran some tests. The results came in: he had cancer. He went back into the hospital immediately. This time he was really scared. I flew back down to Florida to be with him.

Rich had been living with his girlfriend Jeannie for several years and he called me and said, "Peg, I've decided I want to be married. This afternoon. Take care of it."

Oh, sure. I didn't know a soul in Florida anymore, but I sat there with my pot of coffee and started calling around, found out what the legalities were and what had to be done.

As the result of a tremendous spirit of cooperation among those I called, I was able to phone Jeannie at work at about eleven o'clock. "You'd better come home," I said, "'cause you're going to be married this afternoon."

"What?!"

I was frantic all day, trying to get in touch with his kids from his first marriage, making arrangements with the hospital and the minister. I was Rich's "best man" and I wore blue jeans. Jeannie wore blue jeans too, and I ran out and bought her a big picture hat so she could have a wedding chapeau. Her mother was her maid of honor. The hospital brought in champagne and wedding cake, the AP sent over a photographer, and they got married.

Two doctors were fighting over Rich's condition. One called the entire family in and told us, "I'm sorry, but he's going to die. The cancer is too far gone to be treated. There is no hope." The next day he called us and said, "This has all been a mistake. There is no cancer. Your brother's condition is not what I at first thought it to be." We were on a roller coaster.

Finally Rich said, "Look, get me out of here. Get me into Roswell." They had saved his life thirty years before, he expected them to do it again.

I said, fine, and left for Batavia to make the arrangements.

I assumed that Roswell wouldn't be thrilled to find me at their doorstep again after the hassle I had given them over Dad, so I searched my mind for some way to make this admission happen smoothly. I had an enormous book of telephone numbers by this time, and I thumbed through it looking for some kind of divine inspiration.

Aha! I had phoned everyone on my list of local politicians last time except for the governor. Why not. It was worth a shot.

I called Governor Mario Cuomo's office—I had been in touch with them over the course of the year—and they called Roswell and said, "You will be admitting Mr. Anderson as a patient. We know you will give him the best of care."

Just when I thought everything was set, I got a call from Rich. He was panicked. "They won't fly me," he said. "I've got to be on oxygen and they won't let me on a commercial airliner. You've got to do something!"

Again I sat there looking at the phone, thinking, What in the world am I supposed to do?

I called Governor Cuomo's office again. I had talked to his aide quite a bit and he had been very sympathetic. "I've got this problem," I told him. "Can you help me?"

He said, "Let me make some phone calls."

Within an hour he called back. "We can get you a hospital plane but it may take a while; all of the state's planes are in use. It may take three or four days."

Rich was in bad shape by then and I didn't think he'd make it.

"Do you know anybody at the White House?" the aide asked.

"I know Ollie North."

"Well, why don't you call him and see if there is anything he can do."

It's hard for me to ask for help under the best of circumstances, but I had to do this for Rich.

"Ollie," I said when he answered the phone, "my brother is dying in Florida. He wants to come up to Buffalo for treatment. I can't get him on a commercial plane, we can't get a hospital plane in enough time. I don't know what to do."

Ollie said, "Peggy, you don't have a problem. You have friends. Let me make a phone call."

He got back to me quickly. "Call this man at this number, give him the logistics of how and where you want Glenn Richard transported, and he'll be there."

I almost burst into tears.

They flew Rich to Buffalo in a brand-new, very sleek private jet. When I called Ollie North to thank him and our benefactor for the use of the aircraft, he just passed it off with a "Yeah, yeah." When I told him I wanted to contact the plane's owner to thank him personally, Ollie said, "Forget it, Peggy, you don't even know this guy exists." (The next time I heard of that aircraft company it was when Eugene Hasenfus's plane got shot down in Nicaragua; it was one of theirs.)

When Rich was wheeled off the plane I thought he was a dead man. He was in a wheelchair, huddled in a blanket, looking awful. We rushed him to Roswell and they began treatment.

Rich did have cancer. They kept him in the hospital for several days for further tests and medication, but after that they allowed him to come home. He would have to return to the hospital every few days, but he could stay with us.

Rich knew he was dying. He'd had some experience at it and he didn't want to be kept from the truth. He had beaten his drinking problem, been sober for several months and turned into a much nicer person as a result. It was frightening to have him around the house, this constant reminder of death, but I had really begun to love him again.

Rich wanted to make a videotape. He was on his deathbed and he wanted to appeal to Terry's captors to let him see his brother one more time before he died. The tape was to be aired on Lebanese television in the hopes that the men who were holding him would see it and be moved to let him go.

I couldn't go through it with him. I didn't want to beg anymore. Terry was maintaining his dignity, it was important that we all maintain ours. I had given in the year before, at Senator Jesse Helms's urging, and done a videotape pleading with Terry's captors. I had cried as I explained that "begging is difficult for me, but I have been begging for Terry's life since the day he was taken."

I had never begged for anything in my life, and making that videotape was one of the most difficult things I'd ever had to do. I absolutely hated having to do it, it was such an assault on my dignity, but I made the tape out of desperation for my brother. I *hated* that our pain, our raw emotions were put on public display. We had always been a private family and to have our most intimate feelings revealed in the most public way possible was almost too much to bear.

Rich saw things differently. He had nothing to lose, he just wanted to see Terry.

When the TV crew came to the hospital I left the room. I didn't disapprove of what Rich was doing, but I just did not want to witness it.

Of course the tape didn't air only in Beirut, it was splashed all over the American networks. Rich was incredibly powerful. He was intense and angry—at the captors for holding Terry, at Terry for being captured in the first place, at himself for dying. With an oxygen tube running up his nose and needles in his arms, he truly did look as if he wasn't going to make it much longer. A nurse stood behind him in case he collapsed.

"I have made a vow," he said, "that I would not die before I saw my brother one more time. That vow is coming to an end. Please, let me see my brother just one more time before I die."

At one point on the tape he threw a box of tissues across the room; it could have been a bomb. This was a man in agony, how could the captors not be moved?

The networks were all calling again and the press was going bananas. I hadn't realized the tape would air here. Rich wasn't physically strong enough to handle it. Among others, NBC's *Today* show wanted an interview out of D.C. "You and Jeannie go and do the shows," he said adamantly. "This is what I want. If it's going to serve any purpose, you've got to do it." We went to Washington and made the rounds.

I saw Rich's videotape for the first time, on the air, during our interview with Jane Pauley. I hadn't realized that I would have to watch it and it took all of my self-control to hold back the tears. Rich was an open wound. It just about tore my heart out to see Rich, who had always been the family hard-ass, the tough guy, reduced to this pathetic state. At that moment I wanted to hunt the kidnappers down and strangle them with my bare hands.

As usual when I was in Washington, I didn't want to waste the opportunity to remind some government officials that I was still around, so I wedged in several appointments before plane time. I was an old hand at meeting with officialdom by now, but Jeannie, who had never been out of Florida until she came to New York with Rich, was wide-eyed and totally in awe. After the last of our sessions, as we were driving back to the airport, she looked at Washington passing outside and said in a kind of whispery wonder, "Nobody can ever take this away from me."

Jeannie and I went down and back in a day, which I always think is really risky; you double your chances of going down in a fiery crash. It was a Friday and we got into delays at the Washington airport and finally got back to Batavia two hours late. By the time we arrived at the hospital Rich was furious at us. I was so exhausted I didn't know if I was on foot or horseback, I'd had to deal with my fear of flying, and when Rich started to give me grief I snapped. "I don't need this. I'm tired, I'm going home, good night." And stormed out of there.

The next day Rich wanted to go home to Florida. I don't think he took my blowup personally. It was just that his kids were in Florida, and his life. There was no further treatment for him, and he wanted to say good-bye.

I totally refused to accept the reality that he was going to die. God, I told myself, would not allow this to happen. He would not give me Glenn Richard back after forty years and then snatch him away. It was unfair.

I called Governor Cuomo's office and made arrangements for transporting my brother. At the airport we found the plane was very small and this was the first hospital evacuation for the nurse on board. At Rich's request there were several reporters around and he told them, "I want one of you guys to nominate my sister as *Time* Man of the Year." One of the pilots was reading a manual in the cockpit and Rich joked, "This is not the time to read how-to books." He was in good spirits. "Never mind the crop dusting," he laughed, "just get me home." He gave me a thumbs-up.

The group of us, including my sister Judy and our pastor, Tom Vickers, went out for breakfast after seeing Rich off. I was fully confident that Rich would recover as he had in the past. A couple of hours later I called the airport in Florida to see that the plane had arrived safely.

"No, ma'am, the flight has not arrived yet."

I called again fifteen minutes later.

"No, ma'am. Not here yet."

I kept calling and no one down there knew anything.

When David got home from work I said, "Something is wrong." I was keeping in touch with the airport, waiting for the plane to land. Finally I got word.

"Yes, ma'am, the plane has landed. There is a friend here, I'll let you talk to her."

Jeannie got on the phone. "How did Rich make the trip?" I asked.

"He didn't. He died."

"Excuse me?"

"Rich is dead."

I got hysterical, crying and screaming. David's face paled as he took the receiver I had thrown down and spoke to Jeannie. He had never seen me totally lose control before. My stepson David, Jr. hastily retreated to his bedroom.

Something had gone wrong with Rich's oxygen tank, Jeannie said, and the plane had to hop from airport to airport to refill it. That's what held them up. Rich had been very groggy, nodding in and out of sleep. At one point he'd said, "Well, I'm going to go now," and closed his eyes. Jeannie didn't know he had died until they landed.

CHAPTER

7

I GOT A CALL FROM A MAN WHO IDENTIFIED HIMSELF AS A STATE Department official. He introduced himself as Terry Arnold and said he wanted to come to Buffalo to talk to me. I assumed he was going to give me some good news; people from the State Department don't come to Buffalo, New York, just to talk to you.

We met in the airlines terminal and he got right down to business.

"We don't like what you are saying about the U.S. raid on Libya. It's in nobody's best interest for you to go around criticizing government actions."

I was shocked. I was disappointed that they weren't bringing me some good news, which I sorely needed. But I was a citizen, I could talk to the media or anybody I wanted. I was offended that my government would send a man to tell me to shut my mouth. A good friend at the State Department had already told me that the deaths of Kilburn and Collett had been expected after the raid. Apparently the lives of these men were expendable "for the greater good."

"Let me tell you something, Mr. Arnold," I shot back at him. "I'll

115

tell you what *I* don't like. The government knew where Peter Kilburn was, and the government knew where Alec Collett was, and the government knew damn well they were going to be killed when they staged that raid, and they did it anyway. That could have been my brother. That's what *I* don't like!''

Terry Arnold didn't have much to say to me after that. He delivered his message and went off into the sunset.

Rich and Dad had both pressed me to go to the Middle East, especially Syria. Rich had a black sense of humor. He kept telling me he saw the two of us, he would be in a wheelchair and I would be pushing him through the Bekaa Valley, he'd be coughing up blood and somebody would feel sorry for him and hand over Terry. He said, ''Who would hurt a man in a wheelchair?''

But the Syrians weren't very interested in having me; they wouldn't issue me a visa.

A couple of days after Rich died, my friends started telling me that the best thing for me to do was travel. All I wanted was some privacy, some time alone, but everybody was after me to get out of the house, out of the state, out of the country. I found myself down in Washington, alone in a hotel room. It had been a long, frustrating day and I was exhausted both physically and emotionally. When David called to check on me, I struggled to keep the tears back, to keep my voice from trembling as I assured him I was just fine.

One of the local television reporters, Ed Caldwell, called just to see how I was. David had known something was wrong and immediately phoned Ed and asked him to call and see if I'd tell him. All it took from Ed was a ''How are you?'' and I began blubbering. Words tumbled over one another as I poured my heart out.

''I want to go home tonight and it's after ten o'clock and there aren't any flights and I don't want to go to the Middle East and Dad died and Rich died and nobody's giving me time to grieve and I'm tired and I need to get away from all this and Terry's never going to come home . . .'' My voice trailed off as I began hiccuping into the phone.

Ed thought I was suicidal. He kept me on the phone for an hour, the poor thing, just calming me down. Ed had become a dedicated advocate for the hostages, and a good friend. He said, "Peggy, you need some time for yourself. You need to go home and heal."

The next day I called and cancelled my appointments and went home.

David picked me up at the airport and I told him, "You've got to make some arrangements to get me away and let me have some privacy."

Some friends of ours had just bought a cottage in a small town in Kentucky and they said we had an open invitation to come visit them, so we took them up on it. I spent a little over a week just locking things away. I didn't think about anything; I just put it out of mind. My father dead, my brother dead, Terry blindfolded and in chains. I told myself, "I'll deal with all this when Terry gets out and not before. Right now, I'm going fishing on the lake."

I went home to Batavia and tried to recuperate. About all I had been doing with my life was trying to get Terry back. Everything else paled in comparison. What was I going to do, get a job and start over? How could I be so selfish? All I did for two weeks was rest up for the next push.

The State Department called. Margaret Papandreou, the wife of Greek Prime Minister Andreas Papandreou, had called and asked for my telephone number. I could expect a call.

By this time nothing was unusual to me. Sure, the first lady of Greece was going to give me a jingle.

Mrs. Papandreou is an American. When she called she told me that she was thinking about Terry. We started talking, very pleasantly, and she wanted me to know that she had had a meeting with Syria's President Hafez Assad concerning the hostages, and that he was working on solving the problem.

"Mrs. Papandreou," I said, "I have been trying to get to Syria for well over a year now, and I can't get a visa."

She was very sympathetic. "Let's do this," she suggested. "Why don't you come to Athens. Announce it to the press and they will follow your every movement. We will let it be known that you would like to go to Damascus. President Assad and my husband are friends, and I am sure that with the unspoken pressure and implications, you may find yourself in Damascus."

Greece was having a tourism problem at the time. The Athens airport was being billed as the most dangerous airport in the world. There had been bombings and hijackings and terrorist activity all centered on Athens. So, while there was undoubtedly compassion and humanity involved in her call, this was hardly an act of total selflessness. But I was thankful for every assistance and I accepted her offer immediately.

I had never been out of the United States, and the idea of going to the Middle East had always been theory; I never believed that I would actually find myself there. But once the trip was offered, I had to go; I didn't want Terry to think that there was anything I had failed to do in order to bring him home.

The AP agreed to finance the trip. I packed light, taking three changes of clothes. I figured to be gone for about a week.

Before I left I informed the State Department of my trip. Despite my misgivings about the amount and quality of attention they were giving the hostages, I was still a patriotic American and I felt I owed it to them to tell them what I was doing. I didn't want to find myself in the middle of a situation where they had an initiative going privately and my presence would undermine it. "Will this be counterproductive to anything you people are doing?" I asked. They told me no. I kind of wished they had said yes; at least then I'd have felt they were halfway involved.

I had been in touch with members of the Palestinian Liberation Organization almost from the beginning of Terry's captivity and had made several friends there. The PLO had an office in Washington, D.C., and although at the time it was questionable whether they would be able to help, I gave them a call. Terry had known Yasser Arafat, had interviewed him for the AP, and he had told me that when Americans got in trouble over there they could always go to Arafat; the PLO leader really liked Americans and had the power to get certain things done.

Through a young Palestinian named Said I set up a meeting with Arafat's second-in-command, Abu Jihad, to be held in Amman, Jordan. I was in Washington trying to iron out the details when I got a call from Bob Oakley at the State Department, who always kept me informed. He said, "The PLO has just been thrown out of Jordan." I called Said to offer my sympathies.

"Said," I began, "I'm sorry to hear what happened."

"What are you talking about?"

I hadn't realized that the news had not yet been made public. He hadn't heard.

"The PLO has been thrown out of Amman."

I'll never forget his voice. This was a young man with a new marriage and a young baby, and he said so mournfully, "You know, I will never have a home in my whole lifetime. There will be no home for me to go to."

The Jordanian leg of my trip was canceled.

I also contacted Ollie North. Ollie was enthusiastic about my going to the Middle East. Of course they couldn't send anybody with me, he said, and he wanted to keep me as far removed from the State Department as possible. But, he assured me, "Help is only a phone call away."

If I was going to make that call, I was to use a code to let him know who and what I was talking about. If I was referring to Yasser Arafat I was to use the code name "Uncle Jim." The PLO itself was "food." The Iranians were "drink." Said, the PLO representative, was "teddy bear." Fadlallah, the Shiites' spiritual leader, was "state." Cities and countries had numbers: Beirut was 7; Syria, 3; Cyprus, 6; Tunis, 2; Jordan, 9; Algeria, 0.

Although I never told him, my code name for Ollie was "Colonel Flagg," the secret intelligence agent in *M*A*S*H* who was always coming up with maniacal schemes.

The local Buffalo and Rochester TV stations sent three reporters and two cameramen with us, the "Boys on the Bus," I called them. All of a sudden I was traveling with an entourage.

I had brought a large packet of letters from all of the hostage families which I planned to publish in the Beirut newspapers. If worse came to worst, I would simply stand on the shore of the Mediterranean and shout.

It's a nine-hour flight from New York to Athens, and I don't fly well to begin with. The good news was that we were flying first class. I had

119

never even been *in* a plane that had first class, let alone flown in that section. The bad news was that I had been booked in non-smoking and there wasn't an empty seat on the plane.

Although it was a disgusting habit that I vowed to quit once Terry was free, my intense need for a cigarette drove me to make my way to the back of the plane to the smoking section. One of the Boys on the Bus stood in the aisle while I took his seat and lit up.

Children were running up and down the aisles, babies were howling, and the din of conversation was all but deafening.

I was exhausted from all the last-minute preparations before I stepped on the airplane, and I didn't have a leg under me by the time I arrived. Mrs. Papandreou's press secretary met us and took us into the VIP lounge, where I collapsed in a heap.

We were waiting for our luggage to get passed through customs when I saw a group of nuns in very distinctive habits walking across the room. I asked the press secretary who they were.

"That is Mother Teresa," she told me.

I had by this time met many noted people but I had never been that close to a living saint.

"I would die for five minutes with that woman," I said.

"You don't have to die," the secretary said. She crossed the room, spoke to one of the nuns in the group, and came back.

"Mother Teresa will be over shortly and you may talk to her."

So, huddled together right in the middle of the lounge, nuns and press and fellow passengers on all sides, we spoke. She was completely enveloping, almost like there was only the two of us; it was as if everybody else was not even there.

She was a tiny woman, which I didn't expect. And the strength and tenderness of her hands was remarkable.

I told her about Terry's situation and she told me she was aware of it. She said, "I will pray for your brother and for you. That is the only way and the best way." Our meeting was brief, only a few minutes at most, but when it was over I really did feel fortified. I felt her prayers.

* * *

We were in Greece two days and I spent a lot of the time crying. I am not ordinarily a crier but at the slightest provocation I would dissolve into tears. It finally occurred to me that I had been unable to do that at home; everybody counted on me. I had packed it all away. But now, here I was far away, and I let some of it loose.

But only in private. In public I was going from one meeting to the next. Mrs. Papandreou, who encouraged me to call her Margaret, entertained me at the prime minister's beautiful official residence in an Athens suburb. The sun was shining as we sat in her back garden, the Mediterranean was shimmering. She was a beautiful and charming woman, very sympathetic, and we talked about Terry and the hostages, about Greece. She said that she would see what she could do, and would call me the next day.

She did call the next day and told me to see the head of the foreign service of the Greek government. I went to his office and explained, once again, what I was trying to do, which was to get to Damascus. I had been stiff-armed for more than a year by the Syrian government, which did not want me in Damascus. Why? Because I represented a public embarrassment to them, showing to the world that the Syrians were ineffectual in resolving the hostage problem or did not have the motivation to act. I was not good news for the Syrians, or any other government, for that matter.

The head of the foreign service recommended that I go on to Cyprus and make contact there with the Greek ambassador to Cyprus, who would smooth my way.

I had an unexpected emergency. There I was in Athens, I don't speak the language, and I all of a sudden needed some personal items. All the others in my party were males, and I certainly wasn't going to tell them. I remembered I had met a Greek reporter named Maria who was bilingual. I called her up and said, "Maria, this is Peggy Say. I have a problem."

"No problem," she told me. "I'll pick you up and we'll go find something. Besides, you're in Athens, you should take a little tour of the city."

So we took off. First she had to go to her office, which by chance was in the same building as the Athens AP. We took the rickety elevator up, Maria rummaged around, found what she needed, and we went back downstairs.

Maria was very nice. We got my supplies and then we walked around. She took me to some shops, showed me Athens like a native, and I got a very quick feel of the city.

When we returned to the AP building, the place was full of Greek police going nuts. They were all shouting and screaming, and Maria started screaming back.

Apparently we were being followed. Greece was having a tourism problem, my trip was being broadcast all over the world, and the last thing they wanted was for something to happen to this American with a press entourage. The Greek police had tailed us to the Associated Press building and then they'd lost us. They were pretty upset about it. They were screaming at Maria, "How did you get out of here?" She was yelling something along the lines of "You fruitcakes, there's only one door, how do you think we got out of here! How'd you like to read about it in tomorrow's paper!"

Finally everything settled down, but from then on I had the feeling that if I stopped quickly I'd cause a massive Three Stooges pile-up.

We went from Athens to Cyprus. At the Athens airport I looked around and there were armored tanks everywhere. "What are they for?" I asked. "For any suspicious characters we might see," I was told. "Isn't that a bit of an overkill? What are you going to do, run them over?" A part of me was fascinated by the security, by the need for security—where I come from, people don't just get blown out of the sky—but another part of me was in too much of a daze to pay attention.

We spent two days in Cyprus. We had lunch with the Greek ambassador there, an extremely impressive man who had just recently been ambassador to Syria. He was very intelligent and articulate, and he filled me in on who to see and what to say in my dealings in Syria.

I met the president of the Cypriot parliament and his American wife from Detroit, and they invited us out to their house for dinner. They sent a car for us. It was a rather dilapidated automobile and on the floor in the back was a cache of naked machine guns. The weapons weren't in cases or satchels, they were just lying there waiting to be used in a pinch. If you moved your toe wrong you could squeeze off a few rounds.

Over dinner we discussed Terry, and as we talked it seemed as if a solution to the hostage situation could be worked out somewhere. There didn't seem to be any question of who the kidnappers were, or what they wanted. We were all simply looking for some way to appeal to them. I did have the feeling, however, that this was virgin conversational territory for these people; no one had asked them these questions before, certainly not the State Department.

Cyprus had its own tensions. There were monuments erected to the United Nations soldiers who had been killed trying to keep the peace between the Turkish and Greek Cypriots in 1974. Terrorism was a constant threat. Nicosia, the capital of Cyprus, was a crossroads of espionage and terrorism, mystery and intrigue, in the same way that Beirut had been before everybody evacuated the place when it became too dangerous even for them.

Just as Margaret Papandreou had said it would, my visa for Syria came through. The Boys on the Bus were not allowed in, so they had to stay on Cyprus. They would call me every day for an update, and filed their daily stories from these phone interviews. They had traveled halfway around the world with me and, even when I was tired at the end of a long day, I couldn't turn them down.

At the Nicosia airport, I encountered a novel approach to baggage-handling security. Everybody's luggage was lined up on the tarmac in the blazing sun, and each passenger was made to identify his or her suitcase before it was loaded onto the plane. If a bag was not spoken for, it was left behind. If you were going up with a bomb, you were going down with it too.

The flight from Nicosia to Damascus was white-knuckle all the way. I was the last one on the place and as I took my seat I noticed I was the only person not wearing Arab headgear. I was a Western woman and they just sat there and stared; they couldn't believe that I was flying Syrian Arab Airlines. Neither could I. I don't have a happy time on airplanes to begin with, and the plane had shakes and rattles and rolls that felt like it was taking evasive action.

The trip was made all the more exciting by the fact that in order to fly from Cyprus to Syria the plane had to go north and then inland and then south so as not to be blasted out of the skies over Israel.

We were met at the Damascus airport by several welcoming committees. First, there was a huge swarm of press, all wondering whether I would be successful in my visit. Next, the AP stringer in Damascus had sent his Buick, a huge white American car that was extremely conspicuous on the Damascus streets, to pick me up. The drivers were his two very pleasant but formidable-looking assistants, one of whom wore a shoulder holster with no jacket over it.

Here was an armed man prepared to see me safely wherever I wanted to go. I told them, no thank you, I didn't want to stalk around Damascus with bodyguards. Nevertheless, they politely but firmly insisted that I climb in the Buick and they escorted me to the Damascus Sheraton.

What a place! The buzz that runs through the Damascus Sheraton is the pulse of Middle Eastern politics. Almost every person coming into Damascus for high-level meetings or business is going to pass through that hotel's lobby. The AP has a stringer who does nothing but work the lobby of the Damascus Sheraton.

It is a huge space, broken up into many separate alcoves by pillows and banquettes and tables and chairs. You can sit there and watch as the head of the Lebanese-based Druze Muslim militia, Walid Jumblatt, and a few of his people sit and do business. Syrian Defense Minister Mustafa Tlass holds court there every day. In the summertime there are tables outside, and miniature minarets, and the upper-class political and social life of Damascus passes before your eyes. We saw no other Western-looking faces.

But the pace of Syrian life bore no relation to anything I was used to. Most of the people I saw ate dinner at ten o'clock at night and then went out and partied. As a result, nothing began until eleven o'clock in the morning. I remember Terry telling me how frustrated he would get with the Middle Easterners saying *"Inshallah,"* which translates roughly as "God willing, all in good time," or more accurately, "Maybe tomorrow, maybe the next day, maybe never."

We were trying to set up our schedule and we were getting nowhere. We were completely focused on the Terry Anderson issue and felt we should be holding meetings from dawn to dusk. After all, that's the way it worked in the U.S.

"Inshallah."

But finally we got our meetings going. And more than that, I began to work the lobby. I staked out a sofa right off the bank of elevators and had a perfect view of everyone who came and went. Several of Terry's journalist friends were also working the lobby and they would give me the high sign. They knew my mission and they served as a de facto network. "At three o'clock this afternoon Sheik *X* will be here." And at three o'clock I would just happen to be in the lobby when the sheik and his entourage came through the door.

I always carried a stack of photographs of Terry and I would say, "My name is Peggy Say and I'm here trying to get information about my brother, the hostage Terry Anderson. This is his picture. If you hear anything, I would truly appreciate your calling me. I will meet with anyone to get my brother home."

I did this all the time. If I was hesitant at first, I got braver by the minute until finally I was relentless. With practically the entire political population of the Middle East strolling back and forth in front of me, I would never have this kind of opportunity again.

It began to feed on itself. The local establishment began to seek me out. I met with a number of Palestinian leaders who wanted to make contact. They would go back to their organizations and say, "I just met Peggy Say," and this would get around the neighborhood and the next alderman would say, "I've got to meet Peggy Say." There was a steady stream of people.

On about the fifth day I started toward General Alfeid, chief of the Arab Democratic Party and the head of the Syrian army in Lebanon. I was only a couple of steps away when he said, "I know, I know. You are Mrs. Say, you want your brother out. I have just come from President Assad's office and I am leaving right now for Beirut. I will try to find your brother." He had his hands up, almost physically warding me off, and was backing away as I was trying to buttonhole him. He seemed half put-upon, half amused. I thought, "Pretty soon they're going to start greeting me with a whip and a chair."

Most of the meetings I did have were arranged through the media people I met, usually Syrian or Lebanese. I have always trusted the word on the ground in the Middle East much more than the official pronouncements because these are the people who actually know what's going on.

Tony Touma, who worked for ABC in Damascus, was a friend of Terry's who was especially helpful to me, as were all the members of the media who were working out of Damascus. Terry was one of their own and they went to great lengths to see that I felt safe and had access to the people I was there to see. The man who had been Terry's driver in Beirut had made a special point of offering both his protection, if needed, and his friendship. I was very touched by all these offers and displays of loyalty and began to understand what had drawn Terry and held him to the region.

When I arrived in Syria I told the press that I was hoping for a meeting with President Assad. Assad had never given us any indication that he was willing to meet with anyone connected with the hostages. The way it was explained to me, if Assad met with the family members he would be admitting a connection to or influence on the hostage situation, and since Syria's role in the affair was very iffy and questionable, this was out of the question. That was why the Syrians hadn't wanted me to go to Damascus in the first place. I believe it was the personal effort on the part of Margaret Papandreou that got me into the country at all.

I was allowed to meet with two Foreign Ministry officials. They knew good and well why I was coming, and they knew I wasn't going to get that meeting with Assad, so they were trying to pat me on the head and keep me from kicking up a big public fuss about it.

But there were others who were more helpful and willing to meet with me. I got a call saying that the information chief of the PLO would see me. Terry had covered this man for the AP, and I was prepared to talk to anyone who thought he could help, so I said sure. That's why I was there. I asked an AP photographer to come along to act as interpreter.

So we took off in a beat-up cab down the winding streets of Damascus. I didn't have the faintest notion of where I was or where I was being taken. All I knew was that these people said they could help get Terry out.

We took right turns and lefts and the houses got progressively seedier as we got farther and farther from the center of town. Finally we arrived. The building looked no different from any of the hundreds of others we had just passed. We walked up some rickety stairs and stepped inside. The building, like most in the area, was stucco. You could hear the grit of your footsteps as you came in.

The room was sparse, not large, with a rug on the floor and a large desk pushed away from the window overlooking the street. The man who approached had had three fingers blown off, reportedly by an Israeli letter bomb, and his face was handsome though scarred. He introduced himself as Bassam Abu Sharif.

Abu Sharif greeted me warmly. He had been a source for Terry when my brother had come to Damascus for the AP, and he remembered him with fondness. Before we began to talk substantively through interpreters, while we were still kind of awkwardly establishing our ground, he beckoned to me to stand beside him and have our picture taken. I was carrying a five-by-seven photograph of Terry everywhere I went, and we posed with it between us.

A stringer photographer from Reuters had knocked on the door and was allowed inside by Abu Sharif. He came up and wanted to pose the two of us with a framed photograph that was hanging on the wall. I looked at the photo. It showed four young Arab men, two kneeling, two standing, each with bandoliers across his chest and a gun in his hand.

The Reuters photographer jumped up, took the photo off the wall, and put it in my hands. The AP photographer was almost apoplectic. He didn't want to embarrass these Arab men, nor make them angry, but he clearly didn't want me to be in that shot. "No, no, no, no!" he said as courteously as he could under the circumstances. "We don't want to do this until we know more about it." Abu Sharif understood, and they hustled the Reuters man aside.

When everybody settled down, Abu Sharif explained that this was a group photo of the latest martyrs. In that part of the world, the word "martyr" had a special meaning: one who has given his or her life in some military action against Israel.

It turned out that the photograph was of four Palestinians who just a couple of weeks before had floated in a rubber raft down the coast, put ashore in Israel on a bombing mission, and been killed in a shoot-out by the Israelis. These were the latest martyrs.

For a moment I was breathless. What if, in my ignorance, I had posed for that picture? What horrible propaganda would I have lent myself to? How would it have affected Terry? Again I was in over my head.

Abu Sharif and I began to talk. I asked him if there was any way his organization could help get Terry released. I explained that Terry was a journalist, he had nothing to do with any of the sides in the conflict, that he was only there to tell the true story of what was happening. Bassam tried to point me in the right direction, give me advice, tell me who I ought to see. That was how I made my rounds in Damascus, picking up references.

There was a screeching and squealing of tires in the street outside and all talk stopped. One of the boys in the household ran to the window and shouted something in Arabic. I couldn't understand a word but the AP photographer whispered, "He's saying that Abu Sharif is going to be assassinated."

"Oh, no!" I was about to hit the deck, everything was happening so fast around me, the clash of metal men reached for automatic weapons. The photographer ran to the window and looked down into the street, and I followed.

There was the big white Buick that had picked me up at the airport. It had braked and skidded so that it formed a roadblock across the small street. The doors were thrown open and there were my two saviors, standing with their automatic weapons in the air.

Word went down to the street and came back up. Abu Sharif turned to me and said, "They just wanted to know if you're okay."

I couldn't believe they had been following me all this time. If this was civilized Damascus, what could Beirut be like?

The photographer spoke quickly to Abu Sharif. "You must believe me, you are in no danger. The men are Mrs. Say's bodyguards."

I don't know whether Bassam could have been more injured by a bullet. He looked at me gravely. "You come to see me, you think you need a bodyguard?"

I thought to myself, "Terry, if I ever get out of here I'm going to kill you."

The meeting was over. It was a little tough to talk after that. None of this was real to me. The danger wasn't real, the people weren't real. It was like I was walking through a movie, like this other person was doing all these nutty things and I was somewhere deep inside of her looking out.

People wanted to entertain us. That evening we were invited to dinner at the home of the Greek Consul, Dionyssis Kodellas. But I was very anxious about being wined and dined in the company of diplomats. I was so far out of my element, and so unwilling to admit the truth, that I tried to avoid it. I told myself, "We are not here to socialize, we are here to do what we can for Terry Anderson." But at the same time I knew that the contacts I was making were very important and that I had to go to these functions. Plus, not to go would have been insulting.

My fear was not based on anything other than that I was terrified of making a faux pas, and I stood a good chance of doing it. Everyone around me had all the social graces and seemed always at ease, but I felt under constant social pressure. Every event, every dinner, every conversation was breaking new ground and it scared me.

The other guests at this dinner at the Greek Consul's residence were a British embassy official, Robin Young, and his wife, Katherine, and the sales manager of KLM Airlines and his wife. I had never been to a dinner with people like this before, and in the back of my mind the whole evening was, "God, please don't let me make a fool of myself."

We went into their beautiful house and the socializing was fun. I listened to them talk about the Lebanese black market, how if anyone wanted an appliance, for instance, they would simply put the word out and somebody would knock on their door and they would have this appliance. It might not have the instruction manual but it would be new.

Someone told the story of how one of the various factions in Lebanon had rented the road between Beirut and Damascus one night.

Rented it. The cost was a million dollars, but some black marketeer had bought safe passage for two or three hours and rolled a convoy of trucks with contraband goods out of Lebanon. He'd made back his money several times over.

All of this talk was fascinating, but then it came time for dinner.

My hosts assured me that the food was safe. I had been warned not to eat anything because the water was bad and you could spend a week in the bathroom, and I was not eating anything unless it was thoroughly cooked. Both Mrs. Papandreou and Congressman Bob Dornan had told me that they had become terribly ill after their recent visits. But it was explained to me that here everything was prepared within their home, even the ice cream.

That was comforting, but I had another problem. I had read enough books to know that, concerning silverware, you start from the outside and work in. I looked down. There was silverware across the top. This was trouble.

I figured, okay, I'm just going to watch what everybody else does, that should save me. Unfortunately I hadn't counted on the fact that I was the guest of honor; they were waiting for me to pick up something. It took a long time for the first course to begin. Finally I just made a grab.

I had promised Elaine Collett, who refused to believe that her husband Alec had been killed, that I would try to make contact with Abu Nidal. Abu Nidal and his organization, the Fatah Revolutionary Council, had only recently been blamed for the Rome and Vienna airport shootings in which one hundred eleven people had been wounded and nineteen killed, including the daughter of the Rome AP news editor. He had a global reputation for brutal terrorism. These were the people who had sold Alec Collett and Peter Kilburn to Qaddafi for cash and had them killed. I didn't really know who Abu Nidal was, but I put the word out that I wanted to meet with him. I mean, I knew that the Fatah had just planted a bomb on an airplane which had killed a woman and her baby. But that, too, wasn't real to me. There's only so much a woman can take before the whole thing stops being believable.

I got a call: Abu Nidal's spokesperson would meet with me. Fine, I said, what time is he coming?

The next question was, What do you serve a terrorist? What did I know, I'd never entertained a terrorist before.

I called down to room service for a little pastry cart and pots of American and Arab coffee.

The young man who arrived was in his early thirties. He was casually dressed in slacks and a flight jacket. Clean-shaven. He told me his name was Walid Yusef. He had an abscessed tooth, so his face was swollen and he appeared to be in pain. We talked about that for a while.

Walid spoke English. I wasn't nervous at all because I didn't have sense enough to be. I had met so many people by this time that this was simply another one. It was only a young man sitting in front of me, his mouth hurting so badly that he couldn't eat the pastries.

I had no intention of bringing up Terry's situation because I was meeting with him primarily on Elaine's behalf. I explained to him about Alec's family, and that Alec's execution was a terrible thing that had happened—if it had happened. The tape of his hanging was indistinct and it was impossible to prove that the dead man was indeed Alec. Elaine Collett had never accepted it; as far as she was concerned, her husband was still alive and in captivity. If it was actually Alec who had been hanged, I said, I thought that the humane thing to do would have been to give us his body. If it wasn't, give us a communication that he is still alive, because this is killing his wife and family.

Walid seemed to understand. In a strange way I thought he might be feeling compassion for the woman's uncertainty.

I said, "I would like to talk to Abu Nidal personally."

"So would a lot of other people." He smiled wearily. "As far as you're concerned, you talk to me, you talk to Abu Nidal."

He was the one to mention Terry. "You have letters for him? I may know someone who may have gone to school with someone who knows someone who may be holding your brother. Give me your letters, I will try my very best to distribute them." I had brought photocopies of letters from all the families, and I handed a set to him. I felt certain he would indeed try his best.

Something odd happened. The more we talked, the more we seemed to reach each other. There was a special look in his eyes that I responded to, a gentleness in the way he spoke, the way he explained what he had to do and what I had to do as well. Women in Muslim culture are not permitted the freedoms that Western women are used to. They simply may not do or say the things that I was doing and saying. But there was no mistaking the compassion he felt for me in trying to get my brother out.

Family is very important in their culture, and the fact that I was Terry's sister and I was over there, far away from home, doing everything in my power to rescue my brother, must have meant something to him. I was doing what they would expect any honorable family member to do. In their minds, you don't do anything less.

We spoke for over an hour. When the conversation was over and Walid had gone, I began to unwind.

That meeting left me with tremendously mixed feelings. The more I found out about Abu Nidal and his terrorist organization—he's been called "the bloodiest terrorist in the Middle East"—the more appalled I was at their actions. I have no illusions about the terrible things this group has done. But I found myself liking Walid Yusef. He showed compassion, courage, even warmth, and on a personal level we had a strange rapport.

I have real guilt that I actually sat down and talked with this man who is reputed to be a major terrorist and may have done terrible things. But in our conversation that part of him did not glint through.

I was learning. The biggest problem we've had in the United States when trying to handle the Middle East is that we have tried to deal with them with the Western mind, and you can't do it because you'll get nowhere. You don't have to condone or agree with what they say and what they do, but you'd damn well better understand it. We're on their territory and we're playing by their rules.

From day two I had been calling the Iranian embassy. I had established a telephone relationship with a man who was the second secretary at the embassy. Although always very formal, he did at least accept my calls.

I asked for a visa to Tehran. The secretary seemed disconcerted, and there was a moment's silence before he said he'd have to check. He called back the next day; he was still checking. He called back the next day and gave me "official discouragement." At one point he said, "You know, Mrs. Say, my country and your country do not have diplomatic relations."

"I am quite aware of that," I told him, "and that is why I am here in Damascus knocking on the door."

Finally I decided that, rather than work through the bureaucracy, I would try a frontal assault. Early one morning a friend of Terry's and I went to the Iranian embassy.

I had been told that the reason for the head cover worn by most Arab women was that her hair is a woman's crowning glory and should not be uncovered to tempt the male population. I kind of chuckled as I remarked that what was on this particular head would not tantalize anyone. On arrival in the Middle East I had discovered that neither my hair dryer nor my curling iron would work on their electrical current. I didn't have an adaptor, nor did I think to ask for one, so my hair was strictly "wash and wear" all the way. Not a pretty sight, but acceptable everywhere but at the Iranian embassy.

The guard posted outside the front door looked at me and pulled out a kerchief to put over my head. I was entering the Ayatollah's domain and I was not properly attired. I knew I was a Western woman entering a realm where Western women did not ordinarily go, where women in general had a very highly defined role. I was wearing black slacks and a dark-colored sweater but I had not anticipated the need for headgear. The sentry had. How nice of him to keep a supply on hand for the occasional gringo who happened to come by.

I put on the babushka and walked into the waiting room.

The waiting room was like a porch. There was a roof but the windows were only frames. Inside was a large collection of what I could only describe as wretches. Men. No women. These were Iranians who had business at their embassy. Somebody explained to us later that they were Iranian immigrant workers who were working in Syria and were trying to get back home.

These men were in rags. They were emaciated, without shoes; it looked as though they had spent the night on that porch.

Wooden benches lined the walls, but when I walked in they were all packed, there were no seats. I stood for a moment, trying to get my bearings, and when my eye scanned the benches the men threw themselves in the opposite direction to get away from me. I sat down, my eyes averted. They would not look into my face.

I didn't dare to look at anybody, lest I inadvertently make eye contact, whatever that might have meant. Men stood in bunches a respectful distance from me, and stared. I didn't know whether they had never seen a woman without the proper headdress, or a woman in slacks, or a woman who was not an Arab. Whatever it was, they were absolutely absorbed by the sight of me. I realized that my hands were bare—my flesh was exposed—so I put them between my knees. Seductress that I was, I didn't want to taunt them with my sexuality.

I sat there cowering in the corner for thirty minutes. It felt like days.

In the middle of this politico-psycho-sexual tension a mullah came through the door. A mullah is an Arab religious leader, or more colloquially, a big shot, and it was like a western movie where the gunslinger throws open the swinging door and swaggers into the saloon. This mullah must have had at least a 55-inch waist and was maybe five feet tall, and he had the strut of authority. He threw open the doors of the waiting room and these poor beggar wretches couldn't get out of his way fast enough. They just scurried aside. This was the second threat to their tranquility and it wasn't even nine o'clock in the morning yet.

The mullah swaggered to the front desk and said something we could not hear, and people began running around accommodating him. He was quickly ushered in behind the door that was closed to us.

One man, he must have been the adventurer in the crowd, kept coming up to me and talking Arabic, trying to shove a cigarette in my face. Was that an offer or an insult? I kept saying, "No thank you, no thank you," but he wasn't budging.

I didn't like this place and wanted out. The quicker the better. There was nothing that I could get a hold on; it was completely alien, and this was a very small dose. I began to rethink my eagerness to get to Tehran.

Finally an embassy official came over and asked us what our business was. I gathered up my courage and told him we were there to get visas to enter Iran. I had come this far, I couldn't allow my fear to prevent me from doing everything that could be done for Terry. The official took our passports and disappeared. Another half-hour later he came back. Of course they wouldn't see me, I was a mere woman, so they took my escort in the back—leaving me alone and very nervous— and gave him a brief but firm no, we would not be allowed into Iran.

During my week in Damascus I had become friendly with a woman named Hala Nabulsi, a translator who worked in the Syrian Office of Information ministry. Hala was an attractive, dimpled, dark-haired woman with a pleasant, outgoing personality. I took to her immediately and we became fast friends.

Hala's family home was one ridge over from the Bekaa Valley, which was as close as I could get to the Lebanon border. She made arrangements for a driver to take me there.

Damascus and Beirut are only about fifty-five miles apart. As we were driving up in the mountains we came to a fork in the road. On the left was a checkpoint. Beyond that outpost you were in Lebanon. I found that fascinating and a little bit frightening; beyond that line we could be dead in an instant. We headed to the right.

Hala's family made me immediately welcome and I was enchanted by her young adopted Palestinian daughter. As is usual when a guest comes, platters of food were brought out and I was urged to eat. Even though I knew it would be impolite to refuse, I was hesitant to eat what was set before me.

Through Hala, the only bilingual person there, it was explained to me that the food was absolutely safe; particular care had been taken in the preparation. Apparently Arabs were used to American squeamishness at the dinner table. I felt very much at ease and when offered a cup of Arab coffee, kiddingly told Hala's mother that we put syrup on our pancakes at home, we didn't drink it. They had a great laugh when that was translated, and the afternoon was a very pleasant break from the intensity I had been living with.

On the way back we retraced our route. Or we thought we did. Over a rise was an army roadblock. They pulled us over and immediately I thought, "They're going to kidnap us!" My escort was a journalist, just like Terry; if they wanted another one, here he was.

All I could see was our driver screeching to a halt and soldiers surrounding the car, hollering at us in Arabic. I was terrified. Had we made the one wrong turn that would cost us our lives?

It turned out we were still in Syria. The border guards knew that hostages were often transported in the trunks and undersides of cars, and they were checking to see that none came through. But for that one moment I just about stopped breathing.

Hala took me to the top of a hill overlooking a valley. It was the Bekaa Valley. I looked east. My brother was out there somewhere in chains. I looked south and I could see Mount Hermon, the big snow-covered mountain on the Lebanon-Syria border just north of Israel. I walked by myself for a while. I felt very alone.

I said a prayer for my brother. I thought of Dad and Rich. Here I am, guys. What do you want me to do now?

Tony Touma was not only a friend of Terry's but a Syrian with excellent connections. As we were sitting in the lobby of the Damascus Sheraton mulling over possible appointments he asked me, "Would you like to meet General Tlass?"

General Mustafa Tlass, Syria's defense minister, was one of the hundreds of people I had written to, and his written reply, while not encouraging, was at least an opening. I said, "Sure, I would love to meet him."

"Be out at the pool tomorrow at noon and we'll arrange it."

The pool at the Damascus Sheraton was *the* outpost of Western paganism in the middle of Islam country. There was a large and busy bar, and the pool was fairly teeming with two-piece swimsuits. This fleshy display of femininity was very unusual in a Muslim state, and General Tlass went there every day to admire the sights. I was told that even at the height of the 1973 war with Israel, Tlass always found time each day to go to the pool at the Sheraton.

At noon precisely, Tony came over and said, "General Tlass is ready to meet you."

We spoke briefly at his table, but because the day was so busy the general invited me to his home that evening.

When you're invited to someone's home in a Muslim country, chances are it isn't for drinks; alcohol is forbidden in Islam. You will be served Arab coffee or soft drinks. I was very pleased at the invitation.

When we arrived, Mrs. Tlass was engaged in an intense conversation with a man whose appearance startled and fascinated me. He had an absolutely gorgeous face, but was missing an eye. He did not wear an eye patch and he was dressed in a flowing white caftan. He was the kind of man you would expect to see in *National Geographic* with a falcon on his wrist. We were told later that he was Mrs. Tlass's religious counselor. We had to wait for their private talk to conclude before we could be announced.

I found General Tlass to be a very serious and impressive man. He was totally at ease and very talkative, and though he did not speak English, even with an interpreter he came through warmly.

I mentioned that Terry had interviewed him not long before his kidnapping and I could see the general trying to remember. I was not bashful in making a connection between the two.

His home was attractive, and his hospitality gracious. Tlass, an army general, was the author of several books on flowers and gardening; it would seem such an unlikely hobby, from a distance. But that evening it didn't seem like much of a stretch at all.

I had already worked our visit to the Iranian embassy into a conversational set piece. Every time I told it, it sounded more bizarre. I spun the story for General Tlass, and added that we were also serious about getting to Beirut to try to meet Terry's captors.

"Oh?" he said. "You want to go to Iran? I'll see that you can go to Tehran. You want to go into Lebanon? I will personally send an armored car to take you into Beirut. You will be safe. I give you my word."

Tlass was the head of the Syrian army; they controlled West Beirut. If he told us we could go into Beirut and gave us his personal pledge of safety, he was the man who could get it done.

In the car on the way back to the hotel that night I thought, "I have three choices: I can go to Lebanon, I can go to Tehran, or I can go home. What do I want to do?"

I was exhausted, I was homesick, I was in this strange land and it was only going to get stranger.

That night I wanted to go home. But I knew I'd think about it again in the morning. I was getting through this one day at a time. I'd decide about tomorrow when tomorrow came.

I went to bed completely torn. I would be risking my life in both Tehran and Beirut, but Terry's life was at risk all day every day. I was trying to press forward, but no one would tell me anything. I was meeting a whole world of powerful and important people, but I hadn't met the one who could free my brother. I didn't know how much more I could do.

The phone rang early the next morning. It was one of the Boys on the Bus, calling from Cyprus. He seemed very excited.

"Father Jenco is out!"

CHAPTER

8

FATHER MARTIN JENCO HAD BEEN A HOSTAGE FOR 564 DAYS, SIXTY-
seven days longer than Terry. If Terry couldn't get out, it was fair and
just that it was Father Jenco. I called the Jencos in Joliet and told them
the news. "I really think he's out," I told them, "it's just a matter of
finding him." There was some question because the captors announced
Father Jenco's release at eight in the morning but no one had actually
seen him. The family said, "If you see him, you give him a big hug
from us."

I called David back home and told him. Then I just sat there. I was
sitting in my hotel room in Damascus and I had no one to call. Room
service arrived with my coffee and I began running on to the waiter,
telling him that a hostage had been released and it was Father Jenco and
wasn't this just the best news. He smiled brightly. "Yes, missus. Yes,
missus." I was bursting and he didn't understand a word.

Finally the local media started buzzing on the phone and coming up
to the room. We were all milling around, waiting for word, trying to
figure out exactly what had happened.

Tony Touma suggested that we go over to the Foreign Ministry. It was as good a place as any; they would at least have some information there. So we all trooped over to the Foreign Ministry building and waited in a pack outside.

The atmosphere was unreal to me. Frantic, as if we were waiting for the Pope to appear in our midst. I had been at press conferences where cameramen jockeyed for position and reporters angled for eye contact, but this was all that in spades. Rumors flew through the crowd like puffs of smoke. It went on for several hours.

I couldn't cry because it wasn't Terry. Terry's turn would come. This was Father Jenco's turn. He was out! I felt nothing but joy for his family and him.

A military car pulled up in the courtyard and delivered its passenger. A large, pale man stood blinking in the sunlight. The crowd surged, almost lurched toward him.

Father Jenco looked dazed, like a swimmer who had been pulled from the surf. He looked at this sea of faces and said, ''Show me the sister of Terry Anderson.''

We rushed at each other. He threw his arm around my shoulder and we were jostled and shoved by guards as we stumbled inside the ministry.

Inside, he was laughing and crying and shaking, touching and tugging at me. I was so thrilled to be sitting next to this man who yesterday had shared a room with my brother that my mind was skipping around like a flat stone on a smooth stream. Almost before I could get one question out, another had formed. I was trying desperately to concentrate. I knew we had a limited amount of time together and I didn't want to forget the important questions.

''How is Terry?''

He had seen Terry that morning. ''He's okay. He's holding up.''

''Did they move you a lot?''

''Honey,'' he laughed, ''they moved me so many times, when I see a car now I automatically head for the trunk.''

We only had fifteen minutes together and he was so emotional we had to allow time for him to cry and laugh and tremble.

''I have brought out a videotape,'' he said. In the excitement he seemed to be scared that he'd forgotten it. ''It must be played on

140

television by midnight or they are going to kill the hostages. I don't know what happened to it. I was supposed to give it to the Associated Press, but the Syrians took it away from me.''

Before I knew it, the Syrian foreign minister came in and escorted Father Jenco away. The American ambassador, William Eagleton, was coming to pick up Father Jenco, I was told, and they would call me when he arrived and take me along with them. So they whisked Father Jenco away.

I didn't know what was happening. One moment I was with a man who had seen my brother ten hours earlier, the next I was sitting with two Syrian soldiers in the silent office of a Damascus bureaucrat.

One of the soldiers was the man who had escorted Father Jenco out of Lebanon. He didn't speak very good English but he did tell me that Father Jenco was wearing a set of clothes that he had given him.

I sent word outside for the AP to track down and get hold of the videotape.

I waited and waited and waited. Finally someone came in and told me the American ambassador had taken Father Jenco. I was not going to see him.

They let me out of the Foreign Ministry back into the front plaza. Where an hour before the place had been a madhouse, now it was deserted. No crush of press, no crowd, no nothing. I couldn't even get a cab. I had to turn around, knock on the ministry door, and ask them if they could please find a way for me to get back to my hotel.

The lobby of the Damascus Sheraton had its usual buzz going, but nothing more. A hostage release didn't change the pace of the city. I hurried past the businessmen and officials and all the entrepreneurs. I didn't know where the videotape was. I was becoming increasingly alarmed and nervous that the tape wouldn't be found in time for the midnight deadline.

Finally the AP called. "Look, we're going to get the videotape. The Americans have it and we're trying to get it from Eagleton. They want to make copies of it, they want to study it.''

"It has to get on the air,'' I cried. "They said they're going to kill the hostages!''

I was waiting and pacing and crying in my hotel room. I had come so far, been so close. I was joyful for the Jencos but feeling more than a little sorry for myself.

There was a major confrontation but finally the AP got the videotape from the ambassador. Tony Touma had come up to my room, and when the AP called to say they had the tape we rushed to the television station. There was only one station in Damascus. The tape would be pool material, which meant that all stations and networks would have equal access to it, and it would be aired immediately. There would be no delaying, no territorial infighting for an exclusive while the hostages' lives were on the line. The tape had not been screened. We would all be seeing it for the first time.

The station was in a concrete bunker-like building. Of course, nobody was paying any attention to me, and rightly so; this was international news unfolding before our eyes.

The tape was a message from another hostage, David Jacobsen. Things looked very bad. David was saying that the captors were going to kill the hostages. There was nothing I could do. I just leaned up against the concrete wall and cried.

I stayed up all night with the AP correspondent, who was transcribing the tape so it could be put on the AP wire. I hadn't eaten all day and was exhausted, totally drained. By the time I got back to the hotel I was pretty much in shock. I ordered breakfast, but when I tried to eat it I couldn't. I got into bed, clothes and all, and pulled the covers over my head.

Sometime later one of the journalists called. "Do you want to go to the airport? They're going to put Father Jenco on a plane."

"I don't want to go anywhere."

"Are you sure?"

"It's his family's time, it's not time for me."

He rang off and I fell back into bed.

Later he called again. "You'll never guess who was at the airport with his arm around Father Jenco."

"Who?"

"Terry Waite."

Terry Waite was a British envoy of the Anglican Church whom I had met several months earlier. I knew that he had not been in Lebanon this past week; he had in fact been in Amman, Jordan. But here he was insinuating himself into this hostage release. It struck me as more than a little strange, but I couldn't put my finger on just why.

With Father Jenco's release, my trip was blown out of the water. If another hostage was going to come out, they would have been released together; the captors certainly weren't going to let Terry go now. I had packed three changes of clothes and been away seventeen days. I had seen a part of the world I had never even dreamed of. I had hoped against hope that somehow my being there might shake Terry loose from his captors. I didn't know if I'd done one bit of good. It was time to go home.

I didn't have any idea what was going on back in Batavia, I was a little busy with other things. But when I got cajoled into sitting down and watching the tapes my friends had made of the newscasts, there I was. The Boys on the Bus had been filing daily reports on all three local channels, and my trip had been the lead story every day I was gone.

"Peggy Say is in Athens." "Peggy Say is in Cyprus." "Peggy Say has arrived in Syria. Film at eleven." It was as close as our town had ever come to being involved in international news and, since the stations had spent all this money to get the Boys on the Bus over there, they went all-out promoting the story. I know if I had been living in Batavia at the time, after seventeen days I would've been awfully tired of hearing just exactly where Peggy Say had been that day.

After having slept most of the first day I was home, just catching up, I was sitting in the living room with Melody and Randy and David, discussing a contracting job that David was about to start up. As he was heading out the door to go to work, David said to me, "Honey, I'm going to be late tonight, don't put dinner on until later."

Dinner? You get that from room service. Why are these people talking about something other than Terry Anderson? For three weeks I had lived, eaten, breathed Terry Anderson. Everybody who had talked to me was concerned with Terry Anderson. And all of a sudden my own family is concerned about what ladder to use on a roofing job? This doesn't make sense. I was extremely resentful of my family for going on with business as usual.

But once I figured out that it was just a problem of reentry, I got back in control. I began to think of it as living in two worlds. I returned from Damascus on a Thursday and was giving my daughter a baby shower that Sunday. On Friday I went to Washington for Father Jenco's reunion, which left Saturday to make all the party preparations. I did, and it went off beautifully.

I'd catch myself in oddball moments. I used to keep my appointment schedule posted on the kitchen wall on one of those note boards that you write on with crayon and rub off with a paper towel. I kept it up where I could see it, but reporters who came to the house used to look at it so much that I finally had to take it down. They'd always laugh, and when I looked over their shoulder I had to laugh too. It would say things like "Get groceries. Make appointment with Syrian ambassador. See State Department. Pick up dry cleaning." That sort of thing kept me grounded.

The journalists who had traveled with me were going through the same sort of thing. They had just come back from almost three weeks in the Middle East; they had stood on the White House lawn with Sam Donaldson; then they were back at the local affiliates and their station managers wanted them to go cover the sewer plant in Tonawanda.

I thought I was ready for some time off. I thought I had earned it, that I had explored every avenue to bring Terry home. Every time something major happened, like the meeting with Bush or the meeting with Reagan, I would think, "That's it. I have done this, now there is nothing left to do." It would leave me both frustrated and relieved. It was finally out of my hands.

But within a few days I would get a second wind. And something always presented itself.

The Associated Press organized an afternoon in Joliet, Illinois, where the Jencos lived, for all of us to sit around with Father Jenco and talk to him at length, to find out what we could about Terry and about what it meant to be a hostage.

Father Jenco was good with details; after 564 days in captivity they were fresh in his mind. He told us that the hostages were permitted to wash and go to the bathroom only once a day. Other than that they had to use jars to hold their urine. In the beginning of his captivity, his captors made him balance his urine jar on his head and stand there until he fainted. The hostages used their left hands to wipe themselves because they had to have one hand clean to eat with. This was the way they lived.

Several times, when being transported, Father Jenco had been bound from head to foot with tape, with only his nose left uncovered. They then tied him into the wheel well of a truck and drove to their destination. But the roads in Lebanon are not all well paved. Once, they hit a rut and the bridge of his nose hit the bottom of the truck and started bleeding. His mouth was taped shut and he couldn't breathe. In his panic, blind and struggling, he had thought he was going to drown.

Father Jenco and Terry were unusually close. It was clear from the warmth of his conversation that he really liked my brother.

When Terry was first brought in, Father Jenco had been living in a closet in that room for several weeks. There was a crack in the closet door and Father Jenco said that as he dozed off and on in the closet, each time he woke up he would immediately peek through the crack to make sure Terry was still there. Even though they didn't know one another and were forbidden to speak, Father Jenco was comforted at the sight of another American. Later, when they were separated into cubicles they could hear when someone new had entered, and they could hear the tapping on the bathroom walls when each man was finished with his fifteen-minute ablutions. So the men knew they weren't alone, but nothing more.

Each of the hostages had been asking the captors to allow them to come together to hold a prayer service, and finally the guards relented. "We were brought into a room together, still blindfolded and still dragging our chains, and we were allowed to hug one another, but we weren't allowed to talk," said Father Jenco. "When we hugged, we whispered our names in one another's ears. And we had our prayer service."

Terry had asked to be allowed some privacy with Father Jenco to give his confession. The captors didn't understand what confession was, but they did let Terry and Father Jenco go into a room together. "When I pushed up my blindfold to see the face of this other human being, and Terry made his confession, at that moment we all believed we were going to die. And we were ready."

In their cubicles they could hear William Buckley pass toward death. The U.S. government contends, because it serves its own purposes to do so, that Buckley, the CIA station chief in Beirut, was tortured to death by his captors. Buckley may have been tortured earlier but Father Jenco maintained that Buckley was never tortured, period; he knew for a fact, he said, that Buckley died of pneumonia. They were in the same room with him and could hear him failing. In fact, Father Jenco said he heard Buckley say in the midst of his delirium, "I'd like poached eggs on toast, please."

Buckley wanted water and Father Jenco was begging the guards to give the man water. He and Terry were praying for Buckley. One night they heard what he said were the "obvious sounds of death." The guards came in and dragged Buckley out. That was the last they heard of him.

The guards became very frightened; they hadn't intended for Buckley to die. They brought in a doctor, a very compassionate Jewish doctor who was being held by the same captors with two other Jews, and made him examine the remaining hostages. Suddenly their living conditions improved.

They heard a short time later that all three Jewish hostages had been put to death.

Some time later all five hostages—Terry, Father Jenco, David Jacobsen, Tom Sutherland and Ben Weir—were put together. There were five men of extremely diverse personalities living day after day in an underground eight-by-ten concrete room.

Terry, said Father Jenco, was the one who found it most difficult to live without news. He was a newsman and it drove him crazy. One time he went on a hunger strike for three days to get a newspaper. "I said to Terry, 'They don't watch us eat anyway. Just *say* you are on a hunger strike.' But Terry said, 'No way,' he would not eat until they brought him a newspaper. So after three days they gave him a newspaper. It was in Arabic."

"Ha, ha," the captors would say, "here's a story about you." And they would laugh. "We're not going to read it to you." Little cruelties. Father Jenco reminded us that these guards were kids, eighteen to twenty years old. Some were kind to them, some were unbearably cruel.

Terry would wrestle with one of the guards. Of course, he had to keep his blindfold on, and he was always very careful to lose; there was no telling what fate pinning your guard would bring you.

Looking for any means of diversion, Terry wove rosaries from fibers he pulled out of the mattress he slept on, and passed them out to the other hostages. He made chess pieces out of the tinfoil their cheese came in, until the captors took them away, saying that chess was forbidden in Islam.

He made playing cards out of the pages of books they were given. The guards would confiscate them, but he would just make another set. "Terry was a vindictive hearts player," Father Jenco told me. "Nobody could beat him because he had a photographic memory. When Terry got out the cards and started looking for his victim we would all get very busy. Nobody wanted to play with him. But Terry would harass us so badly that somebody would finally sit down and play.

"One of our jokes was, when the guards would ask if there was anything they could get us, we would always yell, 'A taxi!' " When his captors pushed Father Jenco out of their car as he was being released, one of them threw several Lebanese pounds at him and snarled, "Call your taxi now!"

Terry and David Jacobsen, he said, fought constantly about politics. "Every time Terry got bored, we knew David was in trouble."

Every day the prisoners were taken out, one at a time, and allowed fifteen minutes to go to the bathroom, wash their clothes, wash themselves, their utensils. "That was the opportunity for the rest of us to talk about the one who was gone.

"Terry became the Felix Unger of the group. This is a guy who argued because he wanted to hem my pants. He mended everybody's clothing, he swept the place.

"Every once in a while they would give us pens. Terry would use up the ink out of everyone's pen. We had to hide them. He was always writing stuff down. For me, I'd get up in the morning, I'd go to the toilet, that is my day. I'm in captivity, what is there to write about? Not Terry. Scribble, scribble, scribble all the time.

"For the rest of us, when we were told to do something, even if it was bizarre or undignified, we did it; it wasn't worth the argument. Not Terry. He would never do anything he did not want to do. His attitude was, 'Beat me, kill me, whatever you want to do, but I'm not doing it.' "

They lived mostly in their underpants, Father Jenco said. "We called it our three-piece hostage suit: blindfold, chains, and underpants. Every once in a while the guards would come in and check our undershorts for contraband. Me, what do I care? Not Terry. No way were they going to look in his underpants. And they didn't. He was adamant about it."

"It was not so much surviving captivity," he laughed, "as surviving Terry Anderson. Our only hope was that every time Terry would get involved in a new project, he would drop it and move on to something else. About the worst one was when Terry took up jogging. Now, I love your brother dearly, but we were not allowed to shower. And we were in a very small space. Everybody complained because of the noise his feet made, slapping on the floor as he ran around the room. And you can imagine what he began to smell like.

"But, so as not to offend anybody, Terry got a pair of socks and sewed pads on the feet so when he ran around the room his feet wouldn't make any noise.

"He had been learning Arabic from Ben Weir, but then Ben got out. Tom Sutherland was the dean of agriculture [at the American University of Beirut], so Terry took an interest in farming. He would get a project in his head and build it. He and Tom built a farm, cow by cow, building by building. They calculated how many cows they needed, how much milk they produced, how much they needed to eat, how many acres per cow.

"When they finished the farm, Terry went on to a restaurant he was going to build. You were going to cook, Peggy."

"Father Jenco," I said, "not even for Terry Anderson would I go back to cooking."

"Whenever the guards gave us a book," he went on, "Terry would read it over and over again. He'd read that book all through the night. There would be Terry with his candle, because he never knew when they were going to snatch it from us. Of course, that left the rest of us with nothing to read."

They gave him a Mr. T puzzle and Terry worked until he got it down to the very minimum time that any human being could put that puzzle together. "He constantly sought diversion for his mind," said Father Jenco. "It was the hardest thing for him to contend with."

When Father Jenco had greeted me in Damascus he said, "I have a message to you from Terry's captors: They send condolences on the death of your father and brother." But they'd never told Terry. They did tell him, in Father Jenco's presence, something to the effect of "Boy, your sister really sticks it to the government."

Father Jenco is a gentle soul; he wants to believe that he turned these people around, that some of the guards loved him. One of the guards, a boy by the name of Said, was kind to him, even went so far as to bring him popcorn. Father Jenco said, "Peggy, you must forgive these people."

I said, "Excuse me, Father, but I don't call people compassionate who bring you popcorn one day and kick you in the stomach the next. I'm sorry, it doesn't compute with me. I'm not a priest, I don't have that kind of forgiveness in my heart."

CHAPTER

9

In my dealings with so many embassies, I met a large number of people involved in international affairs. Most of them were cordial, but promised nothing except that they would take my requests into consideration. Every once in a while, though, I would strike up a relationship with someone who seemed as though he cared.

A diplomat at one of the embassies took Terry's situation to heart. "Every time I see Peggy," he told a mutual friend, "I'm depressed for days." I didn't want to depress him, but I did want him to do his absolute best for Terry.

On August 19, 1986, not long after I returned from Damascus when Father Jenco was released, I met with the diplomat in his office. He told me he had a plan.

The diplomat prefaced his comments by telling me that his government didn't like the idea that Terry's captors were pressing the United States for the release of the Kuwaiti prisoners. Not only was it not right or just that those prisoners be released, he said, but if Kuwait gave in to American pressure it would seem to be a tool of the United States.

Kuwait was an Arab country and this would make them look bad in the Arab world.

Then he said something I didn't fully understand. He said he was aware of the deal that had been cut in May of that year, 1986, between Terry Waite and the captors for the release of Shiite prisoners held by the South Lebanese Army in trade for the American hostages. I hadn't heard of that deal. He said one of the reasons the deal had not gone through was that it had been too private. If the Shiite community had known about it, they would have demanded that the captors make the trade.

He suggested that I take back to American officials his suggestion that the U.S. leak to the Shiite people the news about the abortive May deal, that the captors had refused it. Even though this idea was coming from him as an individual, he said he was confident his government would play a role if asked by American officials.

The diplomat said that once the leak had taken place, his government would go to Hezbollah, the Islamic fundamentalist movement with ties to Iran, and say they had heard about the Waite deal in May and if Hezbollah didn't accept that kind of deal, they would go to Nabih Berri, the leader of the pro-Syrian Shiite forces in Lebanon, and tell him of the Hezbollah selfishness. Turning down the freedom of a hundred Shiites in preference for one brother-in-law would not sit well with Nabih Berri.

All of these forces were armed. The Hezbollah was organized into militias of between 6,000 and 10,000 men, plus around 4,000 Iranian Revolutionary Guards. Nabih Berri's forces, the Amal militia, had been cultivated by Syria and were even larger.

Under the diplomat's theory, Berri would then pressure the Hezbollah to release the Americans. He stressed that the leak must be made for the scenario to work. He also told me he was skeptical that the United States would make the leak; it would show that the government was in fact wheeling and dealing on behalf of the hostages despite the public U.S. posture against deal-making.

The diplomat went on to suggest that an American official go to his capital and present the plan to his government as if it were an American plan. He asked me to take this plan to the U.S. government and get back to him.

I went back to my hotel and immediately called Ollie North. We set up a meeting in his office for eight o'clock the next morning.

"Ollie," I told him the next morning in his office, "I don't know if I'm going crazy, but it looks like we can get the hostages released." The first thing I told him was that the whole plan hinged on the ability of the U.S. to spring the Khiyam prisoners. These were Shiites being held by the pro-Israeli South Lebanon Army as "suspected terrorists" in Khiyam Prison in southern Lebanon. Their detention had long been a sore point with the Arabs, but Israel always kept a spare few hundred who could be used as trade bait in situations like this.

Ollie seemed extremely enthusiastic about the diplomat's proposal. He said, "On the surface, nothing in the plan presents any problems for the U.S. government."

"You understand, Ollie, that this deal depends on your ability to get the Shiite prisoners held by the Israelis free."

Ollie looked at his watch. "What time do you want them?" No phone call for authority, no time for consultation. Just "What time do you want them?" I was very impressed.

There were two other U.S. government officials in the room with us, neither of whom I had seen before. Ollie was always efficient, and as he repeated back the details of the plan he asked me to take notes for the record. The plan recorded that morning contained the following points:

1. I would return to the diplomat and tell him that I had met with White House officials that morning, that my main contact was Colonel Oliver North, who worked on National Security Adviser John Poindexter's staff. Colonel North answers to President Reagan and is the top man in the hostage situation. If confirmation is needed on my authority to relay this, he will provide it immediately by phone. The State Department is not, repeat *not*, to be contacted.

2. White House officials are very interested in the proposal.

3. Everyone must recognize that Shiites held by the South Lebanon Army are not under the control of the U.S. government.

4. However, the U.S. government is willing to undertake a very private and confidential discussion with those who have influence over the SLA to determine the feasibility of releasing the Lebanon Shiite people detained in southern Lebanon.

5. The White House officials noted that this plan must remain a very private matter between the U.S. government and his government.

6. The White House officials also noted that the Islamic Jihad organization holds an Israeli infantry officer and doubted that the plan would work unless the Israeli was also released.

7. The White House officials do not want to use the American ambassador as the go-between and will notify the diplomat's government of the emissary they do wish to use.

8. Leaking presents no problem, but what timing does his government prefer and how extensive should the leak be? Need clarification of how the leak is to be used by his government.

Ollie's initial evaluation of the scenario was that it seemed too well thought out to have originated with the diplomat. When I disagreed he intimated, with a "We have our ways" wink, that he *knew* it came from higher up.

Ollie told me to tell the diplomat that I had overheard Ollie and two U.S. government officials whom I didn't know talking among themselves about the 1985 TWA situation. In reality I hadn't, but Ollie was very keen on conveying to the diplomat that the White House was drawing an analogy to something in that episode. I didn't understand; I was just very glad to see that they were all so upbeat about the proposal.

Later that morning I shuttled back to the diplomat's embassy, told him that I had been asked to read him the list and get his response. The only point that seemed to concern him was the one involving the Israeli army officer; he said it might present some problems.

The diplomat seemed pleased. He suggested that the families of the hostages stage a news conference, once the scenario had been agreed upon, and that we make an emotional appeal to the captors. This would give the captors something to respond to, without making it seem as if any kind of deal had been cut. He then asked that a high-level American official travel to his country to present the entire package as an American initiative.

I went back to my hotel, called Ollie and told him that the diplomat thought the Israeli might cause difficulties but that he had signed off on the proposal. Ollie said things sounded good.

"Peggy," he said, "call the man back and ask who in his capital we should get in touch with."

I called. The diplomat named an official in his government. I called Ollie back. Fawn Hall answered his phone. I gave her the message.

I met with Ollie several times during the course of this initiative and I began to observe him in action. Whenever the State Department gave me the runaround, Ollie would talk to me one-on-one. Whatever his quirky personality, he would always talk to me. He impressed me with his sincerity, his empathy with Terry. Here was a man, I thought, who would move mountains to get Terry out. And that kind of dedication was exactly what I wanted to hear.

I was in his office one time when the phone rang. Ollie picked it up, straightened, said, "Yes, sir," and put the receiver down. He stood up.

"I'm sorry, I have to go," he said. "I have to meet the Vice President." He said it in an Ollie kind of way, as if he had saluted the phone. He did like to drop names. He would put a name out there on the table and just admire it. Like, "Gee, I have come a long way, haven't I?"

I found this call particularly interesting because, just the day before, Vice President Bush had returned from a trip to the Middle East. One of his aides had written a memo detailing a meeting Bush had had there with the Israeli prime minister's adviser, Amiram Nir. According to the memo, Bush and Nir talked about how many missiles it was going to take to get a hostage out. It was the closest Vice President Bush got to getting caught in the wringer. And here, the next day, Bush was calling Ollie into his office. From earlier hints of Ollie's, I felt there was a particular relationship between Bush and Ollie, and I could only guess at what they talked about at this meeting.

I had already heard State Department scuttlebutt about Ollie's suggestions to release the Kuwaiti prisoners, then put something in their food so that two weeks later they'd be walking down the street and drop dead. He was the guy who wanted to treat hostage ransom money with chemicals so that it would disintegrate. He was definitely "Colonel Flagg."

On one visit I had to wait an unusually long time outside his office before he let me in. Ollie finally came out of his office and apologized. He was grim of face and shaking his head. He told me, "In this business, you have to deal with some unsavory characters."

I was exhilarated by all the secrecy and high-level intrigue I was right in the midst of, but I was also beginning to frighten myself. I didn't know what I was getting into. Shouldn't the diplomat's initiative, this kind of international dealing, be done by people who knew what they were doing? Wasn't that what the government was for?

"Ollie," I said after my last trip to the diplomat's embassy, "I've had it, I'm going home. I'm going to foul this thing up. I'm scared. Let me out. You take it from here on in."

Between the time I was running between Ollie North and the diplomat, and the families held our press conference, two more men were kidnapped in Lebanon. On September 9, Frank Reed, the director of the Lebanon International School in Beirut, was taken; on September 12 they grabbed Joseph Cicippio, the acting comptroller at the American University of Beirut.

On September 16 a letter was released from David Jacobsen saying, "We feel homesick, our bodies are sick and our psychological state is bad." It included a "special hello to Peggy Say." The language was stilted and there were misspellings and grammatical mistakes, and the State Department questioned whether Jacobsen had actually written it. But to me the letter was a desperate call by the Islamic Jihad for negotiations to free the hostages. They wouldn't have put the message out if they hadn't been asking for contact. I was encouraged that they were communicating, but I was frightened and discouraged by the fact that they seemed to be running out of patience.

On September 25, the day of the press conference, we held an impromptu hostage reunion. Rev. Weir and Father Jenco hadn't spent time with each other since Beirut and over dinner they and Jerry Levin, the Cable News Network bureau chief in Lebanon who had been a hostage in the same building and had escaped, started trading stories. It was fascinating to watch.

Father Jenco said to Levin, "Sure, after you escaped they took me out of the kitchen and I couldn't raid the icebox any more. They put me in a new room and I found the rope that you braided and stuck behind the mattress."

"Remember old mean Said?"

They were reminiscing about the guards.

Father Jenco and Rev. Weir had spent time together in captivity but with Jerry they were asking, "Who did you see? Who did you know was in there?" They all remembered the three-tap code on the bathroom door.

For me the evening was heartwarming. When I spent time with ex-hostages Terry seemed closer. I pictured Terry sitting with them, telling stories. The former hostages knew how important they were to us; they were proof that people do come home, they do get out all right.

A strange thing happened after our press conference. *I* started to get press. I'd been interviewed a million times, but always for stories on Terry. Now the articles started to be about me. *USA Today* did a story on me in its "Weekend" section, under the headline "A Hero of Circumstance." My picture was on the cover in living color. The story was lengthy and full of photographs, and I found it tremendously embarrassing.

I was not the story, my brother was the story. But a lot of these profiles started coming out. I was already sensitive about publicity because of the grief I'd taken from my own family. I was guilty enough that, for all my best efforts, I had not been able to get him out. Now all of a sudden I was becoming a quasi celebrity.

What I was most uncomfortable with was being written about as if I were the hero and not Terry. During interviews I always insisted on telling the stories that I knew about Terry from the former hostages. I complained that the press was missing the real story here, the courage, the dignity, the faith and determination of Terry and his fellow prisoners. I felt that if all of America knew what I did about these men they would immediately rise to their feet in outrage and demand that our President do something to bring these incredible men home. The interviewers would usually nod in sympathy and then ask some silly question about my past, or the most frustrating, "What have the last two or three years been like?"

The other sore point for me was the implication that somebody had offered me a choice here. There never was a morally acceptable alternative for me in this situation. How could I have kept silent in the face of the obscenity that I was witnessing? Innocent Americans were being kidnapped and tortured and hanged and shot. The lucky ones were living in dirty basements, chained to walls, blindfolded, isolated, living in their own filth. As Terry's sister, I had no choice but to plead for his freedom. As an American, I had to lay the human rights abuses before the public. To do anything less would have shamed me emotionally and spiritually.

Sometimes I won the battle with the press and Terry's story would be told, but mostly it was an exercise in futility and I would reluctantly accept defeat. If, through their profiles of me, Terry Anderson's name stayed in the public mind, then I felt I had done my job.

One of the benefits of becoming known, however, was that some doors began to open. I finally got to meet Governor Mario Cuomo. He had helped me so much with Rich and the hospital plane and had marked Terry's anniversary by declaring it "Terry Anderson Day" in New York, but I had never met him personally. All of our communications had taken place through staff members.

We met in Buffalo. One of his aides came in to brief me and said, "Look, the governor talks a lot and you'll find it difficult to interrupt, but it's what you have to do."

"Not to worry," I told him. "I've been down this road before."

When Governor Cuomo entered, I was struck by the thought, "This is an incredibly handsome man." His coloring was wonderful, the charisma was almost bouncing off the walls; the room seemed to shrink when he came in.

By this time I'd had a lot of experience with initial meetings and first impressions. Many times it's the intention of the person I'm meeting with to do me the courtesy of shaking my hand and then get me off his back. I knew Cuomo was in town on other business and had been kind of corralled into seeing me. His aide had already warned me that we would have very little time. But I was going to speak my piece if I had to hang onto his coattails while I did it.

First I had to get past the amenities. You know, the "I'm concerned about the hostage situation. I want to help in any way I can. Thank you very much for coming." I had heard a lot of that from official sources in the past year and a half. This time, I stepped in.

"Excuse me, sir. All that is fine, but I need you to understand what's happened to my brother. Do you understand that my brother lives in a dirty basement? He's chained, he's blindfolded, he gets nailed in coffins or trussed up like a mummy and thrown into wheel wells when they want to move him around." People are always shocked by that. I don't know what idea they have in their heads about how these hostages live, but always they are shocked by the details.

"Terry Anderson is one of your people," I said. "He's from New York State, you're his governor. He's been in captivity over eighteen months. His father and brother have died. His daughter has been born, she's learned to walk and talk, and he doesn't even know her name. He hasn't seen the sun shine since the day he was taken. Can you picture the man? He pulled fibers from his bed and weaved himself a rosary.

"Do you remember who Peter Kilburn was? You know he was executed. Bill Buckley died in Terry's room. Terry could be next. You've got to help me."

I made him listen to me. And something wonderful happened. I could almost see the moment that Mario Cuomo got caught up in it. I could see it on his face; this wasn't just an issue anymore, he confronted the fact that Terry was a human being.

Once he took it personally, Governor Cuomo was extremely responsive. He was ready at that moment to put a letter in the Beirut newspapers saying essentially, "I'm only Mario Cuomo, the governor of New York, but I want to help Terry Anderson. Tell me what you want me to do."

One of the things we were trying to do at the time was get a fully equipped hospital into Beirut, hoping this humanitarian gesture might lead to the release of the hostages. He said, "I've got a lot of friends with money. Let's work on this."

I had already prepared a letter for the Beirut papers, so I asked if he would wait a little while until we saw what effect our letter had. He said sure. This was more than lip service; he was truly willing to do whatever he could to help.

Four days later the captors released two videotapes, one of David Jacobsen and one of Terry. It was the first anybody in the West had seen of my brother in over eighteen months, and he looked terrible.

"My name is Terry Anderson," he began. "I would like to send my thanks and those of my fellow prisoners David Jacobsen and Tom Sutherland to all those in America who are working and praying for our release. My special thanks and love to my sister Peggy and to Father Martin Jenco, Pastor Ben Weir and Jerry Levin for their efforts."

He knew I was working for him. I felt a rush of tears and relief.

"But I must ask you all and my government how long our suffering and that of our families will continue? . . . After two and a half years of empty talk and refusal to act on the part of the Reagan Administration it hurt to see the propaganda and bombast with which that Administration solved the problem of Mr. Daniloff, a citizen like us who was imprisoned only a short time.

"How can any official justify the interest and attention and action given in that case and the inattention given ours? . . .

"We are surprised that the American government has put pressure on Arab and European governments not to negotiate in such cases as ours, but surrendered itself on the Daniloff case. . . .

"How long must we stay in captivity? How long will the American government not pay attention? . . . If our captors did not allow us to send these messages we would soon be forgotten by all but our families."

Terry's face was drawn, his voice was dull, he looked beaten. Watching him was horrifying; it forced me to think about Terry as a person and to picture exactly what was happening to him. I had tried to keep those thoughts out of my head, to make his freedom an intellectual issue. The tapes made it emotional again, he looked so awful.

I listened to him hard. Some of the language of his statement sounded like he might have been mouthing his captors' sentiments, but a lot of it sounded just like Terry and I didn't believe he would say anything he didn't want to say.

President Reagan couldn't ignore this, he was forced to respond. In a familiar scene of the President rushing to his helicopter for a Camp David weekend, Reagan never stopped moving but shouted over the whirring rotors, "There is no comparison between the two situations. . . . There has never been a day that we have not been trying every channel to get our hostages back from Lebanon. But . . . we don't know who's holding them."

That was utter nonsense. Terry Waite didn't seem to have any trouble locating the captors, and I was certain that our intelligence agencies knew exactly who was in charge.

Then Reagan said something that really made me mad. As he turned to go, over the roar of the engines, he shrugged and called out, "I have a feeling that they were doing this under the orders of their captors."

Did President Reagan really think that Terry needed a gun to his head to plead for his freedom, to ask how long the hostages and their families had to suffer? That about made my blood boil.

I wanted to know why the same effort wasn't being exerted to free these hostages that had been exerted in every other hostage situation, most recently for Nicholas Daniloff, who had been arrested on espionage charges by the KGB in Moscow a month before and freed—clearly in a swap for a Soviet physicist, although the U.S. did its best to deny it—earlier that week. I had the strong suspicion it was because there were no cameras in Terry's cell to awaken America and embarrass the President.

On October 21 a writer named Edward Tracy was kidnapped in Beirut.

I scheduled a meeting with Ollie North to get an update on the diplomat's initiative. It had had several months to move along, and as far as I was concerned I had fulfilled every part of our bargain. I walked in and said, "Okay, Ollie, when do you pick up the hostages?"

"Peggy," he said as I sat down, "I'm sorry to tell you this, but the diplomat's initiative is a dead issue."

"What!"

"That government has their fingerprints on the Pan Am episode in Pakistan and the terrorist episode in the Turkish synagogue, and we aren't going to do anything that makes them look good in the eyes of the world. We don't deal with countries that sponsor terrorism."

I couldn't believe it. I started to object, but then his phone rang. I sat in front of him and stewed while he took the call. For him to trot out that old line at this late date was not plausible. Nothing that the diplomat's government had done since the start of this initiative had caused the U.S. to say, "We don't deal with terrorist nations." They'd been feeding me that line about "We don't deal with terrorist nations" for almost two years. It was the same government it had been when they'd sent me running over to its embassy in the first place. There had to be more there than met the eye.

When Ollie got off the line I said, "I don't understand. How can you say that? You have dealt with Iran, you've dealt on the *Achille Lauro*, you've dealt with Russia over Nick Daniloff. Where do you come off saying this?"

"Peggy, we've got some other things going," Ollie said, and took another call.

In between Ollie's phone conversations I tried to express my outrage. In the nineteen months since my brother had been kidnapped I had assumed that no one's hands were too dirty, no motive too corrupt, to enlist their help in bringing Terry home. I would have met face to face with the captors if I thought it would help, and you can assume that I have fundamentally different values than they do.

I was painfully aware of the outrageous discrepancy between Ollie North's bottom line and the Administration's droning assertions that they would "go anywhere, talk to anyone, pursue any possibility to its limits, explore all options" on behalf of my brother and the other American hostages.

So the phone was ringing and Ollie was distracted and I was sitting there waiting for him to settle down so I could get into the reasons why he had abandoned us. I was trying to come to grips with it. I said, "Ollie, you and I both know that Terry Anderson is going to be one of the last released. We knew that when Ben Weir got out." There had just been three more taken. It had been a year between Ben Weir's release and Father Jenco's. "If you continue to do what you're doing, maybe in five or six or seven years I might see Terry Anderson. That doesn't hack it.

"You're operating right out of your hip pocket. You're the only one who seems to know what the hell you're doing. For God's sake don't go out and get hit by a car or we're sunk. You say you've got other things going, why can't you do this initiative too? Why can't you do two things at once?"

I finally burst into tears. I was furious at Ollie. When he saw how devastated I was, I think he began to feel bad; he was not used to dealing with me crying. What with interruptions it was well over an hour's meeting before we were finished.

Ollie always used to give me a hug and a kiss when we met and again when I left. "I promise you, Peggy," he said as I stood up to go, "I'm going to get Terry out of there."

"Ollie," I shot back, "your promises aren't good enough for me anymore." There were tears in his eyes as he tried to kiss me but I was just throwing myself out the door, wanting to throttle him.

I had put so much into that initiative, all my hopes and efforts and contacts. I had been scared to death that I'd foul up the communications and really cause Terry harm. I'd been made to play high-stakes poker, and for what? I began to think I'd been had.

My government had let me keep my self busy running back and forth with a proposal they had no intention of ever putting into action. I had been a public reminder that they weren't getting the hostages home, and I had gotten quite good at my job, and they'd wanted to silence me. My trip to the Middle East had gotten a lot of attention, my TV and newspaper and radio interviews were keeping the issue in front of people. I was refusing to let the government allow Terry to sit in his basement while they dawdled or wheedled or actually did nothing. I was getting the government a lot of bad press, and now they had kept me out of circulation and off their backs for two months.

The worst of what I felt was a sense of betrayal. Had I been used and made a fool of by the man whom I had trusted so much? Whatever Ollie had done, I knew that he was Terry's strongest advocate and that he was fond of me. I couldn't believe he would have hurt either of us on purpose.

I had already scheduled a meeting with Richard Murphy, Assistant Secretary of State for Near Eastern and South Asian Affairs. The ambassadors to the Middle East reported to him, and he reported to Secretary of State George Shultz. I had gotten the feeling that it was Murphy's job basically to sit in front of me and allow me to get the anger off my chest so I would not criticize the State Department in public. By meeting with me, the State Department could take the edge off my assault on them. They brought me into the tent—now I couldn't accuse them of not seeing me—but they weren't about to do anything. It was Murphy's job to tell me nothing, and I knew it. But one hope had abandoned me, now I had to try another.

Ambassador Murphy's office was impressive. He had Persian rugs all over the floor, Persian rugs on the wall, and lovely Turkish coffee sets on display. Here was a man steeped in the quality goods of the Middle East.

It started out as a normal meeting. The families' State Department liaison, John Adams, was there, as well as the regular bunch of non-descript bodies and note-takers from this desk or that. The State Department had assigned the families official hand-holders. Their job was to anticipate what our next move would be, and be there to head it off. My job was to get around them and get things moving.

I asked Murphy what's going on, what news do you have. He gave the impression of being almost totally uninformed, as if he couldn't give me any information even if he'd wanted to. He was giving me the usual "Blah, blah, blah . . . quiet diplomacy . . . working behind the scenes . . . everything we can . . ."

I had really agonized over whether to tell Murphy what Ollie had done, but I'd finally decided that I had to put Terry's life and freedom above my personal reluctance to get Ollie in trouble. I breathed a silent "Sorry, Ollie," and plunged in.

"I need to know, Mr. Ambassador," I began, "who dictates foreign policy for this government, the State Department or Oliver North?"

Murphy looked truly angry. His face kind of paled and his jaws clenched.

"What are you talking about?"

I gave him a brief overview of the past six weeks, the diplomat's initiative, the press conference, the backing out. Murphy was definitely not happy. I got the feeling that he was more angry at the suggestion that Ollie was in charge than anything else. I was reasonably sure that this was not the first time that the four-star colonel in the White House had stepped on State Department toes.

Murphy also seemed quite bewildered at the idea that I had been walking point for this operation. Not hard to understand; so was I. He asked me to write up my experience with Ollie and the diplomat's initiative in a detailed memo while he investigated it. I said I would.

The next day I got a call.

"Peggy, this is Ollie. I have been ordered to call you. I have just had my ass chewed by the *highest* authority. I am to have no further contact with you without a State Department representative present."

He wasn't nasty or unpleasant, and ended by saying, "If I can help you in any way, just give me a call."

Part of me was feeling bad for the guy; he was clearly implying that President Reagan had bawled him out personally. But another part of me suspected that Ollie was a loose cannon, and I hoped that this incident would cause them all to get a grip on just what the devil was happening. I felt bad for Ollie, but I felt worse for Terry. If these guys didn't get their act together, the hostages would never get out.

Why would Ollie lie to me? What's the point? He had told me I could trust him, and I did. He was the government, and I'd had faith in him. If I couldn't trust the government, then I was in real trouble.

I wrote my detailed memo and had it delivered to Ambassador Murphy. When we met again several days later, Murphy had clearly heard Ollie's side of the story.

"Colonel North tells us that you were crying," Murphy said. "You were emotional, perhaps you misunderstood what he meant."

I'd had enough. I said, "Let me tell you something." I looked at John Adams, whom I thought of as an actual human being, as opposed to a State Department automaton, and whom I had been working with almost since Terry was taken. "These people have been involved with me for two years now," I said, "and they have never seen me cry. Even when my father and brother were dying, they have never seen me publicly shed a tear. So you know damn well if Ollie drove me to tears, it had to be serious.

"Do you have any idea what this has done to my credibility? I am now left to go back and tell the diplomat's government that I am not as good as my word. Ollie has totally undermined me in their eyes. I feel like a fool. They're never going to trust me again."

Having failed to convince me that I'd simply been confused, Murphy said, "Give Ollie ten more days. If nothing has happened by then, you come back and we'll talk about the diplomat's initiative."

"Well, then, you're telling me that by my brother's birthday, October 27, his feet are going to be on U.S. soil?"

Murphy repeated, "Just give us ten days."

I hit the road doing interviews again. I did *Face the Nation*, the *Today* show, *Donahue*. On October 21 I was asked to address the

Associated Press Managing Editors annual meeting. This was a very big deal to me. Terry had addressed the convention of AP bureau chiefs and editors some years before, when it was held in Monaco. When he called and told me, he'd been oh-so-casual about it. Like, "Oh, yes, I must fly off and talk to princes and publishers." But I could tell he was thrilled. Now here I found myself in front of the same kind of audience.

Every important paper in the United States was represented, including the *Wall Street Journal*, the *New York Times*, the *Washington Post*. In France, the French hostages were being mentioned on every broadcast, in every day's paper. Here, unless there was a death threat, videotape communication, or family demonstration, the hostages were a forgotten issue.

AP vice president and executive editor Walter Mears was on the panel with me and Father Jenco and Eric Jacobsen. All I could think of was, Terry would find this whole scene unbelievable, and he would cringe if I said the wrong thing.

One of my journalist friends was in the audience and he told me later, "I knew when you set your speech down and just looked out into the audience that somebody was in trouble."

It was the first day of the three-day convention and the room was packed. Standing room only. When I got to the podium I was standing there trying not to see faces, especially not to see Louis D. Boccardi sitting there in the front row. Mr. Boccardi is the president of the Associated Press, a very powerful man, and although they were extremely generous in paying for my travel and phone bills, the AP supported "quiet diplomacy"; it seemed they were willing to let Terry sit while the government "did all they could." I was supposed to have boundless and unquestioning faith in both the Administration and the Associated Press. I had a hard time summoning up that faith when the AP treated me about the same as the State Department did; little or no information. "Trust us" did not do much for my confidence in their methods, especially as Terry's time in captivity stretched on. This was the first time I would be confronting the AP members and I was very shaky—I didn't know if I felt worthy to go up against such eminent men as Louis Boccardi—but I was determined to force them to put some muscle into their efforts.

I basically said to this crowd of important newspeople, "Look at what you've got here: you've got a young man, a housewife, and a middle-aged priest, and we're all the hostages have. You're the people Terry Anderson put his behind on the line for. You're the smart guys . . . the ones who know how to ask the right questions. You know who to go to. You know how to make Terry Anderson an issue.

"I have yet to hear anyone confront President Reagan and ask, 'What is quiet diplomacy? Prove to us what you are doing.' There has to be a time when we force the Administration to acknowledge that quiet diplomacy isn't working. . . . How long are you going to let Terry Anderson suffer?"

I read to them from Terry's speech at Monaco telling why he was there. I said, "When Father Jenco got out, he went through the Catholic Relief Services files to find out what they had done to get him out. You know now what Terry Anderson was doing for you. Eventually, Terry will come out and he's going to ask, 'What did you do for me?' "

The first guy who stood up in the audience asked, "Okay, Walter, what's in the files on Terry Anderson?"

Walter Mears said, "I'm here today to admit failure. Not much."

I was told afterward that for the rest of the convention Lou Boccardi was "dodging bullets." Everybody responded.

Eric Jacobsen and I just kind of looked at each other. "We've done it! We have motivated the movers and shakers!"

The APME hand-carried a letter to President Reagan, basically saying, "What are you doing?"

The answer came back: "We are doing everything we can."

They shot off a telegram in return, demanding a better explanation.

They were going to make a case for us. After two years of trying, we finally had a powerful ally.

Eric Jacobsen and I were commiserating before the convention that this is our life, all we are ever going to do is run around giving speeches everywhere. Well, Eric did a beautiful job and afterward we dared to believe that we had finally hit the key, we had talked to the right audience, they were now going to make an issue of this.

Newsweek was putting together an up-to-date overview of the entire hostage situation. They had researched it extensively, and I went over to their offices and talked to the man who was writing the piece, Rod Norland.

President Reagan was still shrugging his shoulders and saying he didn't know who was holding the hostages or where they were. We knew that wasn't true. In a television interview, Lesley Stahl had asked Eric, "Are you saying the President is a liar?" At the time Reagan was like a godhead, and Eric was savvy enough not to come right out and say it, so he answered, "Well, all I'm saying is that he would have to have his fingers in his ears not to know who they are, because I know who they are."

Now so did *Newsweek*. They named Mughniyah, told the background of the political situation, and gave the story six full pages. They were planning to put it on the cover.

Then the editors had second thoughts. What would be the repercussions? Could airing all these details harm the hostages? *Newsweek* was sitting on a very hot and controversial article, and there were other publications that wouldn't have hesitated to publish it and damn the consequences. I was deeply impressed by the *Newsweek* editors and staff. It was probably the hardest decision I had to make, but finally I decided it was important for everyone to know just what was going on. I pleaded my case to several editors and had them view Terry's last videotape, in which he had begged for action on behalf of the hostages. They finally decided to run the story. Enough of "quiet diplomacy," we needed some action. If President Reagan tried to get away with "We don't know where they are," we could simply tell him, "Read *Newsweek*."

They were within hours of locking the story onto the cover when the Reykjavík summit between Reagan and Gorbachev fell apart. We still got our six pages and a cover headline banner, but we lost the cover.

I read the article and it was, all in all, quite balanced and accurate. But they had some facts wrong. For example, they said Terry was beaten so badly he lost part of his hearing. That was Father Jenco. Rod Norland wouldn't tell me who his source was. I couldn't figure out where they had gotten this information; it could only have come from

Father Jenco. I spoke with him and he was at a loss; he hadn't told them anything about his ear problem. In fact it caused a moment of friction between us; he thought perhaps I had been the source. It wasn't until later that it came out that Ollie North had been the Deep Throat on that one.

CHAPTER

10

ON NOVEMBER 2, DAVID JACOBSEN WAS RELEASED AND IT ALL HIT the fan.

Rumors had been in the wind: somebody was going to be set free. I don't know how they got their information, but a caravan of press had heard and they were camped out on my lawn. I was literally barricaded inside my house for three days, but I had good news to warm me: I had gotten a phone call from Ollie North's office; Terry Anderson and David Jacobsen were coming out.

The family gathered and we were waiting for the phone to ring. It got later and later, and finally people started drifting off to bed. Not me. If it was nighttime in Batavia, it was morning in Beirut. I wasn't going to sleep.

In the wee hours of the morning John Adams, our State Department liaison, called. "Peggy . . ." he said. Already I didn't like the sound of his voice. "Now, don't be upset. It's not Terry who's out, it's David Jacobsen."

I was devastated and angry. "Don't be upset, John? How the hell am I supposed to feel!" I was crying, out of control.

It was so unfair. It was Terry's turn. He had been in there longer than Jacobsen. We had done everything they'd asked.

I was overwhelmed with guilt. Maybe I had done something wrong. I had already been criticized and it hurt: "If you'd just keep your big mouth shut, he would get out of there." All of these cruel things.

I waited before waking anybody up. Just sat there by myself, crying about it, knowing it was all my fault.

Eventually, David got up and he woke the others. I knew that I had to go out and face the press camped outside my door. I put on my best face and expressed happiness for the Jacobsens.

But there was more to this story, it turned out, than simply a hostage release. A newspaper in Kuwait revealed that, a month earlier, former national security adviser Bud McFarlane and Ollie North had visited Tehran and offered U.S. military hardware in exchange for a cessation of Iranian support for terrorists and security guarantees for the Arab states. They had come bearing gifts: a Bible signed by President Reagan, a set of Colt pistols, and a key-shaped birthday cake "to open U.S.-Iranian relations." The cake was reportedly eaten by airport security guards.

Ollie North's office called. "Peggy, you've got to call off the press. We're still hoping for Terry, but the press might blow it for us."

I said I'd do my best, but after I hung up the enormity, the impossibility, of the task hit me. There was no way I could pull the media off the scent on this one. They smelled blood and it was Ronald Reagan's and Ollie North's. Besides, it wasn't the American press that had blown open this story, it was the Kuwaiti press.

I was stumped, I didn't know what to do, so I called Lou Boccardi for advice.

"Peggy," he said, "there is nothing you can do about it. The story is out, it's out of control."

So Reagan had been lying. It *was* arms for hostages.

Which was fine with me. I would give them anything they wanted, just send Terry home.

* * *

The hostage families had developed into a close-knit community, and one of the hardest times was when one family got their prayers answered. Each time a hostage was released they were filled with joy, but their joy was diminished by the knowledge that the rest of us had been left behind.

When David Jacobsen was released he was first flown to Wiesbaden, Germany, for debriefing. It was that way for all the freed hostages. I knew that Eric would contact me immediately, even from Wiesbaden, to tell me that David had seen Terry and to give me the news. I knew I could count on that, and that's exactly what happened. David was then to be flown back to the States, where we could all get a chance to talk to him directly.

The day of the homecoming the rest of the hostage families were gathered at Andrews Air Force Base to wait for his flight. We were all sitting in the VIP lounge right off the runway where the plane was going to land. The press was massed behind barricades, State Department people and American University of Beirut officials were there. When something as overwhelming as a hostage release happens, you'd be surprised who crawls out of the woodwork to say, "Yes, we were doing everything we could."

In my immediate party it was just me, my sister-in-law Penny, an AP representative, and Sis and Jerry Levin.

When the plane landed, the State Department entourage started toward it, and we started with them. "Sorry," said State Department security, "you are staying here."

We represented failure. Our men weren't coming home. They wanted to welcome this hostage as a shining example of their successful diplomacy and we were standing there, a reminder that, hey, this is still going on.

It generally takes me a moment to react, so I stopped. I mean, I had been told to stop, so I stopped. Then I muttered, "To hell with this," and out I went.

Everybody followed behind me. I had come this far, there was no way I was going to let them ignore me now. I knew that David Jacobsen's boys expected to see me on that tarmac and, by God, that's exactly where I was going to be.

David Jacobsen was whisked off, but we were to meet at his hotel the next morning for the obligatory returning-hostage reception. I hadn't had a chance to talk to him at all. Eric had already told me, "Yes, he saw Terry. Yes, Terry is okay."

Eric also told me about coming face to face with Nancy Reagan. Eric had been a vocal critic of the Administration's nonaction, and a firm friend of mine. When he met the President's wife and she shook his hand, she'd had tears in her eyes. "You see, Eric," she'd said, "we did care."

"You know," he'd told her, "caring is not enough."

I was very anxious to meet David Jacobsen, even though I have found that first meetings are generally not as productive as ones later on when the hostages have had a chance to sort things through. It is a difficult time for everyone; we all feel we have to say and hear everything at once. At the same time there is a frustrating reluctance on the part of other hostage family members to pressure the hostage. On the one hand, he's just gotten out and needs time to adjust to his freedom. On the other, the rest of the families need to know everything they can about their men. It's hard. They have brochures and programs for returning POWs but none for returning hostages. You've got to make it up as you go along.

My meeting with David Jacobsen was very emotional. One part of me was happy for him and his family and the other was grieved for Terry and me.

Jacobsen told me some interesting things about his release. In Cyprus, where he stayed briefly before going to Wiesbaden, he was debriefed by a team that included Oliver North. David told me that he saw this guy sitting by the wall with his head in his hands, sobbing. He didn't know who it was at the time but he later learned that it was Colonel North. He was crying because he did not have Terry Anderson. I later heard that North was throwing people up against the wall, saying, "What the hell happened here? The deal was for Jacobsen *and* Anderson!"

This is what I have pieced together from reading the papers, from people's books on the subject, and other sources:

On the infamous trip to Tehran, Robert McFarlane was offered two hostages and walked away from the deal. I am told that one of the hostages was Terry. McFarlane's orders were to come home with all four hostages or none at all. The U.S. was prepared to fly a planeload of weapons to Iran in exchange for the four men.

But when North and McFarlane got there they discovered very early on that the Iranians had no intention of following through, so McFarlane ordered the shipment stopped. "Turn the plane back, we're getting out of here, I've had it with these people." That sort of thing. Then he turned in for the night.

Unbeknownst to him, while McFarlane was sleeping, Ollie North continued negotiations. North reached an agreement with Manucher Ghorbanifar, an Iranian arms merchant, under which two hostages would be released immediately in exchange for the planeload of armaments, and two other hostages would be released sometime later in exchange for more of the same. North made a phone call, and had the plane rerouted to Iran. The next morning, when he found out about it, McFarlane cancelled the entire mission. That scotched the contact completely.

In reading McFarlane's justification for doing what he did, I have to say it was probably the right decision. He wanted all the hostages, not some drop-by-drop squeeze play. And he wanted it guaranteed.

Ollie North was by that time reluctant to stop the initiative. In fact he was determined to keep it going; the middle-man profits made in the sale of arms to Iran was going to fund the contras in Nicaragua.

Anyone who had been around Ollie for more than two minutes knew that he had two political priorities in his life: the contra rebels and the hostages in Lebanon. Having stumbled into a major initiative that could conceivably have resolved both dilemmas, Ollie rolled up his sleeves and started dealing.

I don't believe that Ollie would have deliberately prolonged the captivity of the hostages, but as long as he could keep that channel into Iran, grossly overcharging the Iranians for military supplies and diverting the excess to the contras, Ollie was loath to end it. That the hostages were being peeled out one at a time—and with months or years between the releases—wasn't enough of an obstacle for Ollie to give up the game.

Ollie North didn't happen in a vacuum. There were officials in high places who made the decision to "let Ollie do it." Before Iran-contra, every official approached on the subject claimed to be "working behind the scenes'' for the hostages' release. When the scandal broke, these same officials ran for their political lives. Some ran so fast and so far they're probably still panting.

It was the most blatant display of cowardice I've ever witnessed and I was embarrassed for those ''behind the scenes'' statesmen who were now whimpering that they'd had absolutely no idea what was going on. But they can't have it both ways; either they were up to their elbows in Iranscam or they were lying all along. Either way, it smelled to high heaven.

Ollie North is neither good nor bad; he's like most of us, a combination of both. Who among us, given the power and authority that was dumped in Ollie's lap, wouldn't have used that position to affect the things we cared about? Who hasn't nurtured the thought, If I was in charge I'd (a) fire everybody in Congress and start all over again; (b) cut off all foreign aid until there wasn't a single hungry or homeless person in this country; (c) provide free medical care for everyone and see that every child had a college education; (d) all of the above; (e) fill in the blanks with whatever bugs you.

Ollie North was the creation of an administration that couldn't come up with the right solutions. ''Let Ollie do it'' became the grateful cry of those who didn't want to exert themselves. Tired, overburdened, and slightly crazed with power, Ollie *did* do it. Had he succeeded, he would have been everybody's dream. In failure, he became Washington's worst nightmare come true. At least Ollie accepted his part of the blame, which is more than I can say about many of his compatriots. He's been called many names: a madman, a power addict, an egomaniac, a liar. But never a coward.

What began as a botched negotiation ended up as Iran-contra.

There had been rumors floating around for months but the implications just seemed too bizarre to be based in truth: the U.S. selling arms to Iran through Israel? A low-level State Department functionary had mentioned it to me, so I assume that, if they were telling me, it was an open secret around the State Department.

Ambassador Murphy had to have known that Ollie was up to something. He had spent an afternoon telling me to shut my mouth and stop blasting the Administration for another ten days. "Give Ollie ten days," he had told me, in front of several low-level note-takers. Clearly the State Department was more wired than they were letting on.

The first story we were hearing was that this was an attempt to establish a dialogue with Iran. I didn't say anything publicly because I've always been careful of protecting my own credibility. That had been hammered into me: Be credible, don't go off half-cocked. So I refused all interviews when Irangate broke.

Phil Donahue called me one day. I am a big Donahue fan and he had been very kind to me when he'd had me on his show. He was putting together a program on the hostage situation and basically wanted to know what was current. "What do you think about what's happened?" he asked me.

"Well," I told him, "if it was really an attempt at establishing dialogue with Iran, I think it was a good thing."

"What are you saying publicly about it?"

"I'm not saying anything."

"Why not?"

"I don't want to get caught up in the controversy."

"It's no secret to anybody that I'm no Reagan fan," he said, "but my feeling is that if it's a planeload of arms they want to get the hostages out, send them the damn planeload and get it over with." Mind you, at that time Reagan was saying it was just a teeny little planeload of supplies.

After I hung up with Donahue I got to thinking. My bottom line through all of this has always been, What would Terry want me to do? Would he approve of what I'm saying? Of what I'm doing? The more I thought about it, the more I knew I was really acting in a cowardly way. All along I had been encouraging the government to get the hostages home by any means necessary. Now, when the government had taken an initiative and was coming under fire for it, I didn't want to get involved, I was hiding.

I wrote an open letter to President Reagan, which I phoned in to *USA Today* and they published:

I extend to you my support and deepest gratitude for the risks you have been willing to assume on behalf of my brother, Terry Anderson, and the

American hostages held in Lebanon. I apologize for not speaking out in strong support sooner, and feel a deep sense of shame at trying to evade the controversy surrounding this initiative. . . .

"Arms for Hostages" is a gross oversimplification of what has gone into this initiative, but the next time somebody asks me if I want my brother back under those circumstances, instead of taking the cowardly way out and saying "No comment," my answer will be "You're damn right I do!"

President Reagan had never taken any real heat before. He was so powerful and so well-loved that people refused to believe he could do anything wrong. *He* couldn't believe he'd done anything wrong. People found it difficult to criticize President Reagan. They had no such difficulty castigating the hostage families and me. Somebody had to take the blame and the families were convenient, and I was the spokesman so I became the number one target.

It was as if we personally had strong-armed the President into defying national policy, or breaking the law. I'd been trying for twenty months to get the government even to listen to me; now I was being blamed for running it into the ground.

The day before Thanksgiving my phone was ringing constantly. Everybody wanted a comment, but I had said all I was going to say. I took the phone off the hook and was trying to clean house for the next day's family dinner. I was on my hand and knees, my jeans rolled up, waxing the kitchen floor, when my son's fiancée asked if it was all right to use the phone. Okay, I said, but leave it off when you're finished so I can get my work done.

The phone rang. Dammit. She ran in and grabbed it, then came into the kitchen. I looked up at her. "Missy, I told you to leave the phone off the hook."

"But," she stammered, "it's Air Force One. The President wants to talk to you!"

I pulled myself off the floor.

It really was the President.

"Hi, Peggy, this is President Reagan."

Wiping my hands on a dish towel, I said, "Hi, how are you?"

"I just wanted to thank you for the letter in *USA Today*."

"Oh, you're very welcome, Mr. President."

"I want you to know that I don't care what anybody says, I am going to continue to do my best to get your brother and the rest of the hostages home."

I thanked him and wished him a happy Thanksgiving and he got off the phone.

I'm never prepared for these bolts from the blue. There are always a million things I think I should have said, but they all come to me after the moment is gone. I get in the presence of all that power and authority and I'm overwhelmed.

When I thought about it, Reagan had made a very strong statement. And, since he was speaking from Air Force One over the airwaves, anyone could have monitored the call.

This was before anyone knew that the money from the Iran arms sales was going to fund the contras. I don't know if President Reagan knew about it; he has denied any knowledge of the scheme. But when that news came out, the hostage issue was dead in the water.

Funding the contras by overcharging the Iranians. I have come to understand that such machinations are standard in international politics and finance, but Terry Anderson didn't have anything to do with Iran-contra.

Try telling that to the American people. I got hate mail that made me wince. Editorials, letters, comments to me in the street—all blaming the families, some even blaming the hostages, for what President Reagan had done.

I couldn't handle it.

It had been hammered into me so often that Publicity Will Prolong Their Captivity. The government wanted me to believe it; that's what "quiet diplomacy" was all about. Here was a question so complicated that heads of state hadn't been able to resolve it, but Joe Blow walking down Main Street kept telling me that if I'd kept my mouth shut they would've been out of there long ago. Even though I'd tried to harden myself against their criticism over the years, it's hard to do when you've never been under this kind of onslaught. It hurt.

There were times when I'd been engaged in conflict with bureaucrats, but I had never in my life been a personal target of the hate and vindictiveness that was flying my way now. Lots of people didn't like to see a woman have strong opinions and stand up and fight like I did.

Batavia, our hometown, had become divided, about half for me and half very much against. I knew that not everyone in town supported what I was doing when someone spray-painted on a viaduct over an underpass, for all the world to see: "Trade Peggy for Terry." David was outside our house getting the mail one day when a little old lady drove by in her Chevy and shot him the bird.

After having lost Dad and Rich, and now with Iran-contra, I was emotionally unstrung.

If enough people tell you you're wrong, you start to believe it. Particularly when it comes from your own hometown. I think that when someone criticizes you, you need to look at yourself and say, "Is it possible they are right? *Am* I doing the right thing?" I began to question myself. I would get upset about it, and then I'd tell myself, "If you can't stand the heat, get out of the kitchen!" That only went so far. I couldn't get out of the kitchen; I lived there.

The only people I had to guide me, to tell me what the right thing to do was, were Terry's friends and the ex-hostages. If there was any indication that publicity prolonged their captivity, the ex-hostages would be the first to say so.

Ben Weir and his wife Carol were going to speak at a church service in Syracuse, New York, and I made the lengthy drive to see them. The press was milling around their hotel lobby and I walked up the back stairs so I wouldn't be seen.

Carol Weir had been vocal in pressing the government to get actively involved in getting the hostages released even before Terry was taken. She was out there a year before I was. I had taken up her mantle. Now I sat down with them and poured my heart out. "Carol," I asked, "if you had it to do over again, would you have gone public?"

She said, "Absolutely. That's why Ben is sitting here today."

I trusted Ben to tell me the truth, as I knew he would. I asked him if he had any reservations, any regrets, if he ever thought that Carol's being as public as she'd been had kept him in captivity.

"Peggy, it was absolutely the right thing for her to do, and it is absolutely the right thing for you to do. You must keep up the fight."

But even that didn't completely convince me. I was so hurt and guilty and vulnerable that I couldn't risk somebody calling me names. I hid on the fire stairs landing and made my husband go out and scout for the press before I would leave the hotel. I felt that if another person said something nasty to me I would completely disintegrate.

Right after New Year's, 1987, the State Department called. "Give us three or four weeks," they told me, and maybe something positive would happen. I didn't know where they got their information, but I was overjoyed to hear it. There had been a flurry of stories in the news recently, most of them revolving around Terry Waite.

Terry Waite was a figure of some mystery to a lot of people involved with the hostages. An Anglican Church envoy who seemed to have access to the captors and many segments of the Arab world, Waite went in and out of Beirut more often than seemed healthy.

I had first met Terry Waite when my father was in the hospital and I was grateful that somebody was doing something while I was just totally out of it. Waite was a giant of a man, very tall and imposing, and he was extremely closed-mouthed. He wouldn't tell anybody anything. I thought that was admirable, that this was the kind of person we needed. Just go and do the business.

Waite had been in Beirut in December. He wouldn't tell anyone in the press what he had seen or heard, but I figured when I met with him privately that he would tell me. He was in Canada and one of the local upstate New York camera crews had driven me up in a nasty storm to see him. Waite took me into a private office and the first thing I asked him was, "Did you see Terry when you were in there?"

He refused to tell me. He said, "I can't say that. I *can* promise you he is in good health, he is fine."

In the meantime I'd begun hearing from various sources that Terry Waite was not to be trusted, that I didn't want to have anything to do with him, that on his most recent trip he had been given 24 hours to leave Beirut or he was dead meat.

But Waite's reputation was on the line. He had been nominated for the Nobel Peace Prize. His star was still shining on the horizon, though it had been more than slightly tarnished by rumors that he was a front for the U.S. government. Waite and Ollie North, the story went, had been involved in a mutually beneficial scheme. Waite allowed himself to bask in international glory as a front man to divert attention from the U.S. government's behind-the-scenes activity. When Terry Waite showed up with a hostage, like Father Jenco, it was assumed by the press and the general public that he had negotiated the release. Waite, North, and the government allowed that assumption to flourish; it camouflaged the fact that the deal was actually an exchange of hostages for weapons. Because of these accusations, Terry Waite was going to go back in and prove they were all wrong, that he could do it all on his own.

In the world of the hostage situation there are rumor hot-lines, and a big one came across the wire: Because the U.S. government owed Terry Waite—because he had covered for them and then ended up getting smeared with the Ollie North brush—a prewritten scenario had been developed. Waite would go into Beirut in December and come out again. Meanwhile, a deal had been worked out involving Kuwait and assets and captors and hostages. Waite would go in again and this time he would come out with Tom Sutherland and Terry Anderson. The U.S. government was going to allow Waite to be the hero because they owed him.

High-level sources were telling me that Terry was coming home. Based on what we believed to be credible information, David and I decided that when Waite went to Beirut the second time, that was the time for us to leave and go someplace so I would not be accessible to the press. I didn't want them in our front yard again, and I knew that as soon as the story broke they'd be right over.

So we hid out in a hotel in Virginia. Everybody was telling us it would be a couple of days and then Terry would be free.

It was January 19, 1987, when Terry Waite went in. A blizzard hit the Washington area and everything came to a standstill. David and I were stuck in our hotel for two days, then three days, then four days, just waiting.

On January 24 four professors at Beirut University College—Alann Steen, Jesse Turner, Mithileshwar Singh, and Robert Polhill—were kidnapped.

All of a sudden nobody was hearing from Terry Waite. As I recall it, the man at whose Beirut house Waite was staying was a pediatrician. He had been called to the hospital on an emergency and had told Waite not to go anywhere. When he came back, Waite was gone.

Rumors started to come out of Lebanon that maybe Waite was not going to be coming out. The Church of England was still insisting that he was in there negotiating, but by about the tenth day it became apparent that we had a big problem on our hands. Waite had gone in on January 19. On the thirty-first David and I were home again. We had no Waite, no government, no hope.

On February 2 the Islamic Jihad released a picture of Terry. He looked thin and tired and bewildered, but even at that, better than I expected. I felt like such a failure. He obviously depended on me to do *something*, anything, to get him out. I just couldn't find the solution and I wanted so badly to apologize, to tell him how sorry I was that I couldn't help.

My world had become one continuous nightmare, broken only by episodes of wishful thinking: It would soon be over . . . Terry would be out soon . . . This must mean it's going to end. No hope, no rumor, no idle speculation was so wispy that I couldn't grasp it and hang on for dear life.

All over Washington doors were slamming in my face. I would call for appointments and suddenly everybody was tied up or out of town or too busy. For a moment I was startled, but then I figured out the only two reasons that made any sense: first, the whole hostage issue had become poisoned; second, I was the only person who could connect these people with Ollie North, and they knew it.

"I have to see these people," I told myself. "I can't be frozen out by my own government." So I wrote the State Department a letter saying, in effect, "I have proven in the past that I know how to keep my mouth shut and I suggest that it might be in your best interest to meet with me." Only I worded it more diplomatically. There were stories they didn't want me passing around, and I had the feeling they would see me rather than see those stories in print.

I finally got a return call. I was to come to the State Department, but I was to come in the back door. Don't let anybody know you're coming. I seriously thought about buying a trench coat and turning up the collar.

I was in touch with Bruce Laingen, who said, "Would you like to meet with the new CIA guy on the hostage case?" I said, "Sure." He said he'd set it up for me. He called back and said, "I talked to a CIA officer who tells me there is already a CIA guy going to attend the State Department meeting."

Aha! It was time to play Spot the CIA Guy.

The meeting was filled with the usual players and then this new man came breezing in late and was introduced. When he opened his mouth he proved to have a lot of knowledge about Iran. In fact, I liked some of the ideas he was setting forth; he was active and encouraging in ways that no one else around there was. As the meeting was breaking up I said to him, "By the way, do you have a card?"

"Oh, gosh, I don't have one with me," he said. Hardly a surprise. He typed his name, his telephone number, and "Department of State" on a piece of notepaper. I wanted to say to them, "Come on, you guys."

State Department personnel started getting shuffled around so fast that all of a sudden there was nobody I knew anymore. Bob Oakley disappeared to an invisible White House staff job and resurfaced sometime later as ambassador to Pakistan.

Our liaison, John Adams, was off the case, replaced by a man named Michael Mahoney. I had no illusions. Michael's job was going to be the same as those before him: keep the families in line, keep them silent. I had no intention of making his job easy, and I had the sense that he had been warned of that.

Mahoney told me bluntly that the hostages had been "devalued." A new policy was in effect, I was told, a two-pronged policy. First, the hostages would be "devalued"—a word I found totally disgusting and demeaning. The point of the exercise was to convince the captors that the lives of the hostages had no value to the U.S. government. That's how you stopped terrorism. Second, the families would never again move up the line and gain access to high-level Administration officials. They called it "bracket creeping." The only conclusion I could draw from that was that they were blaming us for Iran-contra; we had driven poor Ronald Reagan to his desperate deeds.

So it was no longer a covert operation, the State Department's effort to keep a lid on the hostage situation; it was overt.

I told several reporters about the "devaluing" and they were aghast; in fact, they had a hard time believing me. "Call the State Department and ask them what their policy is," I told them. It took only a few phone calls before the State Department started hesitating over the word "devalue," but they didn't repudiate the concept. All of a sudden my brother's life wasn't worth as much as it had been two months before.

There was another State Department meeting not long after Iran-contra broke, and of the five or six people there I wasn't acquainted with any of them. I had just spent two years building a relationship of trust and confidentiality and here I was back at square one. These people didn't know me from Adam, and now they were not going to tell me anything anyway.

It appalled me that none of them had any Middle Eastern experience. They introduced me to the new guy on the Lebanese desk, a young fellow, and I asked him, "Oh, how long has it been since you've been in the Middle East?"

"Well," he said, "I've never actually been there."

"Oh," I said. "What horrible thing is it you've done to be put on the Lebanese desk?"

He didn't answer, he just sat there and looked embarrassed. I felt a bit ashamed for taking a cheap shot at this pleasant kid.

So my government had put me on notice: from now on I was going to get nothing of value from them. I had to go elsewhere for information and action.

I went to the Israeli embassy.

I felt uneasy talking to the Israelis. What would happen if the captors found out? They are literally mortal enemies of Israel. What would they do to Terry? But I knew the reputation of the Israeli intelligence network as the best in the Middle East, and I was hoping they could tell me something I didn't know.

The first thing that struck me at the Israeli embassy was the security. I had visited embassies of countries that were in conflict with the United States—Syria, for instance—and I would just walk in the door. Most of the time they would simply wave me to the elevator and I would go upstairs by myself. At the Israeli embassy—and the British and the French—you'd better be prepared to show them your birthmark before you can get in the door. A little steel drawer shoots out from behind bulletproof glass, and you put your ID in and they examine it. Then you go into another room and more people eyeball you. And these are our allies. They were probably concerned about attacks by terrorists, not Americans, but still it always seemed intimidating to me.

I met with a man named Oded Eran, the deputy chief of mission, and began to plead my case. Mr. Eran seemed to suggest that the person to go to was President Hafez Assad of Syria, since Syria quite possibly needed more financial help than Iran was providing and might therefore be willing to intercede. However, he said, if Syria were to confront the Hezbollah it would be confronting Iran as well. Since Iran was supplying Syria with a certain amount of money each year, this did not seem a tremendously promising line of inquiry.

I said, "I don't understand. What could President Assad do if he wanted to?"

"I can assure you," Mr. Eran told me, "if President Assad wants to play hardball, the man knows how."

Mr. Eran recommended that I continue to push Iran; they were major players, he said. When I explained to him that I could get neither a visa to Iran nor an appointment with any Iranian officials, he suggested that I ask Ted Koppel to intervene.

I had been hounding the Iranian embassy for years and couldn't get in. I called Ted Koppel, whom I had met several times when I did his *Nightline* show, and explained the problem. Ted Koppel is a really nice person. He said, "Peggy, when do you want to see them?" and he made the arrangements.

The first week of March I went to New York to meet with the Iranians. Although David often accompanies me on these trips, I don't encourage him to come to the meetings with me. I think the perception of a woman alone is much more effective than if you have a man there with you.

I had written a letter to the Ayatollah which I was going to present to embassy officials and ask them to pass along. When the meeting began, I spent a half hour discussing the wording of the letter. At one point I had written, "I have no weapons that I can trade for my brother."

"We never traded arms for hostages," I was told by the official.

"We paid, and we paid dearly for those arms. Any deal for the hostages was simply a figment of the United States' imagination."

"I'm sorry, pardon me," I stammered, "I'm just a sister of . . . I'm sorry I even . . ."

He wanted to know who had written the letter.

"I did," I said.

He didn't seem to believe me.

"Is your government interested in the good will of the American people?" I asked. I was assured that it was. "Well, President Reagan has told me personally that he intends to pursue reconciliation with Iran, and if I can be a small part of that movement I would be more than pleased to do whatever I can."

He seemed interested in that vein and mentioned that he knew I was very popular with the American media. He seemed to warm up as we discussed potential good will and finally he asked if I would like to see his superior. Which was when I discovered I wasn't already talking to the man in charge.

I had been dealing with an underling, and it was quite possible that he had not intended to pass me along at all. He went in another room for about five minutes and I was then ushered into an inner office.

The diplomat I met there was very stiff and formal at first. He reinforced his assistant's statement that there had been no exchange of arms for hostages, that that was simple wishful thinking of those involved. He got really wound up over the money owed to them, Iranian assets that had been frozen by the U.S. government. A deal was a deal, he said, and the U.S. had betrayed them.

The diplomat seemed about to write me off, when I made one last effort to get past the political rhetoric.

"This is an innocent man," I pleaded. "He has lost so much. His brother and father have both died of cancer and he doesn't even know it. He's never seen his daughter. He is a dedicated journalist whose job is to tell the true story of what is happening in the Middle East. He works for no government and represents no political or religious cause. He deserves mercy."

"I don't see what I can do to help you," said the official.

"There is tremendous public relations good will to be gained if Iran responds to a humanitarian plea," I told him. "We could make it very clear via the media that this was a human and not a political response. People don't see that side of Iran and I think it would make most Americans think much more positively of your country."

The diplomat seemed to warm to this point. But, he made clear, Iran had no control over the captors.

"We know the Hezbollah have my brother Terry and Tom Sutherland," I said, "and they are a pro-Iranian group."

He didn't argue the point. Instead he said that if the hostages were to be released, the captors would have to receive something in return.

We were finally engaged in a true conversation, rather than a pair of monologues. We sat there in his office thinking. Since we were both considering only Terry Anderson at that point, the diplomat intimated that a lesser price might be possible; they did have other hostages.

"Would you consider a trade for the Khiyam prisoners?" These were the suspected terrorists being held in southern Lebanon by the Israeli-controlled South Lebanon Army. I told him I had met with Israeli officials who had suggested that they would be amenable to such a trade. This was certainly a far different private posture than what they would admit to publicly.

The diplomat seemed genuinely enthusiastic. He suggested that I mediate the trade.

There was no way I was going to mediate a hostage trade. First, I didn't know what I was doing. Second, the captors would not accept dealing with a woman.

The diplomat then suggested that a Dr. Mohammad Mehedi of the National Council on Islamic Affairs be the broker to the captors and that I be the contact with the Israelis.

"With all due respect," I said, "I think the Israelis will want something in this deal too. Maybe they will settle for the good will of the United States. The captors have other prisoners as well . . ." The official didn't deny it. ". . . and perhaps they might be persuaded to release an Israeli hostage as part of the arrangement." He didn't comment on that at all.

The diplomat promised to contact the Lebanese government to see if the captors would be open to pursuing this entire line of possibilities. He also said he would contact Dr. Mehedi, who the last time he went to Beirut was mugged in his hotel room and robbed of all his money and swore he would never go back. The diplomat recommended that I not get back to the Israelis until he found out if the deal was feasible. He also suggested that I take the same initiative to the Lebanese ambassador, since the Lebanese contacts with the Hezbollah were very good. The more pressure to get this done, he said, the better the chance of success.

I needed the Israelis to sign off on this deal too, so I ignored his advice and went straight to the Israeli embassy. I was extremely embarrassed. I mean, who was I to be mediating a deal between the Arabs and the Israelis? Get serious. I knew that this was really a stupid idea but we're talking with high Iranian officials here, so I had no choice but to pass it on. I said to Mr. Eran, "I know what you are going to think of this, but I've been asked to give you this message. So here I am."

Sure enough, Eran was really steamed. "He knows how to get in touch with me if he wants to talk to me. He doesn't have to use you to do this."

When I got back to the hotel that night David said, "What happened?"

"David, you don't want to know. I promise you, you don't want to know."

I couldn't believe it. I still can't. So many times I've been involved in situations like this, met so many important people, and I just stop and wonder. They send housewives to mediate hostage swaps; they make deals in private, deny them in public, and then renege on the whole thing; they sit there in their suits or caftans and lie to your face. *These are the people who are running the world.* Where do you go to find somebody you can believe, someone you can trust?

In the first two weeks of February 1987 there were nine death threats issued by the various groups of captors against the hostages. In March there were nine more. I was still questioning my whole course of action for the past two years, whether by being so vocal I might have prolonged Terry's captivity; whether by keeping him in the public eye I might still cause his death. The nation was in the throes of Iran-contra, we were being bombarded with editorials and accusations, and I was confused and desperate and just getting beaten down.

The Iran-contra scandal blew the hostage issue out of the water. I continued to make trips to Washington and tried to talk to as many foreign embassies as I could, since it had been made very clear to me that there would be no movement from my own government.

March 16 was the second anniversary of Terry's kidnapping and a ceremony, sponsored by the American Baptist church, was held at the Baptist Convention Center in Valley Forge, Pennsylvania.

There were many people who got personally involved in our crisis. To most Americans the "hostage crisis" is just a phrase, something they hear on the news when a videotape is made public or there is talk of a release. It's not real, it's just another headline, like a fire in somebody else's neighborhood. But some people bring it home, it strikes a chord in them and they hear it all the time. Anne Zickl, Carmella LaSpada, Ray Barnett—these are people I have come to trust and rely on.

Carmella LaSpada is a wonderful woman who is the driving force behind a terrific organization called No Greater Love, a nonprofit, nonpolitical humanitarian organization that extends friendship and caring to families of Americans who died in war or by acts of terrorism. No Greater Love also serves as a support group for families of the hostages, and it nimbly took out of my hands the organizing of events around Terry's anniversary and his birthday. No Greater Love could be counted on to be efficient, effective, and above all tasteful. They knew how to contact the right people and get us sympathetic attention. Carmella can produce a real extravaganza. I was tremendously grateful to her and her organization, and they have continued their valuable help to this day.

When Carmella grabs the bull by the horns I just hang on, because I never know where it's going to take me; she seeks out every opportunity to connect the hostages to other events in the news. I found myself involved in everything from a "Lollipops for Hostages" initiative to packing olive branches for Iran.

On a personal level, if a hostage family needs a ride from the airport, a place to stay, a friend, a meal, a haircut, or even a funeral,

Carmella can be counted on to provide it or find someone who can.

No Greater Love does so much more than keep the plight of the hostages alive, but it is that commitment for which the hostage families are so deeply thankful. I am absolutely convinced that without their help the hostage issue would have been forgotten long ago.

Ray Barnett is the president and founder of an organized prayer network and humanitarian organization called Friends in the West. I first met Ray and one of his dedicated volunteers, Lela Gilbert, in 1986 and have worked closely with them ever since. Among many other initiatives, they provide the POW-type bracelets that we have come to call prayer bracelets. The bracelets have been ordered by the thousands and are stamped with the name and date of whichever hostage is requested and the admonition of Hebrews 13:3: "Remember those in prison as if imprisoned with them."

Friends in the West has founded six orphanages and four literacy schools in Uganda, and cares for almost four hundred children there. Its fund-raising is done primarily through the efforts of the African Children's Choir, which tours the world giving concerts. These are children who are being raised and educated by the organization. Ray's involvement in Uganda began shortly after ruler Idi Amin was deposed in 1979. Ray brought out the first choir in 1984, which funded the first orphanage, and they have grown to impressive proportions since then.

Ray lives in Canada and travels wherever human rights needs are brought to his attention. From his deep involvement with political prisoners in the Soviet Union to the needy of Lebanon after the Israeli invasion, Ray goes wherever his heart takes him. In June 1986 he saw my brother Rich's deathbed videotape plea to the captors and decided that the Lebanon hostages would become a priority in his life.

Ray Barnett has worked tirelessly since then to gain the hostages' release. He has traveled thousands of miles at his own expense and gone into regions where others would have feared to set foot. He is the most spiritual, honest, giving individual I have ever met, and it's that goodness which has gained him access into homes such as Sheik Fadlallah's, the spiritual leader of Hezbollah. He is welcome wherever he chooses to go, and I know that his efforts will not cease until every last hostage is out. Like me, Ray recognizes the possibility that, in the end, nothing he's done may have made a difference, but spiritual responsibility dictates that we have to try.

Ray arranged a World Day of Prayer for the hostages on May 28, 1987, with evangelist Robert Schuller as the spokesperson. My pastor from East Bethany Baptist Church in Batavia, Tom Vickers, accompanied me out to Los Angeles for the ceremony.

My son Edward and his fiancée Missy were expecting their first baby any minute, and I was hoping I would get back to New York in time. We knew from amniocentesis that it was going to be a boy; he was going to be my second grandson. My other grandson, Randy, had been born the previous September and had lightened our hearts and somehow lessened our burden. After the death of two men in our family, it was going to be wonderful to welcome another male into the clan.

The day before the Day of Prayer was to take place we had gone over to the Crystal Cathedral and run through the ceremony with Mrs. Schuller and the staff. Afterward a big crowd congregated in my hotel room and we had snacks sent up. I was doing a telephone interview when Tom Vickers came in and motioned that he wanted to talk to me. I finished up the phone conversation and walked over.

Tom looked solemn. I knew that one of the people in his congregation was very ill and there was a possibility he might get called back to do the funeral and be with the family if the person passed away.

Tom took me into the other room and closed the door.

"Eddie's baby died."

I started shouting, "No! No! It can't be! Why, God, why? What are You doing to us? Oh, no! No!" I felt as if someone had ripped my heart out.

Tom was stunned. He had no words to comfort me. He told me that the umbilical cord had wrapped itself around the baby's arm and cut off his circulation.

I buckled. When something like that happens my body rebels, and I just felt like the whole world was collapsing.

I had to hold that baby. I was determined to get home and hold that baby in my arms before they buried him.

We took the red-eye back to New York and went straight to the hospital. Missy's parents were flying in also, and we held a dedication service that night.

David could not go in the room to see the baby. He just couldn't handle it. I don't know how I did.

When I leaned down to pick up that child, what struck me was that this little boy was a miniature of my son. He had black curly hair and beautiful coloring, just like Eddie. They were going to name him Edward; before he was born we had already started calling him little Eddie. "How's little Eddie this morning?" "Let's feel little Eddie kick." Now that child was gone forever.

My parents had a double headstone at the cemetery, and when Rich was cremated we placed his ashes between them. My son decided that he wanted the baby buried beside my brother. I looked down at those four graves and said, "My God, what is happening to my family?"

Tom Vickers presided over the funeral and he said something that was particularly meaningful to me. My daughter had been working for months on a needlepoint for me, and when she finally got done with it she said it was so pretty she couldn't give it up, she was going to keep it for herself. When we gathered at the grave for the cemetery service Tom said, "When a child dies, especially a baby, the tendency is to say, 'Ah, this was a beautiful baby,' as Eddie was.

"We've all had the experience of working on a craft for a long time, and when it was done it was so beautiful that we kept it for ourselves. Well, that is what God has decided to do with this baby. Little Eddie was so beautiful, God decided to keep him for Himself."

For the first time I didn't have any answer for my son. He kept asking, "Why?" and there was no comfort I could give him. There is none I can give him today. The best you can hope for, I said, was that someday you will be able to think of it without bending over in pain.

When something like this happens you ask God, "Why did You do this? Why did You allow this to happen?" But I believe deep inside myself that God doesn't do those things, He helps you to cope with them when they do happen. But when I was standing at the grave site I think I knew that this was the moment when I was either going to lose it completely and say, "There is no God, there can't be a God who would let this happen to my family," or I would resolve, "I'm not going to understand it, but I will accept that some things happen that will never be explained or made clear."

Little Eddie's death was not God's will, it was an accident. A terrible and senseless accident. There was no one to blame, only more pain to endure.

I walked away from that cemetery feeling that no matter what happened to me from then on, I would keep going. I used to feel that if anything happened to my husband or kids I would die, I would go crazy. At that moment I knew I would survive.

CHAPTER

11

I DECIDED TO STEP BACK. I HAD WALKED POINT FOR THE HOSTAGE families for two years, and what with all sorts of people telling me to take it easy and let the government handle things, I was too burned out to fight anymore. From the beginning of Iran-contra, in November 1986, for almost a year I lay low. I would still make the rounds of the Middle Eastern embassies in Washington, and I kept in touch with the other hostage families, but I stayed out of the public eye. I hoped the government was pursuing every opportunity, as they said they were, but I didn't press them to find out if they were keeping their word.

I'd get up in the morning, put on a pot of coffee, and sit at my desk going through the mail. (I've written back to everybody who has ever written me, and sometimes with the volume of mail it gets pretty hairy.) Then David would leave for work and I would go about cleaning the house, doing the wash, getting groceries.

I was always circulating something. I would compose a letter and send it to every senator, or mail a newspaper clipping to key congressmen. There was never a day that I wasn't involved in something, but I tried to keep out of sight.

There were four people I talked with almost every day: Carolyn Turolla of the Associated Press in New York; Anne Zickl in Batavia; and Bill Foley and Bonnie Anderson, journalists who had known Terry in Beirut. Whenever something happened we would have a telephone round-robin trying to figure out what it meant.

Batavia is between Rochester and Buffalo, and there are seven affiliate television stations within driving distance, so whenever anything happened they would charge out to my house to get my reaction. I thought that was pretty silly. Why should anybody pay attention to what I think, it isn't as if I'm a Middle Eastern expert or anything. Of course, neither is practically anyone else.

I saw the Israeli ambassador to the U.N. on television one night and he said something that struck home. Essentially it was that the so-called experts on the Middle East don't know what they're talking about. Someone took a trip to the Middle East for one week two years ago, he said, and today that person sits on television and talks to you like he knows what's going to happen. Well, he doesn't.

The ambassador was absolutely right. Lebanon changes from day to day. The factions change, the alliances change, everything changes, and if you're not over there you just don't have a handle on it. Which makes it hard to get advice or input. At the State Department I was shocked to find that none of the people I spoke with had ever been to the Middle East, so after a while I didn't expect them to know what was going on.

Father Jenco came to Batavia that summer of 1987. He said he had made a commitment that when he got out of captivity he would come see the property that Terry and I owned together, because Terry had talked so much about it. The hostages, he told me, would take each other on journeys. Tom Sutherland was Scottish-born and he would take them on a mind's-eye tour of Scotland and recite Robert Burns's poetry in a wonderful brogue. Terry took them to Japan, and to this property. Father Jenco said when he got there that he knew the landmarks, he knew what the land looked like.

In July, ABC correspondent Charlie Glass got kidnapped. He was in Beirut on leave of absence, writing a book, when he was taken. All I could think was, "How could he have been so stupid!" It was a stupid, stupid thing to do. I knew Charlie Glass. He had seen what happened to my family and to every other hostage family, and he went over there and put himself in danger anyway. He should have known better, but being kidnapped was much too high a price to pay for stupidity.

His captors sent a video out of him confessing to being a CIA spy. In July there were threats against Glass, against Terry Waite, against four French hostages as well. There was no way to know why this flurry of potential violence was taking place.

Charlie Glass was a close friend of ABC anchor Peter Jennings. The story immediately became a hot news item on all four networks. The history of hostage-taking has shown us time and time again that publicity gets it resolved, and there was a major effort to get Charlie out of there. A delegation of well-known journalists, including Peter Jennings, went to the Syrian embassy on Charlie's behalf. Now, none of this had ever happened for Terry and I was on the outside looking in and wondering why. What was it that all of us missed that would trigger this kind of attention?

There was no day-to-day publicity about Charlie coming out of Beirut—no continuing threats, no string of communiqués. The journalists made a case for him. And a little less than two months after he was kidnapped, Charlie Glass was released (or escaped, or was allowed to escape, it's never been clear).

I was furious. Where were all these people for the two years that Terry had been chained to his bed? And I was really guilty; why hadn't I been able to mobilize enough attention to get Terry free?

The frustration for me was not only seeing what publicity had done in other cases, but knowing that—no matter what the government policy says—if a jetliner was taken tomorrow they would find a way to get the passengers home. And the press would be right in the thick of it.

Like TWA. That was my Waterloo, that my government did something they had told me they would never do—and I watched them do it. First it was, "We don't negotiate with terrorists." Then they got the TWA hostages back. What about Terry? "We don't negotiate with terrorists." Then the government used muscle and the *Achille Lauro* passengers got off. What about Terry? "We really mean it this time;

we don't negotiate with terrorists." Then Nick Daniloff came home. What about Terry? "We really, really mean it this time. No kidding around. We don't negotiate with terrorists."

I had to develop an attitude of calmness. In spite of my frustration at the lack of action, when I talked to journalists and would have liked to grab them by the throat and say, *"Why aren't you doing something!"* I stifled all of those emotions because you lose your credibility if you stand up and shout. You've got to be steady.

Terry turned forty years old on October 27, 1987, and I had to go public again. I had given it a year and we were no farther along than we had been a year before. AP vice president Walter Mears had said, "I have nothing against quiet diplomacy as long as it is active quiet diplomacy and so long as it isn't covering up inaction. I continue to hope and trust that this is not the case and that there is a continuing process." I continued to hope, but I had completely lost my trust.

No Greater Love organized a ceremony in Washington and I swore to myself that I would never again be silent, I would never again question my own actions.

The appalling thing to me was that, in the kidnapping of the TWA people, seventeen days was seen as a long time. The holding of the hostages in the embassy in Iran for 444 days was almost inconceivable. But now another full year had gone by for Terry and it was seen as nothing. Few people paid attention, few really cared.

The first week in November a South Korean diplomat named Do Chae-Sung, who had been held hostage in Lebanon for two years, was released. UPI reported that he had told South Korean officials that sometime during the previous August he had slept in the same room with a "famous Western journalist," who we assumed was Terry. I immediately went to the State Department to get more information. Terry hadn't been sighted in a year and here was a man who had been in the same room with him.

The State Department stonewalled me.

When hostages get out of captivity they are almost immediately thrust in front of the press, and many times they will say things which, after their debriefing or after the government has got ahold of them, they will withdraw. That was obviously what had happened here.

I said, "Come on, guys, I know exactly what's happening, it isn't as if I don't have any experience in this. You have decided that he is not going to say publicly who he saw, but it's important to me. I don't need to know the details, I just want to know if my brother is okay."

They refused to tell me. Terry and the others had been "devalued," and they weren't going to do anything that could bring his name back into the news. I would have agreed to just about anything, including secrecy, to have some firsthand news about Terry. But they would not tell me. It was so needlessly cruel.

I went to the South Korean embassy and met with the chargé d'affaires there. He was very kind to me; I think they were kind of worried that I would rave and rant. In fact, it seems that any time a government official meets me he is stunned by the fact that I'm *not* a shrieking maniac. I explained to the chargé that I wasn't asking them to share any of the details with me, I just needed to know if Terry was all right. He promised to get back to me.

Not much happens in Washington that the State Department isn't aware of. I was back home the next day when I got a call from Michael Mahoney. "Oh, guess what, Peggy," he said, "I was going down the hall and Paul Bremer [the man who replaced Bob Oakley in Counter-Terrorism] mentioned to me that, yes, it's true, the South Korean saw Terry." I was so relieved to hear that Terry was actually okay that I just went limp and got off the phone quickly. I needed a private moment to absorb the feeling that Terry was safe.

A few days later I called Mahoney for more information. What else had the man said? What else could I know? Mahoney insisted that he'd never told me. He denied the whole thing, said that our conversation had never happened.

What?

Now, why would I make a thing like that up? What would be the logic? It didn't seem to bother Mahoney that I knew he was lying. They are such refined bureaucrats at the State Department that they have it down pat. They know that all they've got to do is turn their back on you and what are you going to do about it. They don't have to explain, they don't have to justify anything to anyone. They simply say it, and from that moment on it's carved in stone. I had been hit head-on by Plausible Deniability. You and I call it lying.

There was nothing I could do. If you try to argue with them, you're

the one who ends up sounding like a blithering idiot. You are sputtering and fuming, and they are sitting there looking at you, the souls of
innocence, like, "You have just totally lost control, lady."

There are plenty of people in Washington like that. I had been in
contact with New York Senator Alfonse D'Amato from the beginning
and he was no help whatsoever. At the outset he had given me the
usual spiel: "I'm here for you. I'll do everything I can. Have your
people call my people." Well, I was in Washington again and I called
saying I wanted to come over and talk. Fine, I was told, the senator
would make time for me.

By the time I arrived at D'Amato's office he had already called the
AP, CNN cameras were there, it was a real show. Now, Alfonse
D'Amato had done absolutely nothing that I know of to get Terry
home, and I was truly angry to see him trying to capitalize on this
opportunity to get some favorable press. I wasn't going to embarrass
the senator by telling him of his shortcomings in front of the media, but
I kept saying, "Senator D'Amato, after the cameras go away, you and
I have to really talk about this." He greeted me with a hug and a kiss
for the cameras, as if we were the closest and dearest of friends.

When the film crew and reporters had gone I said, "We have a big
problem here." Once again, I made my case for Terry and the need for
attention to his captivity.

"Oh, certainly," the senator said. I didn't hear from him again.

Months later, out of the blue, D'Amato's office sent out a form letter
saying that the senator was very concerned about the hostages in Lebanon and "the recent kidnapping of three more victims." Recent?
They had been taken almost a full year before. This form letter went
out to everyone who wrote the senator about the hostage situation. I
wrote to his office and said, "This is an embarrassment. You need to
pull this letter, it is no longer valid."

They sent out another form letter which was even worse, expressing
concern over the whereabouts of Bill Buckley, the CIA station chief in
Beirut. The letter was postmarked May 13, the very day that No
Greater Love had held Bill's memorial service at Arlington National
Cemetery. I finally sat down and wrote him, saying, "You are an
embarrassment. How would you like this to be released to the media?"
Finally I got a note back saying essentially, "Peggy, we really need to

sit down and talk." Not with him; he was a waste of time. There are a lot of people willing to stand up before the cameras and shake your hand and say they will help, and then the cameras go away and so do they. Senator D'Amato is one of those.

New York's senior senator, Daniel Patrick Moynihan, on the other hand, has been very kind and helpful. He inserts articles and information into the *Congressional Record* and he keeps Terry's case alive in the Senate. Even during the time when nobody else would talk to me, Senator Moynihan would call and say, "I just wanted to let you know that I'm thinking about you. What do you want me to do?"

There's a right way and a wrong way to treat people. Even a first-year psychology student can tell you that if you want to keep people on your side you stroke them. The hostage families are so eager to believe, so full of awe and respect for their government, that it would take very little to win our support.

I used to tell that to Michael Mahoney at the State Department. "Don't you see what you are doing to us? The first year Terry was in captivity, they dimmed the White House lights. I got Christmas cards from President Reagan and Vice President Bush." Granted, this doesn't do anything, but it is an acknowledgment: We do exist. "The next year there was a hostage situation going on at that prison in Atlanta and Secretary Shultz called the families of the guards being held hostage and told them he was sorry, it was Thanksgiving and they were having to go through so much pain. Did anybody call us? No. Did we get any Christmas cards? No." And, I said, "why are we being punished for Iran-contra? Why are we being treated like lepers?"

Mahoney said, "You're just looking at it wrong."

"Let me tell you something, Michael. Given these factors, what conclusions would you draw?"

Mahoney said, "Maybe you're right."

December 10 was Terry's one-thousandth day in captivity. Coincidentally it was also National Human Rights Day, and No Greater Love held a ceremony in Washington to mark this particularly grim anniversary. In my speech I said:

"Question: What do the French, Korean and German governments have in common?

"Answer: All three have succeeded in the past ninety days in getting their citizens freed from captivity in Lebanon.

"Question: What is the U.S. government doing for the eight Americans held in Lebanon?

"Answer: If we measure efforts by results, the U.S. government has done zilch in recent days. . . .

"I cringe in frustration at the runaround I get daily from some of our tax-paid State Department employees. I wonder what the American taxpayers would do if they had firsthand experience with the cynicism and arrogance that emanates from some of these so-called diplomats. . . . My thousand-day civics lesson has been a frustrating experience. . . .

"Sometimes in the middle of the day I stop whatever I'm doing and concentrate on Terry. I ask myself, 'What is Terry doing at this exact moment? Where is my brother right now? What is he thinking? Feeling? Is he talking to himself? Is he reading? Is he in chains?' . . .

"How long is a thousand days? Soviet leader Mikhail Gorbachev . . . came to power in Moscow at just about the time Terry was kidnapped. . . .

"Terry's thousand days have included two Christmases. I hope and pray he is free before the next."

Christmas Eve, 1987, I was up to my elbows in sweet-roll dough. My family is big on traditional things, and one of our traditions is homemade cinnamon rolls on Christmas morning. I was making them from scratch, mixing the flour and the yeast, letting the dough rise. I was kneading the dough and punching it down and trying to get everything else organized when the phone rang.

The AP foreign desk was calling from New York to tell me that the captors had released a videotape of Terry.

My first thought was, damn, I've got all these things to do and now the press is going to be on my doorstep. I'm up to my elbows in sweet-roll dough and I've got to stop, the rolls are going to be ruined.

But this was Terry and of course I was ecstatic. As horrible as the captors have been, there have been times when they made attempts to do something kind for the families.

NBC hand-carried a copy of the tape to the house and was gracious enough not to ask to film me as I viewed it. I ducked outside, accepted the tape, went back in and watched it with David.

"To my family, my friends, my countrymen and my government," Terry began.

"To my family, I think of you all and each of you every day. Kiss my beautiful children for me and be patient.

"To friends and countrymen, I know your prayers and messages of good will, your efforts for us. I've seen some of your Christmas cards you have sent. I can't tell you how much your love and concern have meant to us, how much hope and courage you have given us in many dark days and nights, to have you thinking of us.

"To my government, I don't know what to say. I know you are trying to get us out. I don't know exactly what it is you can do. I only know that it hasn't been enough or the right thing. This is my third Christmas as a hostage. Others have been here nearly as long.

"Surely, this is enough. It has to be. Our condition is not great. . . . This cannot continue, there is a limit how long we can last. Some of us are approaching their limit very badly.

"Surely, by now you know what must be done and how you can do it. . . . There have been enough careful conversations called discussions and enough intricate secret maneuvering and more than enough prejudice.

"Mr. President, we in the United States are not absolutely innocent here. Our hands are not completely clean. . . .

"It is time to do something. Mr. President, you and all the Americans celebrate this Christmas with your families, think of us, think of our families. When the holidays and New Year's parties are over, you will go back to work. Remember, we are still here in our prisons and we will remain here until you find a solution. . . .

"Merry Christmas."

My first reaction was relief; Terry was getting our messages. The last thing he had said before Father Jenco was released was "Don't let them forget me," and now he knew he hadn't been forsaken.

He looked a lot better than he had on the first tape. He seemed

201

relatively healthy and, though he still spoke slowly and without a lot of energy, he was clearly all there.

I scoured the tape for some good news, some revelation that things were moving forward. He'd said "I know you are trying" to the government, which I felt must mean something. But I had expected a list of the captors' demands, a charge to our government, some specifics we could give in return for the hostages' freedom. There was nothing, and that was frustrating. The tape gave us no indication of what it was we should do. Just tell us what you want; that's what I wanted to know.

I came to the conclusion that the videotape was an outright gift. No demands, no threats, just a glimpse to say that he was all right. The more I watched the tape, the more even Terry seemed puzzled by what he was doing.

The press went nuts. My initial reaction was, "I'm not going to talk to them. It's Christmas, leave me alone." But it was inevitable; they were going to camp out in my front yard, and if I wanted to get on with my life I would have to talk to them.

We played "Let's Make a Deal." The local reporters were saying to me, "Look, Peggy, we want to be home on Christmas Eve, too. Come out and talk to us and then we promise we will go home and leave you alone. We want to get back to our families just like you do."

The State Department said it was "cynical" of the kidnappers to release a videotape of Terry on Christmas Eve. I think they were annoyed that they had been outgestured.

About three weeks later, around the middle of January, a letter arrived in the mail:

Dear Peggy:

I'm very tardy in acknowledging your Christmas greeting, but it has only recently reached my desk. I thank you and the Andersons for the beautiful card, and I assure you we are praying for your loved ones. We are also doing everything we can and exploring every avenue to bring about their release. Don't mistake silence for abandonment or lack of caring.

I know there are no words that can lighten the grief you all feel or make the pain of those in captivity easier for them to bear. Just please know their plight is of great importance to us. They are not forgotten, nor will they be.

Sincerely,
Ronald Reagan

January 20, 1988, was the one-year anniversary of Terry Waite's kidnapping and the press made it a day of national awareness. Since the hostage situation really only gets attention when there is a release, a kidnapping, or a threat, we need any convenient event we can get to peg our case on. Birthdays and anniversaries are the easiest for rallying the media, so we organize around them. In the trade it's called "anniversary journalism."

I've always had mixed feelings about that. In the beginning I refused to make any plans beyond the next month. By planning events in the future, I felt, we were saying that Terry and the rest of the hostages would not be freed soon. After a while I would discuss the next month or coming few months, but not the next year. In 1986 someone said to me, "Wait until the presidential election and then you'll see some action." I said indignantly, "Do you know what you're saying to me? Maybe *two years* down the road I'll see some action? That's ridiculous." It turned out he was being optimistic.

On the Terry Waite anniversary I did all the morning news shows plus *Donahue* and *Nightline*. By that time I had been interviewed on television often enough that I knew that you get on only every few months, and you've only got two minutes, sometimes only thirty seconds, to say what you've got to say. So you just do it.

It's hard to believe that I could get used to being on television, but I did. After several years of being interviewed I stopped feeling intimidated by the media and started learning to use it.

On the *Today* show Jane Pauley was kind of the designated "hostage person." I sensed in her a genuine concern for the hostages and their families. When she asked a question, she seemed truly interested in hearing the answer. Perhaps it was only that she was very good at her job, but I prefer to think she cared about the people and the issue. I had heard that Bryant Gumbel had strong feelings about the hostage issue, that he didn't have a whole lot of sympathy and didn't want to do these interviews. Some time later I was scheduled to be on the *Today* show again and when I was told that I would be talking with Bryant I said, "Oh, no, he's going to make me look bad." But he surprised me, he didn't put me on the spot and he was very kind.

Phil Donahue, as I've said, I hold in the highest regard. I had read his book and I admired him for bringing up his boys after his divorce. I rarely watched daytime TV—I figured that the day I got addicted to soap operas would be the day I'd hang it up—but on those occasions that I did, *Donahue* was the only show I would ever put on. The first time he had me on, he was warm and caring and showed a personal interest. Another time, he interrupted a vacation to come back and bring the TWA people and the hostage families together. One of his producers told me that these were the shows where Phil could more or less kiss off the ratings but that they were also the shows that let him sleep at night.

I have probably been on *Nightline* half a dozen times. Ted Koppel has very firm views about hostage-taking, and once in a private conversation he told me he'd instructed his family that, if he were ever taken hostage, they were not to go public, they were not to pay any ransom; that would only encourage the hostage-takers. "On the other hand," he told me, "that's not to say my family might not choose to handle it differently in the actual event. But theoretically, I think it's wrong."

I said to him, "Look, Ted, let's face it, we all think it's wrong. But right now the captors have their hands on my brother and I don't have the luxury of being able to give in to my personal feelings. I have no choice but to do what I am doing. Personally, I abhor the thought of giving the captors one single dime. There will come a time when this is over with, when Terry and all the hostages are out, when you might hear a different story."

"Will you do me a favor?" he asked. "When you get ready to tell that story, will you tell it on my program?"

Koppel must have faith in my ability to hold my own. A couple of months later he put me on the air opposite Pierre Salinger, Bud McFarlane, and Henry Kissinger. "I think that my role in this has to be very clear," I said on camera, "especially with the learned gentlemen like you have on the program. My job has to be the voice for Terry

Anderson and the other hostages, whose voices can't be heard. I have to be the conscience of this Administration.

"It's easy to talk about foreign policy and stopping terrorism and all of these things. This is my brother that's being held; these are other American citizens. I have to ask for them, don't they deserve better than being sacrificed to future long-term foreign policy in the Middle East?"

"Peggy, I think that's a little bit unfair," Koppel said, "and I don't think that's precisely what either Dr. Kissinger or Mr. McFarlane was suggesting. . . . I think what they're both suggesting is that if it becomes evident to hostage-takers that they can get enormous rewards for kidnapping people, then they have an incentive to kidnap more people in the future and do the same thing over, rather than bringing an end to the process. Do you at least buy that as a theory?"

"I do," I answered. "I think that these are the kind of gentlemen that should form these theories; it's not up to me. What I'm saying is these are American lives and it seems to me that there has to be a better way. I am told by the State Department that the only issue they will pursue is 'quiet diplomacy.' Now, I'm not sure exactly what that is. I have no reason to believe that it's anything other than a code word for 'no diplomacy.' My brother is entering his fourth year of captivity.

"And I think we also have to keep in mind that every other hostage that has ever been taken, besides these men, has been negotiated for. I fail to see why they are the ones that must be sacrificed. I think there are better answers than doing nothing and just literally turning our backs on these men and saying, 'We're sorry that they're living in basements, we're sorry if they have to die, but we have to stop terrorism.' There has to be another answer."

Bud McFarlane was the first to respond. "I think that she has a genuine point, that her government, the U.S. government, has an obligation to do everything in its power to try to recover its nationals." However, he continued, with Khomeini in charge there was no one in Iran who genuinely wanted a change in relations. "I think it is to mislead Peggy and others to say that, knowing that, that we should literally deal with the devil."

So here it was confirmed. They were doing nothing because it was their considered opinion that nothing could be done. So much for trying to bring the hostages home.

Henry Kissinger weighed in. "First of all, I have enormous sympathy for what Peggy Say said, and if my brother were there I might very well also feel that I had to speak for him and not for the general interest. . . .

"I believe that had we consistently from the beginning taken the position that we would not negotiate that there would be no point for them to hold the hostages. But by starting the negotiations during the Iran-contra thing, and by other nations paying the price, of course the Iranians believe that taking hostages is a good policy with which they can achieve their objective.

"But in any individual case it is very painful and I have enormous sympathy for Peggy Say and also for the dignity with which she presented her case. I don't believe it's in the national interest to pursue the policy that France has."

This was right after the French had paid some $600 million in food and other assets, but not cash or arms, in return for all three French hostages and the assurance that from then on no French citizens would be kidnapped. McFarlane had called it "transparent political expediency." Ted Koppel asked Pierre Salinger, "You're sitting in Paris, French officials will hear what Henry Kissinger had to say today . . . how are they going to respond?"

Salinger went right to it. "I think they will respond by saying, 'Don't give us any more lessons, United States. Because after Irangate, where you did exactly what you are charging that we did . . . where in fact we didn't do that: we did not negotiate with the people who are holding the hostages; we didn't give them any money or arms. . . .' I think they will be quite angry with what they heard tonight."

That ended the show. I was doing the program by remote, and in the earpiece I could hear conversations that were not aired. Earlier they had prepared me for the program, and afterward I could hear the sign-off. It's an odd, kind of distant experience; I had heard Ted Koppel wrapping things up every night, and now, as from the bottom of a well, I could hear him wrapping me up too.

But we were all still on the line. And what I heard Kissinger say, before we clicked off, was "I didn't do a very good job, did I?"

I thought he'd done an excellent job—for my case.

ABC has recently undertaken the journalistic equivalent of Kissinger's policy: strictly hands-off.

It was explained to me by Charlie Glass that a policy decision had been made that ABC would not "give the captors what they want: publicity." I didn't understand. Terry was Charlie's friend. And why had publicity been fine in Charlie's case, which lasted only two months, but bad for Terry? I was getting damn tired of this hypocritical and faulty rationalizing on the part of Terry's peers.

ABC will not air communiqués or videotapes from the captors. They seem to accept "quiet diplomacy" at face value, and they go out of their way to maintain that quiet.

I will never understand that. Terry is a journalist, one of their own. How can they cover a story like this for years on end and not have a personal attachment? I have never gotten a sense of personal involvement from Peter Jennings. ABC News did make Terry the "Person of the Week" once, so I may be doing him a disservice; I hope so. But he maintains a distance that I find disquieting.

It's encouraging in some ways and frustrating in others that when I have run into some of the country's best-known journalists at different functions they almost always make a point of telling me to keep on pushing. I met Mike Wallace and Andy Rooney at a No Greater Love spectacular in New York honoring journalists who had been killed while performing their jobs. Mike Wallace told me, "Peggy, don't let them shut you up. Keep doing what you're doing."

I was particularly pleased to meet Andy Rooney. He had just recently written a column in which he talked about waking up in the morning and looking out his window and seeing a lovely day and lots of flowers. All of a sudden, he'd said, the hostages crossed his mind, and how unjust their captivity was. He had closed in a very poignant way, saying that it didn't seem fair that Terry Anderson couldn't get up and look out his window and see the flowers.

I told him, "I just want to thank you for your column. In fact, I made copies of it and sent it to every senator. Would you mind, if I can do it, if I have it read into the *Congressional Record*?"

He seemed pleased, and I got it done.

Larry King emceed a function we were sponsoring at the Algerian embassy. "Keep in there fighting, kid," he told me. I wanted to say, "If you support what I'm doing so much, why am I not on your show?" I had been on once, during the TWA affair, but not again. Don't tell me to keep doing what I'm doing and then stand there and not help me. One shot doesn't equal a commitment.

I met Sam Donaldson directly after the meeting with President Reagan. The crowd of hostage families and reporters were standing out on the White House lawn and it was pure chaos. The press was grabbing everybody, there was no organization, there was lots of shouting. Donaldson, a tall man, was bellowing at the top of his lungs, "Will you people shut up! Let's get organized!" I was standing right beside him and he turned and looked at me.

"Aren't you Sam Donaldson?" I said.

"Yes, I am."

"Well, I'm Peggy Say."

He just looked at me and said icily, "I know who you are."

I guess several conclusions could be drawn from what he said, but the conclusion I drew at the time was, "This man is no fan of mine."

When I met him several years later and we got a chance to talk, I reminded him of that day. He just laughed. He said he hadn't meant anything personal by it. But I was so struck by it at the time; when someone stares me in the eye and as much as tells me he doesn't like me, I take it to heart. It startles me because I'm not used to it. Maybe by this time I should be.

In February 1987 I had gotten a call from a man who introduced himself as David Aikman of *Time* magazine. It was one of those days when my patience was running low.

"Mrs. Say, I think we should form a journalists' committee to work for your brother's freedom."

I said, "Mr. Aikman, I think that's wonderful but you'll have to excuse me when I ask just where have you been for the past two years."

He was taken aback, but he had this really gentle voice and he started telling me he was sorry but he had been away. He had been *Time*'s China bureau chief, and since he was a committed Christian, wherever he worked all over the world he would start prayer and Bible discussion groups. He had started one in Washington, D.C., and Jerry Levin had attended recently and happened to mention that he would like the group to pray for Terry Anderson. Aikman explained that he had become intrigued with the story and had said, "Well, I think we should do more than pray. Isn't there something more we can do?"

David Aikman didn't have the foggiest notion where to go from there. I wasn't sure myself, but I knew that it was the germ of something, so I called a few of Terry's friends: Bill Foley and Cary Vaughan; Ed Caldwell from our NBC affiliate, who had become a close friend of mine; Steve Hagey, who had worked for UPI in Beirut and was now at the *Baltimore Sun*; Salim Aridi, who in Beirut had been at CNN and NBC and was now freelance; AP's Don Mell. There was lots of fumbling around at first, telephone calls back and forth, but out of it came the Journalists Committee to Free Terry Anderson.

We ended up with a very prestigious group willing to lend their names and their time to the cause. The Honorary Committee included Tom Brokaw, Dan Rather, Bill Moyers, Peter Jennings, and James Reston.

At the time the group was formed, I was running out of ideas. I had contacted everybody, been everywhere, and there was nobody out there who could help me in a real way. That's when the group stepped in. We had a weekly Saturday morning conference call to map strategy and bring each other up to date.

The purpose of the Journalists Committee was to pressure the embassies, pressure the media, pressure Washington—to be a force for Terry. It sounded more impressive than it in actual fact was. We had a money struggle from day one, with people meeting expenses out of their own pockets, but no one had to know that. By this time people had been inundated with Peggy Say communications; write a letter on Journalists Committee letterhead, however, and somebody was going to read it.

When we used that stationery to request meetings with people like the Iranian ambassador to the U.N. we got results. And it was interesting to see how people reacted when we got there.

We had asked several members of the Honorary Committee to attend our meeting with Iranian Ambassador Rajai Khorrasani, but we hadn't heard back from them and we didn't know whether or not any of them would appear. When the meeting started it was the regulars: David Aikman, Elaine Collett, myself, and most of the committee founders. No media superstars. We weren't delivering on what our stationery promised, and there was an almost physical tension in the air.

The beginnings of diplomatic meetings are often quite stilted, and this one was even more so. Things did not look to be going well at all.

All of a sudden Dan Rather walked in, late and very apologetic.

What struck me was how Ambassador Khorrasani immediately snapped to attention. It's sad sometimes that that's what it takes, but that's the real world. It's show business. Like at the birthday and anniversary ceremonies we hold: if we have a big-name star, the press is going to cover it.

Quite abruptly the meeting took on a more serious air. David Aikman was our spokesman, and although there was a lot of tension he was very smooth, very good at making this kind of presentation. We were asking that a delegation of senior-level American journalists be allowed to go to Tehran and meet with Iranian government officials. If there was a successful resolution of the Terry Anderson issue, he said, that would perhaps create a climate in which other U.S.-Iranian problems could be discussed.

Ambassador Khorrasani said, deadpan, "Traditionally, the relations between the Iranian government and the American press have not been very good." There was a pause. I think it struck the ambassador just what kind of a diplomatic understatement he had just made. He tittered, and everybody else in the room started laughing with him. That broke the ice, and from then on it was probably the most productive meeting with an Iranian diplomat I'd ever seen.

The ambassador did tell us that the chances were slim, but that he would certainly do his best to arrange the visit. Unfortunately, it was ultimately not approved.

*   *   *

Dan Rather has taken Terry's situation to heart. Apropos of nothing, he sent me a note saying, "Peggy, I always think about Terry a lot, but lately I can't seem to get him off my mind. I just wanted you to know that. Love, Dan."

On February 17, 1988, Marine Lieutenant Colonel William Higgins was kidnapped. Again I was stunned. He was in an obviously dangerous area, reportedly by himself in a jeep, which was inconceivable to me under those circumstances in which no American was out of danger. The government couldn't even keep one of their own safe, how were they going to help Terry?

March 16, 1988, was the third anniversary of Terry's kidnapping and No Greater Love organized what we called a "Candlelight Ceremony of Hope for Peace in Lebanon and the Release of the Hostages." It was to be held at Holy Trinity Church in Georgetown, which the Kennedys used to attend.

Our list of speakers and attendees was long and notable. Father Jenco and Rev. Weir were coming, along with Tom Brokaw and Nicholas Daniloff. Correspondents from CNN and CBS were scheduled to participate in the service. An Arab journalist would read from the Koran and both Christian and Islamic prayers would be said.

There was a lot of discussion over whether to invite Jesse Jackson. Jesse was running for president and traveled with a swarming entourage of aides and national press. The Journalists Committee was more than a little concerned that his presence would distract attention from Terry and the hostage issue, make the event into a political showcase, and throw the whole thing out of whack. A hot debate went on for quite some time, but finally we felt that as a courtesy we had to invite him. Jesse had championed our cause early and had not backed down, and it would have been a terrible slight not to invite him to attend.

When Jesse accepted, Tom Brokaw was forced to decline. Brokaw had been scheduled to give the opening remarks, but NBC told him that, because Jackson was a political candidate, he would not be permitted to share a platform with him, even though Jesse was not slated to participate. Tom is very caring and very involved, but, apologetically, he told us he could not be there with us.

The morning of the service, as the hostage families and speakers and participants were arriving, the big red Jesse bus rolled up. The church was full of people, and a crowd of kids ran to greet Jesse when he stepped out. It could have been the usual media circus, but Jesse was a paragon. This was a solemn occasion and, dressed in a pinstripe suit, he put one finger to his lips and motioned everyone quiet. Without saying a word he made it clear that he was there to give honor, not receive it. He walked inside, the *Washington Post* reported, "like any other supplicant."

I talked with Nick Daniloff afterward. He had been held by the Soviets and accused of spying, and it took a month of intense negotiating by our government to bring him home. Nick drew an analogy between his treatment and Terry's. At different times during his captivity, he said, he was allowed to meet with his wife and his boss. But when they took him down and put him back in his cell, and the door shut behind him, he would get panicky. He thought he would be left there, he would be forgotten and would never get out. So, during the brief time that he was held captive it gave him a real sense of what Terry must feel. He was quick to say that he couldn't even imagine the terror and abandonment of being held year after year.

What with Iran-contra and the anti-hostage backlash, I felt it was necessary to turn back the mood of the country, so I would speak at church groups and ministries and Rotary Clubs and Kiwanis meetings, anywhere they asked me. I did local YWCAs and Batavia High School. But I was burning myself out. I was in Canton, Ohio, speaking to a local Lebanese-American group and one of the people who was running the meeting said, "We were just amazed when we found out you were going to speak here. We asked our director how he got you to come and he said he just picked up the phone and asked you."

But I was getting really exhausted, and the more tired I get the more emotional I become, and I had to hold that in check. So I decided to cut back. I was out on the edge again and I had to have some time to regroup.

On May 4 three French hostages were released, and I knew I had to see them. Having been through the experience of talking to ex-hostages, particularly with Father Jenco, hearing what they had to say immediately upon release and then seeing how that changed over the months, I was determined to get to the French just as quickly as I possibly could. I knew I couldn't trust the State Department to tell me anything.

I called AP and made arrangements for my travel and for Carolyn Turolla to accompany me. A short time later Pierre Salinger called. He was working for ABC in Paris and he wanted to know if I was coming over. He offered to set up appointments with the hostages for me. I gratefully accepted.

Before I left I got a briefing from the State Department: Terry was fine, but he was extremely depressed. One sentence, that was it.

I had called NBC in New York and asked them to send Ed Caldwell to Paris to present to President François Mitterrand a letter on behalf of the Journalists Committee. They said fine, no problem. We all booked a flight together.

None of us had had any sleep the night before, and we left New York on a plane with a party group who were obviously going to the Cannes Film Festival. They were the most obnoxious, obscene group of people I've ever seen crammed onto one airplane, and they didn't shut up the whole night long. Even the stewardess was afraid to say anything to them. I'm not happy in the air to begin with, and it was one long, raucous nightmare.

So we were up a second night, all night long, and when we got into Paris I hit the hotel and there was former hostage David Jacobsen with a CBS crew prowling the lobby. I didn't have a leg under me, it was early afternoon Paris time, and David was now part of the media and working hard. He said to me, "You have an appointment to see Marcel Fontaine right now." Fontaine was one of the hostages, along with Marcel Carton and Jean-Paul Kauffmann, who had just been released. He had spent the previous year sharing a cell with

Terry and I was very, very anxious to talk to him. But not right then.

I said, "David, I don't want to see him right now. I'm exhausted, I want to have my wits about me when I talk to this man."

"No," Jacobsen said, "you've got to go and see him right now. It's all set up."

What I didn't know was that Fontaine didn't know David Jacobsen and the CBS crew were coming with me. David and CBS's trade for Fontaine's time was me. But I was tired, I didn't know what was happening. In the meantime Ed Caldwell had gone up to his room, and they whisked me away.

They swept me into Fontaine's apartment, the CBS crew came in and quickly set up their cameras, and Fontaine started talking, although he seemed tired and more than a little bewildered at the scene before him. He was a very nice man and, through an interpreter, he began to say things I didn't think he should be talking about on camera. Fontaine had been a prisoner for more than three years and he couldn't have been aware of the potential damage of off-the-cuff interviews. I said, "Hold it, guys, you are going to have to leave the room now." David Jacobsen and the CBS crew packed up and left. They'd had their coup.

Fontaine and I talked for about an hour. He had shared a cell with Terry from November of the previous year until two days before. In fact, he said, the night before he was released the guards came in and told Terry to pack his things, that he was going home. They took Terry out of the room and Fontaine assumed that he had indeed been released. It wasn't until his own release later in the day that he discovered that Terry had again been left behind.

Fontaine was a French diplomat and a very gentle man. He reminded me in many ways of Ben Weir. Speaking through an interpreter was difficult, there was so much I wanted to ask him and the process was so slow. But I soaked up whatever stories he could tell me.

Fontaine said he'd had a short and reluctant interview with the State Department, telling them nothing of real value. He and Terry had very briefly shared an apartment, not a cell, and the place would have sounded too comfortable, too nice for hostages. Fontaine had worried that if the government heard they were living in such good conditions it would undermine the urgency to bring the hostages home. In fact, the apartment he and Terry shared had had wall-to-wall carpeting, it had its own kitchen. They'd had what they wanted to eat, they'd had a shower and a television. Unfortunately, this lasted only a matter of weeks and then they were returned to being chained to their beds in a basement.

I asked Fontaine whether Terry knew that his father and brother were both dead. He had been in isolation previous to the time that the captors put him in with Terry, but he'd had a radio and had heard about Dad and Rich. So when he met Terry he wanted to get an idea of how much Terry did or did not know. Fontaine said he'd mentioned, in a very casual way, that one of the hostages' fathers had died. Terry had felt very bad for whoever it was, but Fontaine said it seemed not to cross Terry's mind that it was his own. Fontaine didn't tell Terry the truth because he was afraid Terry would commit suicide.

Terry never heard mention of Dad's death on television because the captors monitored their viewing. They were permitted no news shows, Fontaine said. They used to joke that their torture was having to watch endless reruns of *Three's Company*.

Terry did have a temper. Fontaine said Terry had requested of his captors in November that he be allowed to videotape a message to let his family know he was well. The captors told him yes, he could do it, but then they would say, "*Inshallah, Inshallah*." He asked them regularly and that's what he would hear. One day, as Christmas neared, he asked again, got the same answer, and just went out of control. Terry was so frustrated that he began beating his head against the wall. "Think about your family," Fontaine told him, "they love you." But Terry kept banging and Fontaine had to call the guards in to subdue him. A short time later they brought in a video camera. That was how we got the Christmas Eve tape that year.

Terry was not, from what Fontaine said, particularly despondent. Fontaine, himself feeling low one day, had remarked to Terry that he didn't want to die in that awful place and have them throw his body into the sea, as the captors had done with William Buckley. Terry said, "I don't want to die *anywhere*."

*　　*　　*

By the time I had finished talking with Fontaine and gone back to the hotel I had a stack of messages waiting for me.

Pierre Salinger was livid; I had just completely betrayed ABC. CBS had scored the first Marcel Fontaine interview. NBC's Ed Caldwell hadn't been there, the AP hadn't been there, and CBS had themselves a genuine exclusive. It dawned on me that, intentional or not, I'd been had. There was nothing I could do about it except get angry and determine that it was not going to happen to me again.

I got a few hours sleep and we left the next morning for Geneva, Switzerland, to talk to Marcel Carton. I tried to make it up to NBC and I got Ed Caldwell on the plane, leaving CBS behind—so we evened the score a little. There was an AP correspondent as well.

I've got to say that throughout this entire ordeal the Associated Press have never asked for, nor have they ever gotten, an exclusive. They have paid my way, paid my phone bills, and allowed me the financial freedom to pursue Terry's cause as a full-time job, but they have never told me what to say, they have never in any way interfered with my activities. We may have our disagreements over policy, but the AP have never used their connection to Terry or to me to their advantage.

Carton's family was with him when we met. We sat out in the backyard of his daughter's home in a kind of arbor. He wanted to be out in the fresh air and see the sun. Carton spoke very little English but, like so many French people I met, his face was so expressive. "The sun," he said, beaming, "the sky. There is nothing like it."

He was a wonderful man and I felt so bad for him. He was kidnapped six days after Terry and he told me he had virtually no memory of his first year in captivity. "You have to understand," he said through an interpreter, "it was a very emotional time for me. They had kidnapped my daughter with me, then took her away, my wife had just had a heart attack before I was kidnapped, and I didn't know what had happened to them." He told me whom he had been held with and what the circumstances were, and what he knew about Terry. Then we flew back to Paris.

In my room I found that CBS had sent me a huge bouquet of flowers.

On my third day in France, former hostage Jean-Paul Kauffmann held a press conference on the Left Bank. The place was packed, mostly with French journalists. I speak no French but Carolyn Turolla spoke enough to get us through some basic situations, and she was giving me the gist of what he was saying.

I was fascinated just watching him. Three years of total lack of sun had made him almost translucent. He was a large man and his skin was so ghostly white you could almost imagine looking right through him. But he was mesmerizing. I had never seen anybody speak with such expression before. It was all in his face and hands. I couldn't understand a word he was saying but I sat there enthralled.

The French press had been very active on the hostages' behalf; as opposed to the lack of attention in the United States, the hostages were mentioned almost every day on the French newscasts. Jean-Paul Kauffmann's wife Joelle had been tireless. We had been in contact and had teased each other that she was known as the French Peggy Say and I as the American Joelle Kauffmann.

Kauffmann had arranged for a private briefing for us after the press conference. The French hostage families were there along with me, Carolyn Turolla, David Jacobsen, Jill Morell, who was the fiancée of British hostage John McCarthy, and members of the Journalists Committee who had worked so hard on Jean-Paul's behalf. Terry had told Marcel Fontaine that he'd seen John McCarthy, which was a thrill because McCarthy hadn't been heard from in some time and this was the first word that he was even alive.

Kauffmann demanded an agreement from everyone there. Because the information he and his compatriots had would certainly affect the lives of the men they had left behind, he insisted that before the French hostages made this information public they would tell me what they knew about the Americans and I would go back and get the families' permission to release it to the world. Kauffmann felt the decision of what to tell, and to whom, was too big for him to make arbitrarily; people's lives were at stake and he wanted the families of each of these men to decide for themselves. Everything said in this meeting was therefore, for the time being, to be confidential. We all agreed.

The meeting didn't start well. David Jacobsen wanted to play hostage reminiscence and I was trying to interrupt and get more information from Kauffmann. We had maybe a half-hour and I thought we had better things to do than listen to "Remember old mean Said" one more time.

Kauffmann told us about Frank Reed. Reed had apparently tried to escape and had been caught. He was beaten so badly that when they brought him into the cell that he shared with Kauffmann he was uncommunicative. He wouldn't look at television, he wouldn't talk to Kauffmann, he was almost catatonic. Kauffmann was careful to say that Reed had gotten much better, and although once again communicative and responsive, he was still totally frightened of being beaten again.

Kauffmann also said that for some reason the captors had taken a strong dislike to Tom Sutherland, and he had twice tried to commit suicide. All of this was news to us: bad news.

Back at the hotel, I was told that Pierre Salinger had left three screeching messages with the AP bureau. I knew NBC was also not happy with me, although I was trying to make it up to them. And in the meantime I had gotten the word that the Journalists Committee would be received the next day at the presidential Elysée Palace. That was not for public consumption.

I had postponed my original interview with Salinger. I hated to further incite Pierre, but I'd been caught up in trying to arrange the palace meeting. Finally I made it to Salinger's office. I felt bad about his being scooped, particularly after his having taken the time to set up appointments with the hostages for me. I told him, "Look, I'm sorry, I was had. There was nothing I could do, it happened too fast. But it's done. If you want an interview, here I am." I also said, "Off the record, we got the okay to go to the palace." I figured he would like to know.

So Pierre Salinger, onetime press secretary to President Kennedy, got me on camera and did a very arrogant interview, lots of distance, a clear disdain coming off him. Then, with the camera rolling he said, "I understand that you are going to the palace tomorrow."

I was ready to tear my hair out. "Pierre," I said as calmly and politely as possible, "you know that's private."

I thought I knew about journalists, but it was clear that I still had a lot to learn.

At the Elysée Palace the next morning we didn't get to meet with President Mitterrand but with an aide, who graciously accepted the letter from the Journalists Committee. Our trip was complete.

Back in my room, I got a panic-stricken call from Jill Morell, John McCarthy's fiancée.

"Didn't Jean-Paul Kauffmann say that the information from that meeting was private and confidential?"

"Yes."

"Well, David Jacobsen is down at CBS and he's going to tell them about Frank Reed and about what happened to the other hostages. You've got to stop him!" She was in a panic, beside herself. One wrong word could get her fiancée tortured.

I called CBS and got an executive on the line. "I understand that David Jacobsen is down there," I said. "You've got to realize that this was a confidential meeting. He can't do this to the families. You simply cannot do this."

I was told, "Okay, okay."

I called Jill back and said, "I think everything is under control."

My phone rang again. It was CBS and they began raking me over the coals because by now Jean-Paul Kauffmann and his wife Joelle were on the phone with them, taking no prisoners. And now this guy was screaming at me because he thought I had told the Kauffmanns about the Jacobsen interview.

I said, "Look, I do not know who told Jean-Paul and Joelle, but it was not me. I don't even know how to get ahold of them." I didn't want to put the finger on Jill Morell because I didn't want them screaming at her.

I already had Pierre Salinger shouting at me. Now I had all of CBS screaming. These were the conditions under which I left Paris.

I got back in Washington in time to speak at the Arlington Cemetery memorial service for William Buckley. It was a sizable funeral with full military honors. They had the white horses, the twenty-one gun salute. It was only then I found out that Bill Buckley's protege Chip Beck and I were to be the only speakers.

I looked out from the podium and saw sunlight skipping off an ocean of brass. You could smell CIA spooks from one end of that place to the other. I don't remember anything of what I said that day, just that when the bugler played taps it tore me up.

When I finished my speech I went to give my condolences to Bill Buckley's family and saw a phalanx of State Department people swarming toward me. I'd just come from seeing the French hostages and they hadn't even gotten an interview with Carton.

The acting head of Counter-Terrorism, Al Adams, who had taken Bremer's place; Michael Mahoney, all my buddies just smarmed around. There was a reception following the services and Mahoney said to me, "Well, you're coming over to the State Department after the luncheon, aren't you?" I told him I hadn't thought about it.

"I'll be at the luncheon, so you can give me your decision."

At the luncheon I found Michael had been seated next to me. He was trying, not subtly, to find out as much as he could from me to take back to his superiors. I told him, "Michael, I've been on the road, I just got back, I've done what I had to do. Now that I think about it, you'll have to tell them that I simply can't make it. I'm going home."

The more I thought about it the madder I got, and at my next State Department meeting I went in loaded for bear. "The only time we have these damn meetings," I told them, "is when you want something from me. That's not your function. I'm supposed to come here to get information, not give you information. That's not how it's supposed to work." But I gave it to them anyway.

CHAPTER
12

BY THE SUMMER OF 1988 I WAS STARTING TO LOSE MY TEMPER EASILY. I was tired of stupid questions. I was getting to the point that the next person who asked me a stupid question I was going to knock down.

The basic question, every time a hostage was released, was "How do you feel?" How the hell do you think I feel! I was tired of reporters coming out who hadn't done their homework and wanted me to brief them, to give them the full background, to do their work for them. I was tired of standing alongside other families who were being made whole. I was tired of watching everybody else walk out of there while Terry was forced to stay. I was tired of hearing heroic Terry Anderson stories. I wanted to hear Terry Anderson's voice.

But I held my tongue. I told them all, "I'm so happy for [the Weirs/Jencos/Fontaines/Kauffmanns/Jacobsens]. Their freedom gives us all hope." Mostly what it gave me was a lot of rage.

David and I finally had to get out of Batavia, out of New York altogether. I had become so isolated in my own home that I didn't want to go out. The phone was always ringing, people were knocking at my door. I didn't want to go get groceries because every time I went out people would come up to me. Most of the people who stopped me were very nice and genuinely concerned. Often they would be moved to tears, and as heartwarming as that was, it sure didn't help me take my mind off Terry's situation.

There were others who were embarrassingly impressed at running into a "celebrity," who they defined as anyone who's been on television. I cringed at those public encounters.

David and I had little social life because no evening out went unchallenged. No matter what we chose to do—go bowling, have dinner out, have a few drinks and dance—there was almost always some aggressive idiot braying in my face how *he* would solve the situation.

I can remember being at our local newsstand trying to find something to read, kind of crouched down looking at titles, when out of the corner of my eye I could see this guy weaving back and forth who obviously felt the need to make contact. All I could think was, "Oh, God, please don't let him speak to me."

I stopped making eye contact with anyone. If I was out grocery shopping or in the K mart and somebody looked as if he was going to say something to me, I would wheel my cart around the corner and avoid the person at all costs.

Most of the people meant well, I knew that. And I had spent three years going out of my way to get them interested in getting Terry home. But now I was over my quota and there was no escape.

I hadn't realized how sour I had become. I didn't even want family coming over. No company. When I traveled I had to deal with people all the time; I didn't need to deal with them in my house too.

We had to get out of there.

David and I had friends, Chud and Marty Fuellgraf, who lived in a pleasant town in southwestern Kentucky. They had a cottage on a lake where we had gone to fish and recuperate after one or another time that Terry was supposed to come out but didn't. One day they rang up and said they were about to put the cottage on the market and wanted to know if we were interested in buying it. Because they were willing to do some creative financing it only took me and David about twenty minutes to call back and say "We'll take it."

We didn't know how we were going to afford it. I hadn't worked since Terry was captured, and we were basically getting by. We had to sell the plot of land that Terry and I owned together. I was sad to let it go, particularly knowing how Terry talked about it in captivity, but we couldn't afford recreational property.

The lot had been on the market three times before but each time something had happened and we'd end up taking it off and saying we didn't want to sell it. We'd never had a bid on it. This time it sold immediately.

David and I moved down to Kentucky right before July 4th weekend, 1988. We were going to fish and swim and just relax and try to get ourselves together. We had been hearing strong rumors from reliable sources on the ground in Beirut that there was a good chance a hostage would be released that weekend, and that the hostage would be Terry Anderson. So we were sitting on our new porch, listening to the breeze rustling through the pines, thinking, "This is great. A new house, a new kind of life, Terry's coming home. Things couldn't be better."

Sure.

On July 3, American navy men on the USS *Vincennes* thought they had an enemy F-14 in their sights. They fired and shot down an Iranian airbus, killing all 290 civilians on board. The newscasts showed bodies floating in the Persian Gulf, and the Middle East went wild. Two days later an anonymous caller left word that the captors were going to retaliate against the United States by killing the hostages.

I was just settling into my new Kentucky home and here came the media staging a deathwatch on my lawn so they could interview me when Terry got killed.

Terry's life was spared. It is widely believed, however, that Colonel William Higgins was killed during that time. A videotape was released in July 1989, a year later, showing his body hanging, but from what I can gather the captors killed him in anger over the Iranian airbus shooting.

So things started out with an uproar, but after that life in Kentucky was peaceful. First off, there weren't major newspapers in the area, the town was a two-hour drive from Nashville, and our house was hard to find, so we weren't getting the constant barrage we had in Batavia. Also, the people in the area were respectful of our privacy. We didn't come in as local celebrities and they were just as happy to keep it that way. So was I. Several months went by and basically nothing happened. On one hand, I needed the rest. On the other, on every one of those days Terry was in a lot more pain than I was.

I had been told for two years, "Wait until the presidential election, you'll see some action." I expected the hostages to be an issue.

I didn't expect much from the Republicans. It was their State Department, after all, that I had learned to distrust, and Ronald Reagan had given us a lot of platitudes but very little action. He had asked to be taken at face value, but while I found it a sympathetic face I also came to believe it was of very little value.

I expected better of the Democrats. After all, Reagan had come to power on the hostage issue, when Jimmy Carter was stopped cold by the original hostage crisis. Reagan's staff had made contact with the Iranians and bargained for the hostages; they even, according to rumor, orchestrated the release so it fell on Reagan's inauguration day. If the Democrats had any smarts at all, I figured, they would bring Terry's case to the forefront and blame it on the do-nothing Reagan/Bush White House.

But, as with pretty much everything else in that campaign, Michael Dukakis never got it together. I was waiting for the fireworks, for Terry's situation to become a political battleground, but nothing happened.

It came time, once again, to organize an event around Terry's birthday. On October 27, 1988, Terry would turn forty-one. The Journalists Committee, including Sam Donaldson this time, met early in the day with Secretary General Javier Pérez de Cuéllar at the United Nations. I was excited; this was the top of international diplomacy and if anyone could gather all the parties in this dispute and make them work things out, I thought it would be the U.N.

The meeting was friendly and attentive. Pérez de Cuéllar said they were working as hard as they could to get the sides together. I felt encouraged by his words. Then he turned to David Aikman and said, "If you know anybody whom we can talk to . . ."

I was sitting right there and I thought, "What he's saying is that they are not talking to the right people; they don't know who they are." I had learned to listen not only for facts but for nuances, and though no one else picked it up the bottom line here was horrendous: after three and a half years they were still looking for somebody to talk to.

Carmella LaSpada at No Greater Love had organized a media reception in New York on the occasion of Terry's birthday. Terry was a big Garry Trudeau fan because some of the *Doonesbury* strips were set at the Commodore Hotel in Beirut, where all the journalists used to gather, so Carmella asked Trudeau if he would design a birthday card for the occasion, and he did.

Jean-Paul Kauffmann, who had come in specially for the occasion, spoke at our press reception and luncheon. He gave an impassioned speech saying that the French press was responsible for his release. The French hostages were a popular cause with the French; on television every night they broadcast the men's names and the dates of their captivity. Because the French press made their cause popular, the French government was given room to maneuver. The party in power could cut a deal without being subjected to political repercussions; there would be no backlash of public opinion. Jean-Paul told this gathering of editors and publishers that they had bought into the blackmail by the Reagan government; they had swallowed the official line Publicity Prolongs Captivity.

"It may be your government's job to work in privacy," he said, "but it is your job as the American press, the most powerful media in the world, to report what has happened here. And you have failed."

I got emotional when I spoke. "Some of these men are suicidal, they can't take anymore. You have the power, we have to make these men's lives mean something!"

After the event was over, David and I were walking down the street with Terry's friends Bill Foley and Cary Vaughan, and Don Mell and Jean-Paul and Joelle Kauffmann. It was Jean-Paul's first trip to the States and he is a wine connoisseur, so we were searching out a wine bar someone had recommended. It was five o'clock and we knew we weren't going to catch a cab at rush hour so we began trooping through the caverns of Grand Central Station, and I was falling farther and farther behind.

I was also getting more and more upset, but I didn't want to disturb the others. I was thinking, "It's not fair that Jean-Paul should have to come and do this. His life is in Paris, his life should go on, he shouldn't have to come to New York to plead Terry's case." Finally I burst into tears.

The others turned around astonished. I don't think they had ever seen me cry. "What's wrong?" they asked.

"Well, you know," I said between gulps and sobs, "we have been caught up in all these ceremonies and everything, and the rest of you are not remembering that Terry Anderson is spending his birthday chained to a basement wall, and I cannot stop thinking about that. You know, I stand up and tell all these stories all day long, time after time, and I try not to allow it to get to me, I have to stay strong for Terry's sake. But it *does* get to me."

"But, Peggy," said Bill Foley, "you did such a wonderful job at the luncheon. You really made a case for Terry, and they all listened to you."

"Bill," I blubbered, "do you know how many times I've given that speech, and every time there is a different hostage at my side, but it's the same speech over and over again. As far as I can see into my future this is what I'm going to be doing, every anniversary, every birthday, and I cannot handle it anymore."

I don't think I'd ever seen people actually wringing their hands before. They didn't know what to do with me. I went back to the hotel and just cried for a while. In spite of all the good feelings of the day, and the feeling of support from all of these people, in the end I was left walking away, knowing that I just had to wait until the next event to move Terry one day closer to freedom.

Three days later the captors released another videotape from Terry, his third since he was kidnapped.

"I received your birthday greetings," he said, "and as always they helped very much. But as my fourth birthday in captivity passes, as the end of my fourth year approaches, I find it difficult to keep my hopes and my courage high.

"The news I hear out of here tells me that you have not forgotten, and I know you will not. But the difficulties seem enormous. I have been very close to being released several times over the past two years, but each time, it seems that the U.S. uses its influence to stop any agreement from being made, and I don't understand this. I'm not asking President Reagan to deal with terrorists, although both he and Mr. Bush did so in the Iran-contra affair and the TWA hijacking. Our problem could have been solved long ago without such complications as arms deals. . . .

"All that is necessary is that Mr. Reagan—and Mr. Bush, if he is elected—use their influence in a positive way, not a negative one. . . .

"I gather there has been very little discussion of our problem in the U.S. presidential campaign, and this is disappointing, as is President Reagan's complete failure to find a solution during his eight years in office. But whichever candidate wins this election, remember: an unyielding refusal to deal with this matter is not going to make it go away. It's not going to free us.

"I heard on the radio of the generous and ambitious [work] to free three trapped whales a few days ago, and that the president [sent] thanks to the Soviet Union for its help. It's a warming story. That kind of cooperation and spirit is absolutely necessary to bring this situation to an end. Once again, this has gone on too long; it can't continue like this.

"Peg, Madeleine, Dad, kiss my daughters for me. Keep your spirits up and I will try and do the same. And one day—soon, God willing—this will end."

I was stunned. First of all, he looked better than he had in ten years. He was clean-shaven and fit and had a wiry, healthy feel to the way he carried himself. He spoke with snap and fire. I thought, "Gee, Terry, you shouldn't be looking that good; it doesn't help our cause."

He was wearing a Commodore Hotel T-shirt. Terry's friends and I were always scouring the videotapes for a hidden message in word or gesture, and we did a lot of talking about that one. The Commodore Hotel was where the journalists hung out in Beirut. Until shortly before Terry was taken it had traditionally been a safe haven, then it had been shelled, and we were trying to figure if Terry was telling us he was safe or not safe, or whether the T-shirt was just what he happened to be wearing that day.

The videotape led us all to believe that Terry had been prepared for release. Over the years the captors had established a pattern; all of a sudden a hostage would be cleaned up and dressed well and fattened up before a release so he would look decent when he emerged. Terry couldn't have looked better than he looked on that tape.

As far as what he said, I agreed with everything, especially about the campaign. I'd had about enough of "quiet diplomacy" and now here was Terry saying he had, too.

President Reagan's response was basically that "I don't think Terry would say those things." As if Terry was his intimate friend. When the press told me about that I said immediately, "I think I know my brother a hell of a lot better than Ronald Reagan does, and there was nothing in that videotape that would have been alien to what Terry had said before he was kidnapped." In other words, Reagan had a lot of gall.

A distant cousin, Eileen Motter, who lived just outside of Atlanta, had been involved in several projects to keep the hostage issue alive. She and a friend had, through a series of church contacts, set up a meeting with Jimmy Carter.

I didn't know what to expect. I had contacted the former president's office in the first year of Terry's captivity to see if he would help us and had been told that Mr. Carter felt that he would only be a hindrance. Anything critical President Carter would say, his associate had told us, would only be perceived as sour grapes coming from the man who had been run out of town over the hostage crisis. Mr. Carter, we were told, felt he would do our cause more harm than good.

But this was almost three years later, Carter had been out of office almost eight years, another presidential election had come and gone without his participation, and now he had agreed to see us.

I flew down to Atlanta with Ray Barnett and Lela Gilbert from Friends in the West, and we tried to think how the former president was going to respond. We didn't know whether he was actually interested or if he had just been manipulated into a photo op by these two well-meaning ladies.

Whenever I met with important people I had found it best to leave the decision of how to deal with the press up to them: "Do you want press coverage or do you not want it? I will do it either way." President

Carter did not want it. Unfortunately, my cousin Eileen and her friend had notified the press and by the time we got there we had a major media crowd on hand. I was embarrassed and explained to them that after the meeting there would be a photo op only.

Ray Barnett and I knew that in order to have a productive meeting there would have to be privacy, so we decided that once inside, after Eileen had read the opening remarks which she had written, David and Lela would stand up and excuse themselves and sweep my cousin and her friend out with them. I felt sorry for them as they were being led out of the room—they had been very eager to meet President Carter, and they had these stricken looks on their faces, like "I set this meeting up. How did this happen?"—but sometimes sacrifices have to be made. This was not a social occasion, it was a meeting with a very serious purpose.

When we got down to business, Mr. Carter seemed anxious to help. He explained briefly to us that he had a friend who was still in prison in Tehran, who he had been working very hard to get released.

Since leaving the White House, Jimmy Carter has been an unusually progressive force, for a former president. He has been involved with the Center's for Disease Control and many humanitarian causes. Ray Barnett had been trying for a long time to get financing to establish a hospital in Beirut, and Ray brought that project into the discussion. The goal was never a hospital-for-hostages deal, but it certainly couldn't hurt.

I had read a recent magazine interview in which Yasser Arafat said that the PLO had been the contact that cut the deal between Republican U.S. negotiators and Iran to hold back the release of the hostages until after the 1980 presidential election. If the hostages had come home while Carter was still in office it would have been a tremendous political coup, maybe even enough to turn the election around. As it was, Reagan opened his Administration with one of the greatest staged celebrations of all times, the hostage homecoming.

I had heard that story rumored, but I thought it was just so mind-boggling that, if it were true, it would never be made public. The implications were terrible—that time was added to the hostages' captivity *by Reagan* so that he could get elected. The cynicism, the cruelty of it. I thought there would be a huge uproar when this story broke, that the office of the President would disintegrate, but nothing came of it. Not a murmur.

At the end of the meeting Mr. Carter had consented to a photo opportunity, and as he was walking us out the press started shooting questions at him. I watched the man and I could see that part of him was anxious to talk and part of him was reluctant. Finally they fished him in. "The policy of this Administration towards these hostages," he told the press, "is designed for defeat, it is unworkable."

I was asked why I was there. "Isn't it ironic," I told them, "that with history on his side I have come to Atlanta to speak with President Carter because he is now perceived as a successful hostage negotiator? His crisis ended in 444 days, my brother's captivity has gone on for almost four years."

Somebody said to Carter, "Do you regret that your involvement with the hostages cost you the presidency?"

He answered, "I consider my involvement a success; my people came home."

Who's going to go back now and say, "We're sorry we thought you were ineffective"? There's no way you can undo it; what happened to President Carter was totally unjust.

I have gotten several strange introductions during the course of Terry's captivity. People who operate in the peculiar realm of what they insist on calling the intelligence community are sort of generically odd packages, and some have showed up at my door.

In the summer of 1987 I got a series of calls from a man who identified himself as Michael Trumpower. He said he wanted to help get Terry free. To establish his bona-fides he shared details with me of an initiative he claimed to have been involved with which was bank-rolled by Ross Perot. The initiative was highly confidential but, as it happened, I had been in touch with Mr. Perot and Trumpower's information jibed with my own. I called Perot's office for verification and was told that he did not recognize Trumpower's name. Now I was really puzzled.

Over a couple of months Trumpower told me several things. He said that he had worked for the government in the Middle East and that Terry Arnold, the man who had come to Buffalo to call me off criticizing the Administration's bombing of Libya, had been his contact.

Trumpower claimed to have recorded every conversation he and Arnold had had over the past three or four years. He also said he had recorded proof that the government knew beforehand not only that, after the U.S. bombing of Libya, Peter Kilburn and Alec Collett and two other British hostages would be murdered, but also that Qaddafi was trying to buy up the others, Terry Anderson included.

Trumpower also claimed he had tape-recorded evidence of the disinformation campaign and other devious CIA-backed manipulations concerning the Libyan bombing, information that the Libyans would pay dearly for. He said he had reliable Libyan connections.

At this point I was trying to find out just what Michael Trumpower wanted from me. Not an easy task. The guy was a wandering conversationalist and very difficult to get a straight answer out of. He also insisted that if the CIA tracked him down they would eliminate him.

Trumpower claimed he wanted nothing for himself; he simply wanted justice served for his suffering fellow Americans.

Obviously the guy was blowing smoke about his private reasons, and I didn't know what they were. Finally, however, I pinned him down as to what he wanted from me. He wanted me to go to New York and hand a sample of his tapes over to the Libyan ambassador to the U.N.

Trumpower claimed that, although the Libyans would be happy to pay a great deal of money for these tapes, he was going to try to get them to release my brother and Tom Sutherland in exchange for them. Look, I said, the Islamic Jihad detested the Libyans enough to refuse to sell them their hostages after the U.S. bombing of Libya; just how were the Libyans going to influence the Jihad to give these men up now?

"There are ways it can be done," he said.

I don't think I actually shrieked in horror over the telephone, but I did convince him that there was no way I would get involved in his little scheme. Absolutely no way.

Months passed with no contact. Then in September or October of 1988 Trumpower called again out of the blue. He was in Ohio, he said, and needed to see me. He was going to bring some of the "evidence" with him.

I didn't want to see this man, he was too disturbing, too weird. But I figured he must know something valuable and finally I caved in. I started to tell him how to find our house, but he said, "I know."

That made me extremely uneasy. I had only recently moved there; when I'd first heard from Trumpower I hadn't lived there at all. Plus, to get to our house you've got to take a complicated series of rights and lefts off small roads, and people are always getting lost. The fact that this strange man with unsavory contacts knew where we lived scared me.

Trumpower arrived the next day in a rusty 1977 maroon Dodge van and said he'd been driving all night. He didn't seem tired, in fact he appeared rather wired. His hands were dirty and he explained that he'd had car trouble along the way. My husband found it peculiar that he refused any refreshments and seemed careful not to touch anything. Okay, so we'd both seen too many spy movies. Our suspicions were blown when he accepted lunch and handled his glass and silverware.

About the third time I tried Trumpower did, indirectly, give me some sense of why he was there. Without naming me specifically he said that a "credible third party" needed to be involved in his Libyan initiative. The plot was that this party would release half the tapes to the American media at the "homecoming" of Tom Sutherland. A week later, he said, Terry Anderson would be released and then the remaining tapes would be given to the press.

Trumpower had "left the tapes at home." He had not told me what he wanted from me, and I remarked to him that I failed to understand why he had come; there was nothing he had said to me that day that he hadn't already said over the phone. More mumbling and off he went.

Two weeks later he called to say that the Libyans were flying him by private aircraft to Libya and that "things looked good." A few days later he left a message on my answering machine saying that he was going to see "the person in question."

A few days after that I was in the house with the answering machine on. I heard Trumpower say, "Peggy, are you there? This is Mike." Before I could pick it up we were disconnected. I never heard from him again.

*   *   *

Not long after that, Terry Arnold called. He and a writer named Neil Livingstone were working on an article for the *Washingtonian* about scams that people over the years have run on the families of hostages. Now, at the time Arnold called the families did not have a good relationship with the State Department. Our State Department liaison had the dubious distinction of having held that position for about two years without ever having passed on one single useful scrap of information. There was no indication that anyone with authority was doing anything to bring our guys home; there was a big void out there. People were calling the families and offering false hope for a high price; they always wanted financing to go to the Middle East, and none of us had that kind of cash. All we were getting was disappointment, and here Terry Arnold was calling with a sympathetic ear for our problems.

I had just had this experience with Trumpower that made me very uneasy and I really felt the need to express my feelings about what had happened.

"Do you know a man named Michael Trumpower?" I asked him.

Arnold said he had worked with him on some initiatives. "What's Michael up to now?" he said with a sigh.

I spilled my guts. Terry Arnold was so sympathetic and such a willing listener, and I was so vulnerable, that I told him the whole story. Arnold knew just which buttons to push, and in the course of several long conversations I began to feel as if I had finally found a friend, a knowledgeable contact to replace the ones I had lost.

I told him about some of the scams I had heard were run on the other families. These were stories on the rumor mill, they hadn't happened to me. One involved a relative of Ayatollah Khomeini, a man named Hossein Tabatabai. I had met Tabatabai several times and had thrown myself on his mercy, trying to get him to put in a good word for us with the Iranian government. His attitude was "I don't need this, thank you very much." The Ayatollah was still alive, and anyone who acted in sympathy with the Americans was automatically at risk. Finally I found myself near him at a luncheon in Georgetown and pulled out all the stops, told him all the horrors that had happened to my family, literally begged him. He said he'd do what he could.

But according to one hostage family, another Tabatabai—a cousin of my contact—had tried to con them, had offered to deliver a letter to the Ayatollah personally in exchange for two or three thousand dollars. When they related the story to me and asked if I wanted to ''chip in,'' I said, ''The U.S. mail is a lot cheaper.'' I could not verify the story. I told Arnold he would have to take it up with the family in question and see whether they were willing to discuss the scam in public.

I got a call from Terry Arnold in December saying that his article would be out in the next couple of days. Copies of the *Washingtonian* arrived the night before Christmas Eve by Federal Express and I read it immediately.

I was horrified. There were two items in the story which were devastating. There was the entire Trumpower saga, including my own impressions and suspicions. Trumpower came off looking like a wild man, a dangerous spook, and I was the one who had told his story. If he saw this article he would be very angry. Angry enough, I thought, to come looking to do me harm. Oh, great, I thought. This man is going to be highly peeved, he's got frightening connections, he's out on the loose and I've got no one to blame but myself.

And he knew where I lived.

Then there was the story about Tabatabai. Terry Arnold had written that Tabatabai had tried to scam *me*. There I was in print accusing a relative of the Ayatollah of scamming me for chump change.

This was no small deal. I had been told that another of Tabatabai's cousins had been assassinated by Iranian hit men in the employ of the Libyans. This was big-time, we had a major danger here, and I was quoted in print as saying that he was an extortionist.

It was late at night when I read the article and there was no way I could get ahold of Arnold. I was hysterical. I sat at the table and kept saying to myself, ''He couldn't have done this to me, he couldn't have.'' David went to bed and I stayed up trying to find a way to get myself out of this horrible mess Arnold had put me into.

I came as close to breaking down as I ever had. I started to get dizzy, I felt queasy. I went in to David and said, ''Just sit here with me for a while, please, honey.'' Even after my dad and Rich died, David rarely saw me lose control; he didn't know what to do. ''Just stay awake,'' I asked.

When it got light I called Terry Arnold. I was trying not to be incoherent, not to get so upset that I'd babble. I said, "Do you realize what you've done to me? Michael Trumpower has very frightening connections and you've made him look like an ass in print and made me responsible.

"And Tabatabai. These people are in a hands-on situation with my brother. For all this time I have lived knowing that one wrong word could cost my brother's life. Now you have totally discredited me with a relative of the Ayatollah. It's a very simple matter to retaliate against Terry. That story? *It never happened to me!*" I had never felt so betrayed in my life.

"Plus, you have endangered Tabatabai. How do you think that's going to play in Tehran, him trying to scam me for minor bucks. Terry, you know that that incident never happened to me, how could you write that it did?"

"Well," he said casually, "I had the story. I knew that it happened to [one of the other families] but they wouldn't give me attribution and I wanted to use it, so I attributed it to you."

I could barely contain my rage and, after remarking that I was being "overly dramatic," Arnold said, "Let me see what I can do about this. Let me get back to you."

By the time he called back he had a different story. Same kind of turnaround as the South Korean diplomat who first did and then didn't see Terry.

"I'm a very accurate reporter," he began, "and I went through my notes carefully."

"Terry, you couldn't have gone through your notes carefully because it never happened to me, and you know damned well it never happened to me."

"I passed this to Paul Bremer [the head of the State Department's Office of Counter-Terrorism] before publication and he said it was all right."

I asked myself, "What is this man doing running his manuscript by the head of the State Department Office of Counter-Terrorism?" And why in his article did he refer to "a former government official," "government representatives," and "task force officials," when during my conversation with him, all of those people were him?

Although I knew Terry Arnold was still tied to the State Department, I thought that in writing the article, he was acting as an independent journalist. I guess I was naive in thinking that he could both work for the government and retain some level of independence as a journalist. But it really irked me that he was wearing two hats.

What I believe happened was that by writing the story Terry Arnold effectively discredited Michael Trumpower. If Trumpower actually has damaging tapes of the government, Trumpower's credibility had just been destroyed. The more I thought about it, the more I believed Trumpower. What motivation did he have to lie? Why say he had tapes he didn't have? It made no sense. Then I began to think that, if what he said was true, I had quite possibly just severely endangered Trumpower's life.

Terry Arnold joked that his wife recommended that he buy a gun. It wasn't a joke to me. David *did* go out and buy me a gun. I was afraid that Michael Trumpower would come to kill me.

It was the night before Christmas, 1988, and I was sitting at home with this huge seven-shot magnum that I could barely lift. My son Eddie said, "Now, Mom, if you have to reload, you have to be very careful."

"Eddie, if I fire seven shots out of that gun either somebody else is going to be dead or I am."

"Or else you're going to blow every wall out of the house," he laughed.

But it wasn't funny. Bonnie Anderson was our houseguest, and she and David went into town to pick up some final Christmas stuff and basically locked me in. "If anybody comes up the road, shoot him," David told me. I was in no mood for jokes, I was too scared.

But I couldn't just sit there. After a while I made up my mind that I was not going to be paranoid about this, and set about preparing Christmas Eve dinner. I was jumpy but I told myself, "I want to enjoy Christmas with my family and I've just got to set it aside. There is nothing I can do about it, but I will never be taken in by the State Department again."

When David got back we had a serious discussion and concluded that we were being silly. Michael Trumpower may have acted strange but he didn't seem dangerous. He was a hustler, not a killer. I was exhausted and still very angry at Terry Arnold as we gathered some rods and headed down to the lake to go fishing. I had made a pot of coffee to carry with me, as I always do.

So there I was, after a night of terror, walking totally defenseless down this country road. I turned to David and Bonnie and said, "Well, if I see anybody threatening I could just say, 'One step closer and I pour.' " We got real giddy and the tension began to go away.

I never heard from Trumpower again and I certainly never heard from Tabatabai.

The whole Terry Arnold/*Washingtonian* scenario was the most blatant episode of betrayal on behalf of the State Department. I had been unhappy with them, I'd had confrontations, there had been incidents in which I knew they weren't telling me the truth. But this was almost like somebody saying, "What do we have to do to you to convince you that these people are not on your side?" A year after all this happened, I was at the State Department and saw him walking down the hall. He did not meet my eyes.

CHAPTER
13

In January 1989, with the State Department of no help at all, I once again had to figure out what my next step should be. A very reputable source told me he had just gotten a message that the captors wanted to release Terry and Tom Sutherland, and they wanted to turn them over to me. I was to go to Paris for further details.

Ordinarily I would think that the U.S. government were the best people to handle such an offer, but as far as I was concerned my government wasn't there. I convinced the AP that this was a responsible lead, and they financed my trip to Paris.

Unfortunately, in Paris I found that the offer relied on me and the other hostage families writing a letter to Muammar Qaddafi requesting that he buy the hostages and turn them over to us in return for a promise of better relations between Libya and the U.S. I had to think that one over.

I had heard Qaddafi on television recently and I'd had to laugh. He had said something to the effect that, "Well, we only have a few more weeks to deal with this madman Ronald Reagan and then we can deal with President Bush, who must be much more reasonable." Libya's economy was hurting, the country was isolated, and Qaddafi wanted to remedy that with a grand gesture to the West. Wouldn't it be ironic, I thought, if Qaddafi were the one to bring them out.

But I was uneasy. If Qaddafi got his hands on the hostages he'd have a trump card, he could use them as a shield against U.S. intervention in Libya. And by this time I knew our government; if they wanted to stage an action they would do it and to hell with the hostages. They knew, as I knew, the reality that we were living with, that we have always lived with: the captors could stand the hostages up in front of a video camera and blow their brains out and in two days it would be yesterday's news.

So, after giving the proposal a lot of thought and even factoring in the strong credibility of the people involved, I ultimately decided I could not go through with it. I respectfully declined.

So there I was in Paris. There were rumors coming out of Syria that there might be some movement there, and I was already overseas so the AP let me go to Damascus.

The Damascus Sheraton was still hopping. The last time I was there I hadn't seen a Western face, but now there were Americans, Europeans, Orientals, the place had seemed to open up. Unfortunately, the only reason there was talk of the hostages was that I was there; everyone figured that because I had showed up there must be some action. The talk fed on itself but there was really nothing to talk about. I once again worked the lobby of the Sheraton, but nothing was happening and nothing would happen.

When I got back to the U.S. the State Department agreed to see me. Al Adams was now head of the Office of Counter-Terrorism, and they consented to let me have access to them, but only if I did not tell the other families about the meeting. The new Administration's hostage family policy was No High-Level Contact.

It was all very cloak-and-dagger. I had to go in the back door, literally sneak in the back door of the State Department.

I was upset that I had to withhold the fact of this meeting from the other hostage families; it put me in a very ugly position. I was not happy and I told Adams, "I can understand the paranoia after Iran-contra, but this has got to stop. You have got to meet with the families, you have got to make them feel that somebody cares."

They told me, "Don't request a meeting with President Bush. Don't even think about it." Their reasoning was that if we got a lot of play in the American press the Iranians were going to get the idea again that they could hold out, that the hostages were worth something.

I said, "Look, if you don't want us to request a meeting with Bush, then you sit down with the families and explain to them why. You cannot get away with this behavior anymore." I went on and on.

Adams tried to cut me off. "You people have Michael Mahoney . . ."

"He's not enough."

I said it right in front of Mahoney, which was hard for me, but it had to be done. "I'm sorry, but this doesn't work."

Adams shot Mahoney a look that meant, "I was not aware that this was the situation," and I was saying, "I'm telling you it is."

Adams said, "Are you suggesting that *I* meet with the families?"

"Yes, I am."

They conferred for days and days and finally notified me that we would get our meeting.

They scheduled it for March 16, 1989, the fourth anniversary of Terry's kidnapping. The families were gathering in Washington for a ceremony and they had us over afterward.

It was not a good meeting. Adams was not opening a door to the families, he was trying to push us through one. What they wanted the hostage families to do, he told us, was stand united at the podium at the United Nations while the U.S. government presented a hard-line resolution against Iran.

I said, "Excuse me, but if you think I'm going to thumb my nose at Iran and stand up there with you alone—the United States, which has stood off the coast of Lebanon and flexed its pinkie and then turned tail and run—think again. I'm not going to do it, it's too dangerous. If you want us to do this, you line up all of our allies behind us; we'll stand behind you, we want these people to stand behind us."

And, I said, "let's talk about economic sanctions." I was upset that Kuwait, whose ships and oil we had just spent millions of dollars protecting, and which had cost American lives in the Strait of Hormuz, had just reestablished diplomatic relations with Iran. "Canada has just reestablished diplomatic relations, Great Britain had just reopened its embassy there. We can't even hold on to our allies. We've got nobody, we've lost it over Iran-contra. They're not going to support us because we've stabbed them in the back."

It was left with us telling them, "You do your part, you come back to us with a proposal in which you have a unanimous resolution, and maybe we will think about it."

There were several things that disturbed me about that meeting and it took a few days for me to piece it together. I was cleaning the house when it finally clicked into place.

First, some time before, I had been told that the CIA was trying to locate and pick up the original videotapes and letters that had been released by the captors. Someone who had been asked for possible leads told me and I replied, "If they want the original letter, I've got it. Why don't they come to me?"

Then at one of the last meetings I'd had with Paul Bremer of Counter-Terrorism he'd said, "Peggy, you could really help us if you used some of your contacts to get the originals of the videotapes, so we can send them to forensics and find out who these guys are." Give me a break. We know who these guys are, read *Newsweek*. Did he think I was that easily placated that I was going to go running around again; I had done enough makework for these people.

The same week as Terry's fourth anniversary, the same week we met with the State Department again, *Time* magazine came out with an article headlined "The Lost Life of Terry Anderson." The writer, Scott MacLeod, also included a two-thirds-page sidebar headed "The Man Who Holds the Hostages" which fingered, once again, Imad Mughniyah. I had been interviewed by Scott MacLeod for that article and I was impressed by how much he knew. The sidebar told the brother-in-law story, gave detailed personal background on Mughniyah, and portrayed the man as a bloodthirsty terrorist. The gist of it was that Imad Mughniyah was the most dangerous terrorist in the world, grislier even than Abu Nidal.

Now, I'd been through the State Department manipulation of the press over the raid on Libya and knew such detailed information was very hard to come by. Scott MacLeod had to have had high-level help. I could see a pattern developing, but I couldn't figure out what was going on. Finally it dawned on me: they were going after Mughniyah.

I was terrified. If they killed Mughniyah, Terry was dead; that was that. If they pulled him in, he'd be in the court system forever and we'd never see the hostages. Either way, it seemed clear to me that the CIA was planning to strike a blow against terrorism by building up the image of this boogeyman in the media so that when they either snatched him up or blew him away it would look like they had achieved a major success.

I wrote a memo to Lou Boccardi at the AP saying, "This horrible thought has just occurred to me and I'm absolutely sure that this is the direction they're pointing." Boccardi wrote back saying words to the effect he understood my concern, but that our government was never going to do anything that would bring harm to the hostages.

I read his letter and sat there thinking, "Don't you remember the raid on Libya? Don't you remember Peter Kilburn, the two British journalists, and Alec Collett? Has everyone in the world forgotten but me?" I wanted to run around screaming, "The sky is falling, the sky is falling!" But who would believe me?

I went to Washington to plead my case one more time. I had been told over and over again, "Forget going to the White House, you've visited that place for the last time." But I periodically requested a meeting anyway and this time, surprisingly, I was told that, on the stipulation that the meeting remain secret and private, I could meet with National Security Adviser General Brent Scowcroft.

I was stunned. I never expected to meet with someone so highly placed. I went through the White House gates and sat in the waiting room outside General Scowcroft's office, not having the foggiest notion of why I was being given an audience. I knew these guys didn't do something for nothing. What were they going to want from me now?

I had been told that Scowcroft liked to be called "General," so when I met him I made sure I addressed him properly. The conversation was initially stilted but not quite formal. Finally I just grabbed the reins and lunged forward in my usual delicate way. I explained to the general the strange proposition the State Department had put forward and asked him for an explanation.

"General Scowcroft," I said, "this is a blatant bid for the families' loyalty. They want us to line up like good little soldiers behind them while they make this initiative at the U.N. These families depend on me to make the right judgments for them, and before I make that judgment I need to know some things.

"What I see happening now is that you people are after Mughniyah. If we stand up behind the State Department while they take this hard-line stance and you then go pick the man off, you have just hung us out to dry. We'll have no defense. We'll have said to the State Department, 'Do what you have to do,' and we'll be in big trouble. I need to know from you that this is not the reason you are being so generous as to see me."

Scowcroft looked as if I had socked him in the stomach. He was astounded that I had come to my conclusion.

"I'm not going to lie to you," he said. "Yes, we are after Mughniyah. But that is not the reason the State Department is offering you this new initiative. That is not the reason at all."

I started to get rolling. "Terry Anderson has put his life on the line for others by staying in Beirut and reporting the news when the rest of the world was fleeing the danger—"

He cut me off abruptly. "Peggy, as a thirty-year veteran of the United States armed services I put my life on the line every day, and when I signed on I understood that I might be called upon to die for others. Others in uniform do that every day. I do not feel that your brother's act was particularly exceptional."

He didn't speak in a mean way—he didn't seem like a mean person—but from then on, every time I tried to make a point he would confront me. He never let me hit my stride.

"Anderson is a good Marine," the general said. "He'll understand, sometimes sacrifices have to be made."

I was too stunned to make more than a token reply. This man was very cavalier with my brother's life.

"Look," I said, "my brother is a loyal patriot and would make sacrifices for the greater good. But I don't want him to die for nothing.

I don't want him to die like Bill Buckley or Peter Kilburn or William Higgins. What did they die for? Nothing! Their deaths didn't resolve a thing. My brother didn't survive two Vietnam tours to die for nothing in a dirty basement in Lebanon. At least not while there's breath in my body. If he's going to die, by God let it mean something!"

I told the general about Terry's being chained to his bed, blind-folded. I told him about Terry's making rosaries out of fibers from his mattress. I told him about Terry's devotion to duty. And then I told him I wanted to speak with President Bush personally.

Scowcroft looked me in the face and said, "You can sit here and put tears in my eyes and that's okay. But you are not going to put tears in the eyes of this president, because he must be clear-eyed to do what has to be done about this hostage situation. You are not going to do to President Bush what you did to President Reagan."

Of course. This was the same man who, as a member of the Tower Commission, had come to the conclusion that poor President Reagan had been driven to trade arms to Iran because of his great concern for the hostages. Afterward John Tower was supposed to have been ele-vated to Secretary of Defense, Brent Scowcroft was sitting here as National Security Adviser. What kind of deal was going on here?

But more important than that, I had my worst fears confirmed: they *were* going after Mughniyah. They could pick him off and then say, "You can run but you can't hide," and if the hostages paid the price, "Sacrifices have to be made." It would be a real saber-rattling public relations coup. The safety of the hostages was very far down on their list of priorities.

I almost felt like taking an ad in the Beirut papers saying, "Imad, run, hide, bury yourself." Of course I wouldn't do anything like that. I knew that this man had committed acts of terrorism and people had died because of him and he should be caught and brought to justice. But I was also personally involved and if Mughniyah got caught or killed I could kiss Terry good-bye; there was no way for me to separate myself from that.

As it turned out, the CIA couldn't catch him. He remains at large.

My meeting with General Scowcroft took a half hour at most, and from there I was shown to the office of his assistant, David Miller. I was tired of being told no, there was nothing we can do to gain Terry's freedom, and after being stonewalled by the general I took it out on his assistant.

"There is no creative thinking going on around here," I complained. "Nobody can write a handbook for all hostage situations, each one is different, each one takes creativity to deal with. You've got to be prepared, you're dealing with people who are not run-of-the-mill, who don't think like we do. You've got to come up with some new ideas, and nobody around here is doing that."

Miller agreed. "I'm certainly willing to blue sky," he said. "To blue sky"? Must be some new kind of free-form expression.

"I have heard from several different sources," I told him, "that Fadlallah [the spiritual leader of the Hezbollah] might be approachable as the contact person on the hostage issue. He's supposed to have said to a friend, 'We have no negotiator. What do you want us to do?' He was giving indications that he himself would be willing to fulfill that role. Rather than going to Iran and selling arms, nobody has ever gone directly from A to B; why can't you contact Fadlallah, through whatever sources you have, and feel him out about this, see if he's genuinely willing to negotiate. And if he is, you have to be willing to give something back. Negotiations imply both sides giving. We can start at this ground level and see if something doesn't come of it."

Miller said something to the effect that "I love this kind of thinking, I'm the creative thinker you want around here. Feed me information and let's see where we go. Feed me."

He seemed eager, maybe a little too eager, not the serious and authoritative figure I would have liked to see in his position. Leaving his office I thought ruefully, "Ollie North lives!"

Miller appeared at the next State Department meeting. I was accompanied by Carolyn Turolla and the new AP Terry Anderson point man, Larry Heinzerling. It was something less than successful. Once again, when I asked where we were in terms of getting the hostages home I was told basically, "We're nowhere." Things started to get heated. Up to that time I had always managed to keep from leaping up and grabbing somebody by the throat and shrieking in their faces that they're all nuts. But something was said that sparked me off.

"Iran-contra burned out every spark of creativity there ever was in this department." My voice hardened as I listed their sins. "Your paranoia is keeping all of you from doing the least little thing that might resolve this.

"And another thing." I looked over at Miller. This was the first time I'd had a chance to reply to Scowcroft, even indirectly. I knew Miller would take what I said back to him. "I am sick and tired of you people trying to put the blame for Iran-contra on me. You ought to be ashamed of yourselves. I am a middle-aged housewife, I did not cause Iran-contra. The very fact that you imply that I did should be an embarrassment to you."

I had had it. "We're sitting in an office hearing that we are no closer to anything than we were four years ago. Iran-contra has destroyed everything and you are blaming me! I'm sick of it!"

I stayed away from the State Department for more than six months.

In the middle of March 1989 I got a call from a journalist friend who had gone to work for a network affiliate in Miami. He said he had interviewed a man whom I might find very interesting. The man's name was Sarkis Soghanalian and he was strongly rumored to have been actively involved in trying to get Terry released.

Soghanalian was a Lebanese of Armenian descent. He owned an aircraft company and was transporting goods to Armenia for the earthquake relief effort. He was also under indictment on federal weapons charges. In 1986, the AP reported, he was arrested for possessing five unregistered machine guns and two unregistered rocket launchers; in 1987 he surrendered to U.S. Customs agents on charges of trying to smuggle combat helicopters into Iraq. In 1988 the AP reported that President and Mrs. Marcos of the Philippines were rumored to be planning to return to their country aboard a Boeing 707 owned by Mr. Soghanalian.

This was clearly a player. I was given his number and asked not to tell him where I got it.

I called Soghanalian directly and did not have to explain to him who I was. I told him that I understood he was involved in efforts to bring Terry home. He didn't know how to react to my call. He said, "I am not going to give you details over your telephone, Mrs. Say, because we can both assume that your telephone is tapped. If you want to come to Miami I will be happy to meet with you privately. I will only say that talking about Terry Anderson and the hostages raises the hair on the back of my neck. I was involved in an initiative that had every chance of success and it was destroyed by the U.S. government."

I called the State Department. I had many times in the past asked them for profiles of various people, just curious to see what they had on this guy or that. This time I asked, without giving any indication of my involvement with him, "What is your opinion of Sarkis Soghanalian?" I had done this often enough that I didn't think I would be red-flagging him in their eyes.

They told me he was a sleaze; he was an arms dealer, and if he was an arms dealer he was held in contempt. He was an all-around bad guy, they said, don't pay any attention to him.

But it was a mixed message. They also said he was well connected. This intrigued me more. My attitude was, we weren't going to get to the people who took Terry by approaching fastidious Foreign Service types, we would get to them by approaching people with real contact, people with connections.

I called Soghanalian back and told him that I was coming to Miami.

"What name will you be traveling under?" he asked.

"My own."

"When you arrive a bearded man will board the plane and take you off to a waiting automobile."

In actual fact the man had no beard and he met me after I got off the plane and entered the terminal. He turned out to be a CIA agent, retired, who had gone to work for Soghanalian. He had been involved on the wrong side of a sting operation that had resulted in an indictment.

"Don't you find it a little strange to be working for an arms dealer after being in the CIA?" I asked him.

"Hey," he answered, "my government hung me out to dry after all of my service. So, no, I don't have a problem with this at all."

First I was checked into an airport hotel and then I was taken to meet Soghanalian.

His office was in one of the airport hangars. I walked in and felt immediately as if I were back in Damascus. The place was kind of a barn, filled with boxes of relief supplies for Armenian earthquake victims, all being handled by a squadron of Arabs. The ex-CIA man showed me to Soghanalian's office and I walked in.

Sarkis Soghanalian was absolutely gigantic. A mountain of a man, maybe four hundred pounds. I was fascinated by his fingers; they were like sausages, the biggest hands I had ever seen on a human being. I couldn't stop looking at them, he must have taken a size 98 ring, these porkers resting on the table.

He was dressed casually in a pullover and pants, and we spent the first few minutes sizing each other up. I wanted to know what he knew about Terry, I was dying to know how the government had interfered with his initiative; and Soghanalian was basically trying to decide whether he could trust me. We danced around awhile getting a feel for each other and then I started homing in on the purpose of my being there.

"What specifically was it that you were involved in that concerns my brother," I asked, "and how did the U.S. interfere?"

He wouldn't outline the initiative in specific terms, but he did say that he was within a hair of having Terry released the previous October, 1988, and was told by the Administration to back off. Apparently the Administration did not want Terry released before the elections; after the deep suspicions surrounding the Iranian hostage release following the Reagan election in 1980, they felt it would look too contrived. And so the initiative was allowed to fail.

I didn't find that outside the realm of possibility in the least. In fact it was a rumor I had heard the past January when I was in the Middle East. It was one of those things you don't want to believe, but logic tells you that, yes, it could have happened. We had been told by several people out of Washington that all efforts on behalf of the hostages had ceased in the weeks prior to the elections. They were really paranoid, we were told, that the release would have been perceived as a cynical political move—you know, "You could have done it a year ago and you waited to serve your best interests."

I'd been told there were half a dozen private initiatives being undertaken prior to the elections. George Shultz had told us, essentially, "All you people butt out, you're complicating matters. No private initiatives." The best face I could put on it at the time was that the

Administration really did have something going and they were afraid that these other initiatives were going to interfere with it. I mean, how could I sit there and think that my government was going to let good chances to free my brother pass them by just because it might hurt them politically?

I didn't want to think about it, but Soghanalian's explanation was very logical. There was nothing about it that didn't make sense.

So, if my government had betrayed me again, it became a question of "Mr. Soghanalian, how can you help me?"

He made several impressive telephone calls while I was there. He was obviously a man who liked to be in the thick of things and it didn't take much to get him interested. "Do you speak Arabic?" he asked me. I told him no. "Too bad. I would like you to hear this phone call."

He dialed Geneva, Switzerland, and told me he was in contact with the Iranian Revolutionary Guard. He spoke for a while and then hung up the phone.

"You can tell your government that your Colonel Higgins is alive." I had heard enough rumors in the past four years not to jump at even such tantalizing bait.

Then he called the National Security Council. It was mostly just "Hi, how are you? Is there anything I can do?" He was told basically to butt out, which is what he'd been told before, but he clearly wanted to demonstrate that he had enough clout so that when he gave his name his call would be put right through.

Soghanalian asked me to take back to the State Department his request that he be allowed to make an arms shipment to Iran. I looked at him and thought, "Fat chance. You think the government is going to tell me, 'Oh, yes, Peggy, go back and tell Mr. Soghanalian it's quite all right'?" He also wanted them to quash his indictment.

We met again the next morning and I told him that I'd be glad to relay his message but that it was definitely not going to wash. He said, "If you can't do it one way, there are always other ways. But try this."

I left the building and was walking with Soghanalian and several of his associates on the outskirts of the airport, when all of a sudden a television crew came running up.

"Peggy! Oh, Peggy!"

Oh, no.

A young woman reporter I had never seen before came charging over.

"How did you know I was here?"

"We were here covering another story and we saw you going into the building. What is going on? Can we get a picture of you and Mr. Soghanalian together?"

"You can do me a big favor and forget that you ever saw me. Please." That's all I needed, to be on the news with this indicted arms dealer.

The crew was very nice and did back off, but I about fainted.

So, okay, I went to the State Department to deliver Soghanalian's request. As was to be expected, they were somewhat less than receptive. "What are you asking us?" "Are you crazy?" That sort of thing. I figured that was the end of me and Sarkis Soghanalian.

After I reported to Soghanalian the expected "No way" from the State Department, he asked me to write a letter to Terry that included a question only Terry would know the answer to and I gave him one: "What name did you write under other than your own when you were overseas?" Terry had used Alan Lunn, his middle name and our mother's maiden name.

I wrote the question and a brief letter on Journalists Committee stationery, which I thought was pretty smart. I was making double contact: first, the question; second, the fact that he's got stationery with "Free Terry Anderson" and all these notable journalists' names on it, which ought to have made him feel good.

From then on, the ball was in Mr. Soghanalian's court to bring back the correct response from Terry.

I haven't heard from him since.

I was definitely living in two worlds. David would come home from work and I'd say, "Honey, I'm going to Miami to meet with this arms dealer." "Okay, when are you coming back?" "I'm only going to be gone tonight." I'd be packing my stuff and keeping everything in the house clean and cooking him something, which I like to do. I like to take care of him even when I'm traveling, that's important to me; he's got enough stuff to put up with and I want to make things as easy as possible.

I had jumped down to Miami and back and the next day I was cleaning the house when it suddenly occurred to me, "What do you think you're doing? Just what do you think you're doing going to Miami and getting involved with this arms dealer, and now you have to go to the State Department and try to cut a deal. Who do you think you are? Remember, you're a housewife, this shouldn't be your business. You are getting out of control."

For that brief moment I thought, "You've got to cut this stuff out, you've got to end it." That was my decision for the day.

The next day I was booking reservations to Washington.

I have tried to give it up a couple of times, but it has never worked. Generally the thought would hit me when I was away from home, getting ready to go to bed, without my family, in a strange place. I would just get overwhelmed and say, "I shouldn't have to do this."

I guess part of my resentment was toward the AP, in spite of the fact that they were financing me; I felt I was doing a job that they should have been doing. I was doing a job that my government should have been doing. At those moments I would feel sorry for myself and say, "What are they doing to me? Why are they making me do this?"

When I need to figure things out, or to get myself out of a funk, I do housework. Carolyn Turolla of the AP has learned that when she calls me up and I'm waxing the floors, I've got a problem. One day I found myself sitting on the kitchen linoleum vacuuming my onions.

Another friend and I have a standing joke: whenever I'm expecting Terry to come home I start making barbecue sauce. When Terry would come home from overseas assignments he would give me a list of everything he'd been dreaming about eating, and always first on the list was barbecued something or other.

Several months can go by with nothing happening. That's the hardest part. When there is some news or movement, even a potential disaster, it's easier for me to deal with than nothingness; I cannot bear nothingness. When there are no videotapes, when there is no news, when months and months go by and nothing is happening, I don't know what to do. I am left in this terrible void.

In April 1989 Terry's daughter Gabrielle turned thirteen. He hasn't seen her since she was nine.

In May I went to Washington to speak at the National Press Foundation awards dinner. They gave Terry a prestigious award and asked me to accept it for him. This kind of thing happened fairly regularly. The invitation would arrive a few months in advance and I would accept, thinking that by the date of the event Terry would be out and could accept it himself. David kidded me that I always seemed amazed when things finally rolled around and I had to do them.

The National Press Foundation is one of the most esteemed organizations in journalism and they had gathered a fabulous audience. Tip O'Neill was at David's table, that kind of attendance. They gave Terry this award and in his absence he got a standing ovation. Then it was up to me: say, in five minutes or less, why we should care about Terry Anderson.

I told them how he lived, what his work meant to him, what we knew about the lives of the hostages. Afterward people came up to me and said, "We knew Terry. This was very touching, this was wonderful." By giving Terry the award they were recognizing that he is a unique and valued individual. I'd made my speech that night with a lot more hope than I had on similar occasions; these were Terry's peers, they had to care about him or they wouldn't have staged this big event.

I picked up the little plaque and went home, and I never heard from them again.

It happened over and over. People seemed to think that they could pay attention to him for one night and then just let it go.

The same thing happened at the convention of the American Veterans. They gave me their award "AmVet Auxiliary Humanitarian of the Year." I was co-recipient with the country singer Lee Greenwood, who is known for his song, "God Bless the U.S.A." Receiving the award for myself was not as important to me as having this audience of veterans and being able to say to them that Terry is a veteran himself and one of their own. If we could get every AmVet organization in the country to write a letter to the White House or their congressmen or the newspapers, we could make a real impact. The potential was wonderful.

This annual awards dinner was very important to them. As someone told me that night, it was AmVet's Oscars.

Well, right before I was to be given mine one of the organizers pulled me aside and said, basically, "We're running long. Grab your award, say 'Thank you,' and get off the stage."

I couldn't do that. I resisted getting truly angry, but when I was introduced I went to the microphone and said, "This award is given to me because of Terry Anderson, and I can't just take it without saying something about him."

Once again I did five minutes on Terry Anderson, trying to hit on the emotional things, how he's chained to a wall, how he'd been chained to that wall for four years now, and it was high time somebody did something about it. There was a standing ovation, but they were anxious to get to Lee Greenwood because he was going to perform.

People came up afterward and told me they'd been touched. Several AmVet officials told me, "You were so poignant, it was wonderful. We never knew." But by this time I was a little more realistic. I told them, "Please don't just tell me you're going to call me. Terry is a veteran, he's one of you. Please, you have to take some action."

After a couple of weeks went by and I got no response I wanted to go back and say, "Take this award and stick it. I don't need awards, Terry needs your help. You can't give me an award on the one hand and then refuse to help on the other, it doesn't make any sense." Apparently it made sense to them, because there was never any follow-up.

The Overseas Press Club also gave Terry an award, and that was the last I heard from them. The club president had suggested that an ad be placed in the Beirut newspapers telling about the award. The president said he would be willing to strike a deal with the captors: if they'd let Terry out to receive the award, he would guarantee that Terry would return to captivity afterward. Seriously! I wouldn't have believed it myself, except that the suggestion was made during a conference call and several members of the Journalists Committee heard it.

These same Journalists Committee members were surprised to read in the *Washington Journalism Review* that the National Press Foundation was "coordinating the committee's efforts." The article was accompanied by a photograph of alleged committee members, none of whom we knew.

If all of the organizations that gave awards or made a decision to "do something about Terry Anderson" had followed through, publicity would have been the least of our problems. I have more proclamations and declarations than you can shake a stick at, but they only make the giver feel good. It's an easy out for those who need to feel that they did something for Terry; they want to be able to justify themselves when Terry finally comes home.

I'd like to be in the audience when these same people invite Terry to speak when he gets out—which they will—and Terry asks them, "What did you do to help me?" They can always wave a piece of paper in his face and hope that it blinds him to the reality of their efforts.

What I wanted from all of them was to participate in our postcard campaign. We were trying to swamp the White House with mail.

A man named Ezell Harris in Rochester, New York, had come up with the concept. He'd had postcards printed, at his own expense, with pictures of the nine American hostages on them and a religious message, something like "Pray for the Hostages." Anne Zickl asked him if we could borrow the concept and write our own message and distribute the cards. He agreed.

Our message, written by Ed Caldwell, read:

A nation that chooses not to pursue freedom for an innocent captive resigns its own freedom. Those who choose not to listen will themselves cry out and never be heard.

We are your fellow Americans. Hear our cry for freedom and raise your voices, for ours are silenced.

Our hands are tied, yours are not.

The card was addressed to President George Bush, The White House, Washington, D.C.

What started us on our postcard campaign was a remark by Michael Mahoney, the families' liaison at the State Department. He defended the Administration's policy of non-negotiation by saying to a member of the Journalists Committee, "United States policy is dictated by the American people, and frankly the American people do not want the U.S. government to negotiate for the hostages."

Aside from the amazing personal insensitivity of a man saying this to people whose brothers, fathers, husbands, and friends were sitting in cells halfway around the world, we were insulted by his bravado and we were out to prove him wrong. Ed Caldwell, Bill Foley, Bonnie Anderson, and I went on a speaking blitz to bring this campaign to life.

We never had a lot of money to pay for printing, phone bills, distribution. We asked people to buy the cards for about a nickel apiece, the printing cost, and distribute them among their friends and organizations, to create a network of vocal supporters. We now have 375,000 postcards out there and the orders are coming in every day. It seems to have taken on a life of its own.

CHAPTER

14

I SHOULD HAVE SEEN IT COMING.

When I was in the Middle East in February 1989 I had started having physical problems but I didn't want to go to a doctor in a strange country. When I got back I went to my local physician, Dr. Anderson (no relation), who told me I might have an ulcer. He gave me some medication. As with anything else, when you're hurting you'll do anything a doctor says, but when it eases up you let it pass. I began to feel better, and when the medication ran out I didn't go back.

One night in June I had rented two movies and was planning to sit at home and watch them, when I started feeling something like indigestion. This was not an unfamiliar sensation, and I was already drinking Maalox by the bottle.

All of a sudden there was a vice around my chest that just kept wrenching at me. I lay down on the couch but I couldn't get comfortable and I couldn't breathe. Finally David said, "I think I'd better take you to the emergency room." Before he could get me to the car I doubled over and couldn't move. They had to take me to the hospital in an ambulance.

The doctors gave me nitroglycerin pills in the emergency room and finally the pain subsided. I stayed in the hospital for three days and, after examining me, Dr. Anderson felt it was not my heart but just my esophagus that had spasmed, like a cramp in my chest.

A month later I started feeling lousy again and knew there was something seriously wrong. I went to Dr. Anderson and said, "I'm sorry. I know I'm a terrible patient, but if you will give me my medicine back I promise I'll do everything you say."

Dr. Anderson told me he would give me the medication but he wanted me to go in and be tested for ulcers. This meant two extremely unpleasant tests, plus he wanted me to see a cardiologist.

I started trying to cut a deal with him. I would go have one internal test and I wouldn't have to see the man about my heart.

It turned out I had two ulcers. Why should that surprise me? I said to Dr. Anderson, "But I'm under less stress here in Kentucky than I've been in a long while."

"It's cumulative," he told me. "When you think you are not under stress, you still are. All the anxiety is still churning around inside of you and as a result you've got ulcers. I want you on the medication and I want you to see a cardiologist."

Still I resisted.

I was at Dr. Anderson's office one day having my prescription renewed when he said, "It just so happens that the cardiologist is over at the hospital right now. Why don't you get over there and have this test done." At that point I didn't really have a choice, the hospital was about twenty steps away.

I went over, they did a stress test, and the cardiologist told me, "You have an abnormality. I want you to go in for a catheterization." He wanted to put a tube in my heart.

I was leaving for New York the next day, I told him. I had a series of meetings and some kids from the North–Rose Wolcott school district in western New York were presenting a project called "Dear World, a Message of Hope" at the U.N.

"What time does your plane leave?"

I kept backing away. I didn't want to think about this. "Let me go back and talk to Dr. Anderson."

Dr. Anderson was on the phone with the cardiologist when I got back to his office. When he got off he explained what they wanted to do.

"Dr. Anderson," I told him, "my mother died during one of these procedures. I have bad feelings about this. I don't think it's my heart; I have a congenital defect, which is probably what he's seeing, which is also minor, in my estimation. I have to go to New York tomorrow. What if I take the medication and go to New York, and if I have any more symptoms I'll go to a doctor or a hospital there?"

The doctor agreed to increase the dosage and let me go. He said, "I want you to take these nitroglycerin tablets with you. If you feel pain, take one tablet. If the pain does not subside after ten minutes, take another. If you get to the point where you have to take three nitroglycerin tablets, get yourself to the hospital immediately." I promised him I would.

My appointments in New York were scattered over a couple of days, so my pace wasn't hectic. (I am careless about my health in many ways but I'm not a fool.) And the episodes hurt so much I was really and truly frightened by them and didn't want to do anything that might bring on another attack.

The first night in town I was relaxing, watching a movie on television in my hotel room, when the pain struck. I started to get scared but I told myself, "Don't hyperventilate. Relax, take it easy."

The pain didn't go away. It got worse. Finally it got bad enough for me to take one of the tablets. Nothing happened. By this time I was doubled over. Ten minutes passed and I took another.

Now, in my warped mind I was not going to take another nitroglycerin because if I took the third I would have to go to the hospital, and I didn't want to do that. Hospitals were where you went to die; I wasn't going there.

By sheer will power I lay on my bed and made myself take deep breaths, and eventually the pain did ease. I made it through the trip, but I'd had a good scare.

Back in Kentucky, Dr. Anderson told me, "You must give up alcohol, caffeine, cigarettes, and chocolate."

I said, "How about two out of four?" I didn't eat much chocolate or drink much alcohol anyway.

"If you are going to give up one thing, give up the cigarettes, they will tear you up with these ulcers."

"I can't do that," I told him. "If I give up cigarettes I'm dead of a heart attack, because I can't handle the stress without them."

Dr. Anderson was not very happy about it but finally just shook his head and gave up. He continued me on my medication and told me to exercise regularly. I've tried to be diligent.

In June my aunt Gwennie died. She was the third of our aunts to die while Terry was in captivity. Aunt Gwennie was my father's sister and had raised Dad from the time he was eleven, when their mother died. He was always her baby, you couldn't say a word to her against little Glenn. I hadn't known her very well when I was growing up, but after Dad died we had become very close. She and Uncle Ed were the kind of parents I wished I'd had.

Aunt Gwennie was constantly hounding everybody to quit smoking—she and my daughter were the most avid anti-smoking people I'd ever come across. Aunt Gwennie got lung cancer. She called to tell me. "If I have lung cancer," she said, "there is no justice in this world."

It was such *déjà vu*. I had seen my Dad die swearing that he'd hang on to see Terry. I had seen Rich die pleading to see him. Aunt Gwennie was the same. She tried to hold out, to wait for Terry, to see him just one more time.

I didn't want to hear it. I found myself not wanting to visit, not wanting to call her on the phone. I sure as hell didn't want to watch her go. But after I had dragged my feet for much too long, David and I did go see her for the last time.

I cried, and I miss her, and I'm going to miss her some more, but I could not allow myself to feel the pain. You can only hurt so much until you become numb to it. It felt like I was walking through the same desolation, the same dirge, the same funeral, looking at Dad, looking at Rich, and knowing that this is what happens.

It's going to be devastating enough for the hostages to be told of deaths in the family. The mother of British hostage John McCarthy has died. The Cicippio family has already lost a sister and now Joe's sister

Helen is suffering from cancer. She's trying desperately to hang on to
see Joe free. If I only had to tell Terry that Dad had died, I could do
that. But when you've got to say, "And by the way, so did Rich and
so did Aunt Sis and so did Aunt Nora and so did Aunt Gwennie," it's
almost too much to think about.

On June 3, 1989, Ayatollah Khomeini died. We had all dreaded that
possibility because his death could create chaos. There was the feeling
that there would be such an intense and long-lasting struggle for power
in Iran that nothing would happen on the hostage issue until it was
ended and someone emerged, either a hard-liner or a so-called mod-
erate.

But there had obviously been a lot of groundwork laid, because the
transition was incredibly smooth. When the smoke cleared, Iran's
government was being run by its new president, Hojatolislam Hashemi
Rafsanjani.

That was major good news. Rafsanjani was known as part of the
"pragmatic" faction and we saw that as a positive sign; you can work
with pragmatists. It was felt that Rafsanjani wanted to bring Iran out of
its isolation.

On July 28, Sheik Abdel Karim Obeid, a Shiite cleric said to be a
regional chief of Hezbollah and linked to the kidnapping of Colonel
William Higgins, was himself kidnapped by the Israelis. The Israelis
wanted their own hostages returned in exchange for Sheik Obeid.We
didn't know what to think, and were very frightened trying to figure
out what the reaction would be.

Within days the videotape was released showing what one terrorist
organization said was Colonel Higgins, hanging, dead. (Word on the
ground had it that Higgins had been dead for about a year, but that was
difficult to confirm.) There was a deathwatch all over the international
airwaves when the captors threatened to kill Joe Cicippio. For several
days in a row we would wake up in the morning and turn on the radio
to learn whether he had been murdered. It was hell for the Cicippios,
and not much better for the rest of us.

That storm got ridden out, with incredible anguish among the families, when several deadlines passed and Rafsanjani intervened to have the death sentence lifted.

When I first heard that the Israelis had kidnapped Sheik Obeid I thought, "The Israelis are playing hardball." Israeli intelligence is generally extremely good, so everyone figured some movement was in the wind, the press in particular. And then nothing happened.

But it did bring public attention back to the hostages. After reports that the U.S. was prepared to bomb Hezbollah bases if more American hostages were killed, there seemed to be some effort begun to exchange Shiite and perhaps Palestinian prisoners held by Israel for some Western hostages. Rafsanjani said, "The freedom of the hostages is solvable." President Bush's response was that he did not want "to raise hopes beyond fulfillment."

With the Sheik Obeid kidnapping, at least everyone who should have been involved was talking. All I had ever wanted was for all the people who had anything to do with either abducting, holding, releasing, or taking responsibility for the hostages to be in touch with one another. I had asked for help from any person or government that had even looked in the direction of Iran. That included the captors, Iran, Lebanon, Syria, Israel, West Germany, the PLO, the Swiss, the Japanese, the Algerians, the Pakistanis, the United States, and the home countries of all the other hostages. The Reagan and Bush Administrations' policy of never negotiating with terrorists had made talks impossible, but now finally it seemed it was going to get done.

Working together to release the hostages was in both Rafsanjani's best interest and the United States' best interest; people on both sides were involved. I had to believe that they weren't simply going to pack up their tents and go home and say, "We can't work a deal with these hoodlums in Lebanon." In August I really believed the whole thing would be resolved by October. There didn't seem much left for me to do.

Terry's birthday came around again. On October 27, 1989, Terry turned forty-two and there were about two dozen camera crews at the Dahlgren Chapel at Georgetown University for our Mass of Hope. Tom Brokaw spoke, along with Ben Bradlee of the *Washington Post*, Ambassador Bruce Laingen; Chuck Lewis, formerly of the AP, and R. W.

Apple of the *New York Times*. Afterward we met once again with the State Department, but nothing came of it.

I had been lulled back into silence. Hope and faith had shut me up, but when neither of them produced Terry I had to start thinking of more ways to bring him home.

Rumors were flying around the holiday season. Terry would be out by Christmas. Terry would be out by New Year's . . .

Christmas came and went. It used to be that we stretched the holiday season out as long as we could, taking the Christmas decorations down the day after New Year's, but there was no celebration in us and we threw the tree out and tidied up the day after Christmas. It didn't seem right that we should be of good cheer when Terry was still out of reach.

New Year's arrived. Terry didn't. My ulcer kicked up, I felt awful, things did not look good.

Early in January 1990 I got a call from Larry Heinzerling at the AP. Even though he was their new point man for Terry Anderson I didn't know Larry very well and I was surprised when he asked me, "Peggy, would you consider traveling to the Middle East again?"

"Larry, I spent my last birthday in Damascus. Where am I going this year? Libya?"

It turned out that they were developing an extensive itinerary for me. They were talking about a month-long trip that would take me to Switzerland, Paris, London, Tunisia, Syria, and the Vatican. I would be accompanied by Larry and Don Mell.

I told him I'd have to think about it. A month away from home was a long time, I was not a happy traveler to begin with, and I was hesitant to go on a trip this lengthy with two men I barely knew. I called back and told Larry that I'd go but I wanted both my husband David and the AP's Carolyn Turolla to accompany me. Larry talked to Lou Boccardi, who was in charge of financing the trip, and got back to me.

"You'll have to choose between David and Carolyn," I was told.

I was crushed. I couldn't leave David alone for a month. I'd promised him the year before, when I was gone for three weeks, that I would never leave him for that long again. And I didn't think I could travel abroad without Carolyn, who knew protocol, knew who to see and how to present oneself in these international situations. I was in a real bind.

I wrote a letter to Mr. Boccardi explaining my problem. "David and I are neither sophisticated nor accomplished world travelers," I told him, "and Carolyn always smooths the way for me extremely well. There are times and places where a woman specifically needs a woman to understand."

Boccardi responded to my appeal and said yes, they both could go. Bill Foley, who knew the Middle East better than anyone else on the trip, was going to join us in Rome.

When they gave me the final itinerary, I was terrified. I would be addressing the European Parliament and meeting with the Syrian foreign minister, the Archbishop of Canterbury, and Yasser Arafat. And they had arranged an audience with Pope John Paul II! I kept thinking, "What am I going to say? How am I going to carry this off?"

Before I left, I went to the State Department. They were glad to hear I was going to the Middle East again. That was news; they had never been enthusiastic about my travels before. Then I visited the NSC, who told me, "You need to go. You need to go specifically to Syria." I asked jokingly, "Do you have any messages for Arafat?"

"Yes," I was told. "Tell him good will begets good will." This was getting more interesting by the minute.

The day before we left, word came out of the Middle East saying that Westerners could no longer be guaranteed safety there, that any Westerners who traveled to any Middle Eastern country did so at their own risk. I was more than a little bit nervous about that kind of communiqué, particularly since I was going on a high-visibility trip into the heart of that threat. But I decided to go anyway.

The AP had arranged a meeting at the United Nations with Secretary General Pérez de Cuéllar, who told me the same thing: "You need to go. Go to Syria." I grabbed my best international contact, who also worked at the U.N., and he too said, "Peggy, you need to go to Syria, and you need to go now."

We never expected anything like this. Always before, when we announced a trip the powers that be had tried to head us off, had made things difficult, had made it clear to us that we were on our own over there. This time, as David put it, it was like everybody else had read the book and we were only on chapter three.

The omens were good. Shortly before I left I was told that a group from Buffalo, New York, called the Buffalo Area Metropolitan Ministries had come up with an initiative that was now rippling across the United States. Each day of my trip, I was told, groups in each of hundreds of churches would be taking turns fasting and praying for our success. Churchgoers throughout America would be praying for an end to the conflict in Lebanon and peace for the people there, for reconciliation with their Middle Eastern neighbors, and for release of all hostages held everywhere.

It seemed like a huge responsibility, all these people praying on my behalf, and I took it very seriously.

My first day in Europe I met with the U.S. Ambassador to the U.N., the chief of operations of the International Red Cross, and the secretary general of the International Commission of Jurists. I delivered my message about Terry and the hostages without a hitch. It may sound funny but I really felt people's prayers supporting me.

Two days later I was in Rome, about to see the Pope.

I'm not a Catholic and I never in my life expected to be in the papal presence. It used to be a kind of joke in our house; when the phone rang David would say, "It's probably the Pope, he's the only person you haven't talked to." Now I was going to see him.

We had been prepared for a front-row audience. Once a week, we were told, the Pope addresses the public and will touch or bless those select people who have been given special tickets to sit in the front row. As I understand it, these are people who are either very ill or have some overriding reason to be given his attention. That's what we expected to happen.

Well, at the last minute we were told that we would have a private audience. The woman who arranged it, Danielle Simpson, knew people in the Church hierarchy; her daughter had been gunned down and killed in the terrorist massacre at the Rome airport, where her husband and son had also been wounded. She had pressed for a private audience for us and her wish had been granted.

I must admit I went in there rather blasé about the whole thing. I was not intimidated, I was not frightened. Danielle had talked me through a physical description of the sequence ("This is how it will happen.

We will go into this room . . . Don't let the aides make you nervous, because they'll be running in and out saying, 'He's coming,' 'He's down the hall,' 'He's almost here' ") and I had it in my mind that I would do this by the numbers.

We walked into a large, beautifully furnished room and in strolled a huge black man in long, flowing African robes. It turned out he was a Sudanese prince and he, too, had been granted a papal audience. I just started to laugh softly; the idea of me meeting the Pope, and then this exotic-looking man, it was all so bizarre.

I told Danielle that I hoped the Pope would see the Sudanese prince first. I've always felt that when I get my hands on somebody I'm not going to let him go until I've said what I had to say; that has been my strength. If the Pope heard the Sudanese man first, it would give me a little more time with him.

So I was prepared for my meeting, or so I thought. My mind was on grabbing him by the robe and making him listen to what I had to say.

When Pope John Paul II swept into the room I found I was not prepared at all. There is nothing that can prepare you for that moment.

I had learned through sad experience that people you think are larger than life, when you meet them in person they are so much smaller and more human that it's very often a disappointment. It's an old lesson unless you've never learned it. That is what had kept me from being overwhelmed, what had allowed me to function in the presence of all the world leaders I had met without being intimidated. But Pope John Paul is larger in life than he is anywhere else. The face, in particular. It's a face that seems to have lived a thousand years. When you've got him, you've got his total attention; you could almost drown in it.

He went to the Sudanese prince first, which gave me a moment to catch my breath. I watched the prince do what I had been specifically told not to do, which was kiss the Pope's ring. I was told the Pope really doesn't like that, it makes him uncomfortable and he prefers that people not do it.

He spent maybe sixty seconds with the Sudanese prince. Of course I didn't hear what they were talking about, but from a distance it seemed very stuffy. The Sudanese man made what appeared to be a prepared statement to the Pope and that was the end of that. Then John Paul came over to me.

I had been told that the Pope didn't like to use an interpreter. He speaks many languages but English is his poorest, so there might come a point, I was warned, when an interpreter will intervene, but it didn't come to that.

I knew that, as with presidential meetings, I had a very limited amount of time and I had better use it to the fullest. Danielle introduced me to the Pope and I grabbed his hand to shake it, which I had been told was perfectly proper. Larry Heinzerling was standing right next to me, but our conversation began so quickly that he kind of got left there. I felt awkward that Larry had not been introduced, but I was not going to let go of the Pope until I had said my piece.

I first brought him best wishes from Father Jenco, who had met with the Pope after he was released. For a moment John Paul could not remember Father Jenco. It fascinates me that people who speak so many languages must have a process they go through in their mind to change from one language to another, especially to one in which they're not especially fluent. Once we got by the few initial rough edges, John Paul did remember Father Jenco.

"Father Jenco shared a cell in captivity with my brother, Terry Anderson," I told him, "and they asked and asked and were finally granted their request to hold a Mass together. They used bread that they had saved from their meals as the body of Christ, and as Christ's blood they used water because they had no wine. Father Jenco said that Jesus wouldn't mind because He had also turned water into wine."

The Pope laughed softly. "Yes, that is true," he said. "He would not mind."

I told about the rosaries Terry had woven and distributed, and John Paul seemed touched by that devotion. I showed him pictures of Terry's daughters and he was very sympathetic. I did not have to remind him of the Lebanese problem. He said how concerned he was, and I could see the pain in his face. I sensed that he didn't know what to do but pray, as he had been doing for a very long time.

He said to me, "I will be with you in prayers every day. I am with you in prayers for an end to the terrible things that are happening there."

I think we talked for several minutes, but I can't be sure. It seemed as if it were over in almost an instant. Before he made his exit he gave me a rosary for Terry.

I met the Pope on a Wednesday. On Thursday I was addressing the European Parliament. This was all a little hard to handle.

Addressing the European Parliament was the one that had me most nervous. I do best when I have a physical sense of what I'm getting into, and I pictured this huge semicircular auditorium with plush chairs and dark wooden desks; a cavernous room full of very solemn people, like the U.N. General Assembly, and me there at an echoey microphone making my appeal. I really sweated over it, and got on Larry that he needed to prepare me better than I was already prepared.

When we got there, only four people showed up. We sat around a small table in a private conference room and I talked. It was like reading something into the *Congressional Record,* I was able to address the Parliament even though they were not there, and I was able to make human contact at the same time.

I spoke with the Parliament's president, Enrique Baron Crespo, and with Ken Coates, a member of the Parliament and chairman of its Human Rights Committee. My remarks were translated into each country's language and then distributed to the various delegations. For all my worry, it was a very successful meeting.

President Crespo impressed me immediately as a man who meant what he said. There are few people who command almost automatic respect from the moment you meet them, and he was one of them. He gave me the impression that he himself had been a political prisoner. When I told him the kind of terror Terry was living under, he said he knew *exactly* what my brother was going through.

There had been a statement out of Tehran saying that Iran didn't need the United States, that they could just as easily do business with European countries instead. "Well," said President Crespo, "we'll see about that!" I was very exhilarated when I left.

*　　*　　*

Our next stop was Tunisia, where we had been told we would see Yasser Arafat.

The Tunis airport was scruffy, to say the least, and by the time we got through customs it was dark. There were six of us and a ton of luggage, so we divided up into three cabs and figured to rendezvous at the hotel. Everybody took off, two cabs going in one direction and David's and mine going in another altogether.

The driver was demented. We were barreling down the road to We Didn't Know Where, and it was dark and the road was deserted, and he started screaming, *"Deutschemarks! Deutschemarks! Deutschemarks!"* David tried, in English, to make the guy understand that we had no Tunisian currency, let alone deutschemarks. Don Mell had changed money at the airport and was going to pay for all the cabs once we got to the hotel. But the man didn't understand a word David was saying. He was literally half-turned around in his seat, driving in the darkness and screaming, *"Deutschemarks!"*

We didn't know where in the world we were, we thought he was going to slit our throats and dump us out of the cab in the middle of nowhere. It was terrifying.

We got to the hotel finally. The guy had kept up a nonstop barrage the whole way. Apparently he had known of a shortcut, because the other cabs hadn't got there yet. Which meant, of course, that there was no one around to pay him.

I jumped out of the cab and told the doorman, "This maniac wants money and we don't have any until the other cab gets here." The doorman started to pull our luggage out and he and the driver got into a screaming match.

The cabdriver called the police on us. We were in this country solely to see Yasser Arafat and there we were explaining ourselves to the Tunis police. Finally Don Mell, Mr. Moneybags, pulled up in his cab, and we lived to tell the tale.

Our meeting with Arafat had been arranged by Bassam Abu Sharif. The last time I'd seen Abu Sharif was in a second-story den in Damascus, when there'd been a lot of tire-squealing in the street and he thought he was going to be assassinated. This time he was Arafat's right-hand man.

The call came the next morning, saying that sometime later that day we would get a call to go to another hotel, where we would be picked up and delivered to the PLO chief. That call came within the hour.

When we got to the second hotel we found it was much plusher than the one we were staying in. We thought about changing, but then it dawned on us: Arafat doesn't stay anyplace too long because of fear of assassination, and this might be too close for comfort. If somebody was out to get him, we'd really rather not be in the building when it happens.

We had barely gotten comfortable in one of those conversation alcoves that I had come to realize were designed into all Arab hotels, when the call came. In fact I had just said to the AP North Africa correspondent Mike Goldsmith, "What's the longest you've ever waited to see Arafat?"

"Two days," he said.

So I was kind of settling in for a long winter's nap and cursing that I hadn't brought either a book or my needlepoint when the phone rang and they were coming to pick us up.

A few minutes later two cars screeched into the parking lot and a band of PLO guys jumped out and began waving us in. Everybody had an automatic weapon. Some of them balanced it on their hip, others just fanned them around like ushers using their flashlights.

We drove a short way down the road and turned sharply into a compound.

Inside, the security was tremendous. They took our passports and escorted us into the house.

The place was teeming with people. I gather that this atmosphere always exists around Arafat. A few women were in sight but mostly it was young Arab men, PLO security, in casual dress. Weapons but no uniforms.

When I first saw Yasser Arafat he was sitting at the end of a long table on kind of a raised dais. The table was piled high with food and every seat was taken. The room buzzed with activity. To the left was a sunken living room and several couches and chairs, security guards lounging on them while the rest were eating. Arafat waved several people away from the table to make room for us. They moved immediately.

We were introduced, and I was seated on Arafat's left. I was startled to see him without headgear; he was completely bald. Later, when photos were taken, he put on a hat.

In front of me was someone else's meal. They took that away and brought me a fresh plate but left the used cutlery and the smudged water glass. Now, no one had told me we were going to eat and I had already had a big lunch, but there was no way I was going to insult the chairman of the PLO by refusing his hospitality. Arafat leaned over and, with his hands, plopped a huge hunk of lamb onto my plate. I knew the polite thing was, I've got to eat some of this. I did.

It was obviously not the time for a discussion. In fact Arafat was talking to various people around him, not addressing me at all. It was a bit awkward but I was clearly being given the silent instruction that I was not to discuss the reason for my visit at the dinner table.

Arafat made a great show of offering the others at the table, in a way that brooked no refusal, a concoction of yogurt and water and other things that pass for milk in that area. I am not an adventuresome eater and I was very pleased that he apparently forgot me when the pouring got done. I was thanking my stars that all I had to do was eat the lamb, because when people put their glasses down there were curds on their lips.

No such luck. Arafat noticed that I hadn't been served. He took the dirty water glass from in front of me, dumped the dregs into another glass, and started to pour me a large helping.

Quickly and quietly, a woman seated across from me said something in Arabic. Arafat put the pitcher down. "You'll have to excuse our men," the woman said to me. "They have no manners."

Before a fresh glass could come my way, Arafat gave a grunt, leapt out of his chair, and started striding across the living room. I thought, "Now we're going to have our meeting." I got out of my seat and began to follow him. Carolyn and Larry and the rest of our entourage got up and followed me.

Behind one couch was a hallway and Arafat careened on ahead. I was a couple of steps behind, trying to catch up, but at the end of the hall I lost him. There were several doors and I stopped short, didn't know what to do. Carolyn, Larry, and the gang piled into me like the Three Stooges in the Casbah. Behind us the woman was screaming.

"What are you doing! The chairman is going to the bathroom!"

The PLO boys with their automatic weapons were just about rolling on the floor with laughter. The whole place erupted. We kind of ambled aimlessly back from the hall, not knowing where to go, and all the security people were hysterical.

All I could do was laugh. If Carolyn's face had gotten any redder she would have died of a stroke right there. I wasn't so much embarrassed as I was laughing at my own stupidity. By now it's probably part of PLO lore, the time that American hostage lady followed the chairman to the john.

When Arafat emerged, it was indeed time to talk. We were shown into a small alcove and seated around a table. They brought out a bowl of fruit and some Arab finger food.

In terms of the feel of the place it was like meeting with the President, there were security people hovering about, you didn't know who they were. Bill Foley, Carolyn, Mike Goldsmith, Don Mell, and Larry were scattered among several PLO people, and I was seated on Arafat's left. He now gave me his complete attention. We finally began to discuss the reason for my visit.

I knew when I went to Tunis that Arafat was probably not in a position to do anything. But I wanted to meet him, I was curious about him. I knew I had absolutely nothing to fear, no reason to be intimidated. I had tried several times over the years to see him, and it had been a long wait for this moment. I was relaxed about talking with him. After all, I had just suffered the deepest humiliation, it could only go up from there.

I began as I usually did, by telling him the whole story. Bassam Abu Sharif had been a friend of Terry's, so I was going in presold.

"Mr. Arafat, my brother Terry told me when he was working in Beirut, before he was kidnapped, that whenever Americans ran into trouble they could come to you for a reasonable hearing. I am now coming to you in that capacity. As you probably know, I contacted your people in Washington several years ago and have kept in touch with them. I don't know what you can do to help my brother, but whatever you can do will be appreciated tremendously."

Arafat was sympathetic. He said that, over the years, he had done what he could to help get the hostages freed. If we had arrived some years earlier, he said, he might have been able to arrange something. Now, however, the situation was beyond his influence.

Arafat also said that he would be in a better position to free my brother were it in the power of the captors to do so. But the captors basically no longer had a say in the matter. The decisions as to what to do with the hostages were no longer theirs to make; those decisions were being made in Iran.

This was more confirmation than surprise. We had heard that if it were up to Rafsanjani the hostages would have been released in November. There had been a plan to that effect. However, the hard-liner Ali Akbar Mohtashemi, the new political leader of Hezbollah, had made a three-week trip to Lebanon and had in fact physically moved the hostages, taken over their control and moved them out of the reach of Syria.

We had heard these rumors from our sources on the ground in Beirut, whose information was generally reliable. But this was Yasser Arafat, and now they were confirmed.

The meeting was amiable if somewhat restrained. Arafat knew there was very little he could do to help us, and we knew it as well.

Afterward, as Arafat was posing for pictures with various members of our entourage, I said a friendly good-bye to Abu Sharif. As we were walking away I remembered something.

"Bassam, I had a message for the chairman and I didn't know whether to give it to him or not, especially in front of all the people there."

"Who is it from?" he asked.

"It's from a member of the National Security Council."

"What is it?"

"The message is: 'Good will begets good will.' "

Abu Sharif got quite excited. "This is very important, this is very important." He hustled me back to Arafat and said, "Mr. Chairman, Mrs. Say has just told me she has a message you should hear. She did not want to tell you in front of the others."

When I told Arafat the message he seemed touched and extremely grateful. In that brief moment before our departure, the message changed the whole complexion of his commitment. It seemed to mean so much to him. To me it had sounded like a crumb, the very least they could say. But to Arafat it obviously had a lot more significance.

What I wondered was, why did a member of the NSC need me to pass that message along? What if I had forgotten to mention it? Why couldn't the American government just go and make the deal themselves? Did they actually think this was not negotiating?

Who is in charge here?

The trip continued. In Paris we met with Frederico Mayor, the director general of UNESCO, and from there we went to London, where we were scheduled to see Robert Runcie, the Archbishop of Canterbury.

That meeting was very strange to me. The archbishop was extremely amiable and happy to spend a few minutes with me, but when I started to brief him on my trip and what I had discovered he didn't want to hear it. He didn't say it outright, but I got the distinct impression—from his expression, by his changing the subject—that he did not want to hear anything I had to say on the matter. He just wanted to avoid the topic of the hostages, even though they were the reason I was there in the first place.

It was a short meeting. Afterward I met with Archbishop Runcie's secretary for public affairs and with the employer of one of the hostages, John McCarthy, and as I shared with them what I had found, Terry Waite's name was never mentioned. I found that more than a little strange and significant. Terry Waite represented the Church of England, he had been held hostage for over three years, and his name never came up.

A dinner for me and the relatives of the British hostages had been organized at the posh Savoy Hotel that evening by the AP London bureau chief, Myron Belkind. Myron had generously flown various family members into London, put them up at Grosvenor House, where we were staying, and arranged the whole wonderful evening. I immediately forgave him for presenting me with a schedule of interviews that had left me staggering with fatigue.

Tom Sutherland's brother and sister-in-law flew in from Scotland; John McCarthy's fiancée and his dad Pat were there, as were Terry Waite's brother David and his wife. Even Frances Waite, Terry Waite's wife, who never went anywhere near occasions like this—they didn't expect her to show, but she was there.

There were about twenty people at the table. Unlike in the U.S., where the hostages families have made great efforts to see one another and keep in contact, I was surprised to learn that these people hadn't been meeting with each other. I don't know how they do it. There is a common ground among the families, a common experience; we gain great strength and solace from one another.

One of the things I found we had in common that evening was our attitude toward the media. Pat McCarthy told me that his wife had died during the past year. He didn't like to do interviews, he said, but he would if he was cornered; he's too nice a man to say no. Mr. McCarthy mentioned that the last interview he had done was held in his home. The camera crew hooked everything up and the lights were turned on and the interviewer, this nice young thing, said to him, "And now that your wife is dead, Mr. McCarthy, are you lonely?"

David Waite seemed guilty, and I was straightforward enough to say so. I got the feeling he was relieved to be able to talk about it. He said his brother had told him that if he was ever taken, he didn't want anyone to try to get him released. David Waite had been semi-active on his brother's behalf and had begun to doubt himself.

I said to him, "David, I faced that question. If Terry Waite comes out and disagrees with what you've done, well, that's just too bad. You had to do the right thing for you, and that's going to have to be enough for you. You may never get his approval, and you have to learn to live with that."

Terry Waite's wife Frances came at the problem from another direction entirely. She was a shy, unobtrusive woman, seeming almost apologetic for taking up any space at all. We didn't have much of a chance to talk during the dinner, but as I was leaving Myron Belkind came over and said, "Mrs. Waite would like a few words with you."

I walked to the door where she was standing and Frances began talking through clenched teeth. In her English accent it came out like a whisper on a train. I had to watch her mouth to make sure I was hearing what I thought I was hearing, because once she started the words tumbled out in a virtual flood of complaints.

"The bloody press," she spat out. "The next bloody reporter who asks me a stupid question I'm going to strangle with my bare hands. They didn't even know he had a wife, they thought I was his bloody housekeeper."

I was so startled by her outburst that I didn't know whether to laugh or cry. She was obviously in deep pain and desperately needed someone to share her feelings with. I was upset that I only had a moment to give her.

"Mrs. Waite," I said, "you might want to talk to somebody about this."

"I'm talking to you. And I keep thinking if I talk about it I won't do it, but I think I'm going to do it and I think you're going to read about it in the papers."

This was dynamite getting ready to explode. When Mrs. Waite had departed, I said to Pat McCarthy and David Waite, "You people really need to talk with one another. Mrs. Waite is very upset and I hope you'll all keep in contact and try to help one another."

When we finally got to Syria we stayed for several days. At dinner with some friends I had made on my two other visits there I asked about what was going on, outside of the hostage situation. One friend gave me some frank answers and told me about things I didn't think still existed in the twentieth century. For instance, in Syria, he said, if an unmarried woman gets pregnant her father or brother has the right to kill her and not be charged with a crime. Premarital sex is not only out, it's not even talked about, you don't even hint at it.

Most of the needed goods, he told me, are bought on the black market. When anything of value comes on the black market, those people with money immediately snap it up because they don't know when they'll ever see it again. The economy is so bad that young people have to wait longer and longer to get married because they can't afford a house, so you're looking at a whole generation not marrying until twenty-five or twenty-six, if then, and having to deal with all of those emotional frustrations.

As we were sitting in Damascus there were people demonstrating for food in the streets of Tehran. As witness the upheavals in Central and Eastern Europe, there were lessons to be learned.

Dissatisfaction was also beginning to stir in Damascus, my friend told me. The people were hungry, they wanted food, and President Assad was not getting it for them. In a major address to the people, what Assad did instead was to engage in a tirade against Israel settling Soviet Jewish emigrants. He didn't have anything positive to give the people, so he had to divert them.

It was a situation that needed addressing that day. Not six months down the road, but right then. The Soviet Union had its own economic problems and couldn't support the Syrians any longer.

I met with Syrian Foreign Minister Farouk al-Sharaa. In the past, Syria had been referred to as "the taxicab" for the hostages, nothing more than transportation. But now, from everything I had heard from many different sources, I knew that Syria's role had shifted. I didn't understand why, but I knew there had been a major change in their attitude toward the situation.

We were given the meeting with Foreign Minister Sharaa almost the moment our feet hit the ground in Damascus. We called and were told he would see us that evening. Larry, Don, and Carolyn would accompany me.

I had been at the Foreign Ministry before, when Father Jenco was released. It is a big, impressive building, and we climbed the stone stairs to the entrance. It was evening and there was an empty silence to the place, no traffic, only the hot Syrian breeze. Just as we passed the guardhouse a sentry stamped his foot on the stone. It sounded like rifle fire.

I thought I'd been shot. My heart stopped. I was just waiting to fall over.

"That was a salute," I was told, "a gesture of respect. Expect it on the way out."

"Nobody could have warned me on the way in?"

The meeting lasted for about thirty minutes and could not have gone better. I told him, "Mr. Sharaa, I am not a diplomat but I have seen you one time before, in New York in 1985 when you visited the United Nations. At that time I asked you for your help. I am not here to do that now because one cannot ask for that which has already been freely given." But I did come bearing a gift, of sorts, which was the Buffalo Area Ministries initiative, in which Americans all across the country were praying for peace in the Middle East.

Mr. Sharaa was very moved and said, "I assure you that will go directly to President Assad."

Then he made some comments about the terrible injustice of U.S. policy supporting Israel. That will always come up in conversation with Arab officials, but this time it was almost perfunctory, he didn't really push it. We were both so relaxed in this talk that I felt free enough to tell him, "Mr. Sharaa, American policy is dictated by the American people, and I have great faith in the American people. You capture the hearts of the American people and we'll capture the hearts of our politicians."

He smiled. "And you say you're not a diplomat."

Then Mr. Sharaa shocked me. As to the hostage situation, he said, "President Bush is doing exactly what he should be doing."

This was a resounding change. What had brought it on?

"Let me assure you," he continued, "the Syrians are intimately involved in this situation. If there is anyone who wants this over with more than the United States, it is the Syrians."

Larry Heinzerling and Don Mell started pressing for details, and I could sense Sharaa's growing irritation. I told them afterward that what I thought Sharaa was trying to say was, "We're the Syrians, we're not playing games here. We understand the problems and we know what has to be done to resolve them. Leave us to it."

So Syria was entering the battle in full gear. I've always been convinced that if the Syrians found it in their best interest, it would be a very simple matter for them to free the hostages. There was the example of the Russians. Three Russians had been kidnapped and one was killed during the scuffle. Rumor had it that the Soviets then picked up several Hezbollah family members and sent the first one back in sections, packed in dry ice. They reportedly then issued a warning that there would be one delivery a day until their hostages were released.

True or not, the threat worked. The Russian hostages were sent back in short order and no other Russians have been kidnapped. Although American stomachs, including mine, are too queasy to consider such options, there are other countries that don't flinch over fighting fire with fire.

I'd never thought that Syria was helpless in all this, just that they didn't have any special reason for going forward with it. It was not a winning proposition for them, they didn't have any incentive to get intimately involved. Now the incentive existed; their economy was in shambles and they needed help. The Soviet Union had its own troubles and could not give them the financial support they had in the past, and which Syria so desperately needed, so Syria had to make other arrangements.

All of a sudden the Syrians were not passive players, they were active participants.

"I am leaving in two days for Tehran and we are going to end this situation," said Mr. Sharaa.

I was not going to ask what went into the deal. I picked up bits and pieces here and there, and I don't think that anything tangible was going to go from the United States directly to the captors. What Syria's deal with the captors was, I had no idea. But what had happened was that the United States was now dealing with another country, Syria, and Syria was dealing with the Mughniyahs of the terrorist world.

I had requested a meeting with President Assad, but I never actively pursued it while I was in Damascus because it would be self-defeating; they weren't going to give it to me, and I wanted to be able to get back into the country. So I made the formal request but without any real push. At the end of our talk Mr. Sharaa said to me, "You'll get your meeting with President Assad when he gives you back your brother."

"What kind of time frame are we talking about?" I asked.

In the past a question like that would almost always get answered with "Oh, but these things are so complicated." This time Sharaa said, "Sooner rather than later."

True to his word, Sharaa did go to Tehran. After that, things began coming together.

CHAPTER

15

WE WERE FLYING HIGH WHEN WE GOT BACK TO THE STATES. I REALLY had the feeling that I was going to see Terry in the coming weeks. Mr. Sharaa instilled that kind of confidence in me. He knew exactly what was going on, he knew what had to be done to resolve it, and he did not question his own ability to do so. There was no waffling about it. In Damascus, few get to President Assad, so when you go to Sharaa you've gone to the Man.

And then we waited. Terry's fifth anniversary in captivity came on March 16, 1990, and we scheduled a ceremony in Washington. We were very hopeful that this would be the last of these gatherings we would have to organize.

The only time the hostages get much attention is when the captors threaten to kill them or somebody organizes a media event. Otherwise they really are forgotten. There is no one in government whose sole job it is to get these men home. No one. So when the day of the event comes, we've got to go all out to arouse people.

David Miller, the aide to General Scowcroft at the National Security Council, hand-delivered a letter to me from President Bush that morning saying he would not be able to meet with the hostage families. We had expected as much.

Before Miller went back to the White House I gave him a message for President Bush: Even though the President wouldn't be able to meet with the hostage families, it would be very nice if Mrs. Bush could attend the ceremony. He said he would deliver it.

Father Jenco, Bill Foley, and I were in the middle of an interview with CBS when a message arrived, marked Urgent. I was to call David Miller immediately.

The President wanted to see me.

I was surprised, to say the least. This was truly a bolt from the blue. I'd thought that the letter that morning had closed the issue. It had been White House policy to keep the hostage families as far away as possible from any and all bigwigs. I asked if the other family members were invited as well. Miller told me no, it was only David and me. Non-negotiable. A car would be sent around for us in half an hour.

I couldn't believe they wouldn't see all of us. We weren't individuals in this, we were a full group with a wide expanse of needs and requests. But that was the White House's final position, and I did not feel I could refuse. David went downstairs to break the news to the others while I finished up the interview, then I went downstairs as well.

"I feel terrible about this," I told them. "We are all in this together, and I asked that all of us be allowed to speak to the President, but they refused. I won't go if you don't want me to."

Virginia Steen was holding a picture of her husband Alann. She looked right at me and said, "No, you should be the one to go, you speak for all the hostage families." Frank Reed's wife Fifi started crying but said I should go. We hugged and they wished me good luck.

David Miller picked us up. I asked him if something had changed, was there some change in policy, since the White House had never shown us this kind of interest or attention before. He just said the President wanted to see me.

At the White House gates the guards asked us our names and called inside to make sure we were to be allowed in. One of them asked to look in the trunk of the car. David said with a straight face that it was real nice of him to check and make sure we had a spare tire.

We entered through the diplomats' entrance and were seated in an anteroom. Less than two minutes later Mrs. Bush walked in with a man I did not recognize and her dog Millie. She came straight toward me, and as the man began to make the introductions she took my hand and said, "I know who this lady is."

"Someone will be bringing Mr. and Mrs. Say upstairs," she was told.

"Tell them they're going up with me." She walked us to a small elevator and we rode up to the family quarters.

Mrs. Bush seemed like a very pleasant woman and I felt instantly comfortable with her. We began talking about our grandchildren, and our family dogs.

One of Mrs Bush's major interests, I knew, was the Literacy Council, a huge program run entirely by volunteers, dedicated to teaching illiterate Americans to read. I had been involved in the same organization when I was in Florida, adapting the program to teach non-English-speaking migrant workers to read and write. We started chatting about that and other concerns we shared.

After Mrs. Bush seated David and me on a sofa, she poked around between a lamp, a clock, and two framed family photos to find the buzzer to ring for someone to bring us coffee. "Everything is so secretive around here," she said as she found the button. The coffee appeared almost instantly.

Mrs. Bush and I were having such a good talk, and he hadn't been mentioned, so I wasn't sure whether the President was going to join us or not. Then, after about fifteen minutes, he strode in with his daughter Margaret and White House Chief of Staff John Sununu.

The President acted warm and glad to see me, which was not a response I had experienced very often in meeting with officials. I had as much as called the man a terrorist, then called him out to his face in front of the other hostage families; now it was as if none of that had happened. Politics are strange.

We shook hands and he remarked on an article in that morning's *Washington Post* about me, saying he thought it was an excellent story.

"Anyone who can survive a *Washington Post* profile," he said, "can't be all bad."

President Bush unbuttoned his jacket and drew up a chair across a small coffee table from David and me. He had a cup of coffee and some of the pastry being passed around, and he started asking me about my trip. He was particularly interested in my meeting with the Syrian foreign minister, Farouk al-Sharaa. He asked who had said what, and what my feelings were about both the man and what he had said. When I told him that the indicators I had gotten on the trip all pointed to an atmosphere of resolution, he was pleased. However, he said, "I feel it is my responsibility not to give the families of hostages any false hopes, because it has happened too many times in the past." He did tell me that the trip had been a remarkable undertaking.

I told the President about the meeting with Arafat, and how the PLO leader was so very moved by the phrase "Good will begets good will." I told him about President Crespo's comments at the European Parliament, and the meeting with the Pope. He seemed very interested in my assessments of each face-to-face encounter.

"The hostages are on my mind every single day," he told me.

"Yes," added Mrs. Bush, "and he prays for them every night."

President Bush kind of flushed. "You know I don't like to talk about things like that."

Now if this had been President Reagan I would have suspected he was just acting up a storm. But I felt President Bush was sincere. I sensed a total and complete attention; he was interested, and from the questions he asked I felt he genuinely wanted to know.

What did puzzle me, however, was that he knew so little. He was nodding and listening and very eager to hear the details. He seemed to be digesting everything as if he were hearing it for the first time. But high Administration officials had considered the trip important—it had been made with the pressing encouragement of the State Department and the NSC. I had briefed the State Department when I returned, and I simply assumed that the President would have been well aware of what had actually happened.

He knew not the first thing, only the highlights of whom I had met with, not what had been said. Maybe he was just not involved in the day-to-day mechanics, but it certainly didn't seem that there was any particular closeness in his relationship with either the State Department or the NSC. In fact General Scowcroft's aide David Miller, who portrayed himself as such an insider, had to be introduced to Mrs. Bush.

One of the first things the President brought up was the famous phony Rafsanjani phone call. (Someone claiming to be President Rafsanjani telephoned the White House and when the President returned the call it turned out to be a hoax.) He seemed greatly embarrassed by it.

I said, "Mr. President, I was reassured by your willingness to talk to Rafsanjani. I don't find it embarrassing at all. I wish I had a dime for every phone call I've taken that turned out to be nothing." When I told them about the terrorists who wanted money and blue jeans he and Mrs. Bush and Mr. Sununu all laughed and seemed relieved. The President said, "I will still talk to anybody. What have I got to lose?"

I also told the President about my appearing on Syrian television. Everyone I had spoken to recognized the significance of it, but the whole thing was news to President Bush.

Syria wanted the captors to know that enough was enough. They were saying, "If you're going to cut a deal for these people, you'd damn well better do it now because they're rapidly decreasing in value," and they wanted the message to come from me. The Syrian government knew what I would say from the meetings I'd already attended. One can assume, since Syrian television is run by the state, that I would not have been invited to speak unless it was in the government's interest to air my message.

It was to be a taped interview and I was terrified that I was going to say something wrong and get my brother killed.

"Well, then, why did you do it?" President Bush asked.

I said, "Mr. President, when you're in Syria and the government asks you to do something, it's probably a very good idea to do it." Bush and Sununu both laughed.

What I said to the captors during that interview, however, seemed to impress everyone in the room.

"We are the American people," I'd said on Syrian TV. "You have humiliated us and used us and threatened us and beaten us and killed us and finally made us angry.

"The captors ask for ransom. If I had ten million dollars in my hands today and they said, 'Give it to us and we'll give you your brother,' I'd say, 'Not a dime. Not a *dime!* I'm not going to pay anymore. I've paid. My family has paid in pain and heartache.'

"I am not the person I was five years ago and I am no longer willing to give the things I would have given then. I don't think Terry would be willing to do it. He's been chained to the wall for five years and they want a reward? Not anymore. There was a time I would have given them anything. That time is long past.

"I want them to give my brother back, but I'm not willing to reward them for doing so.

"They wonder why their cries for justice fall on deaf ears. They claim that their story is not being told and yet they keep the man that told it best chained to a wall. If they expect us to hear their cry for freedom, then they must first hear ours, and let the hostages go."

I was going to deliver the same speech at the ceremony in Washington that afternoon.

"Wow," said the President, "that's a very powerful message."

It was a turnaround for me. But the times had changed. President Reagan had professed this great concern for the hostages that led him to make a deal with Iran, but after Iran-contra he completely ignored the issue. The hostage families and friends had all thought that our first job would be to make Bush recognize the fact that we've still got hostages. But Bush walked into office talking about the hostages. "It's a priority," he said.

Where Reagan had told the captors essentially, "We'll never give you anything. Give us the hostages," the Bush position was "We'll give you something, but only after they are home."

"Future incentives." In baseball parlance, President Bush would be offering "a player to be named later." It was a policy I could support. I told the President what I'd said on Syrian television: "I stand behind President Bush one hundred percent when he says, 'We will talk *after* the hostages are out.' "

I said, "Mr. President, it feels good, for the first time, to be able to stand behind my President."

We spoke for almost forty-five minutes. I think we would have just sat there and continued to talk if Mrs. Bush hadn't said, "George, Peggy has to be at a ceremony in about two minutes."

The President was very affectionate in leaving. He hugged me and kissed me and seemed very pleased with how the whole meeting had gone. It was not, I don't think, what he had expected. Nor I. He undoubtedly had thought I was going to challenge him; and I was impressed that even though he thought he'd be in for a fight, he had seen me. Besides, I still wanted to believe my President.

The night before the ceremony there had been a statement released by the Islamic Jihad for the Liberation of Palestine, and a picture of hostage Robert Polhill, and a death threat: they were going to kill their hostages. I had had dinner with Virginia Steen, whose husband Alann had been a hostage since January 1987, and then gone back to my room while Virginia went to the airport to pick up Frank Reed's wife Fifi.

Under the door of my hotel room someone had stuck the day's news clippings. Not only was there a picture of Robert Polhill, there was a picture of Alann Steen; the death threat included him.

I felt very badly to be the one to have to tell Virginia, but I tracked her down. I was very upset when I handed her the picture. She knew that Alann's teeth had been knocked out, which was why he smiled with his mouth closed. I told her, "Virginia, given the death threat, I won't say what I was going to say tomorrow if you don't want me to." There was no death threat against Terry, and maybe I was being cavalier with the hostages' safety. Her husband's life was on the line; it was definitely a big risk we were taking.

Virginia was very brave. "No," she said, "give them hell. Enough is enough."

I delivered the speech. I told the crowd what I'd told the President, that if I had ten million dollars I wouldn't give the captors a dime. That we had been blasted one time too many, that the time for ransom was past.

For days afterward I held my breath. I knew how closely they monitor our television, and I prayed that the captors would not send out a statement that they had beaten Terry or any of the others because of what I'd said.

The responsibility was overwhelming and I was scared to death. But I felt, in the present atmosphere, it needed to be said. I knew why the Syrians wanted it said: they wanted the captors to know that whatever the Syrians were offering them, they had best take it because they weren't going to get anything else. The captors were not going to be allowed to drive the families to pressure the Administration again.

CHAPTER

16

OBVIOUSLY SOMETHING WAS WORKING. ON APRIL 22, 1990, ROBERT Polhill was released.

Polhill was one of three Beirut University College professors who had been kidnapped on the same day in January 1987. We had been furious with them for being willful and foolish enough to get taken after so many warnings that it was not safe for Americans to stay in Beirut. All the old accusations—"It's their own damn fault for being there"—had resurfaced, and at the time it had hurt our cause tremendously. But they were hostages and we had added them to our list of men we had to bring home.

I didn't go to Washington for Polhill's release. I knew he hadn't seen Terry and I just decided to stay home.

A few days later Frank Reed was released. Reed had been a hostage since September 1986 and I knew he had seen Terry. I also had met his wife Fifi several times. They'd lived in Boston. From the start his release didn't go well.

When hostages are freed they are flown first to Wiesbaden, Germany, for debriefing and reentry into the outside world. The State Department routinely flies family members to Wiesbaden for an immediate routine. Fifi and her son Tarek had booked a flight on Lufthansa Airlines, and when they arrived at Boston's Logan Airport she found their tickets weren't there. She called the State Department and was told that she wasn't allowed to fly Lufthansa; the State Department would pay her fare only if she flew an American airline. In addition, there was a mob scene at the airport, and Fifi said she was seriously worried that her son would be trampled by the crush of press.

When she and her son arrived in Germany, Frank told her he would have preferred that they wait in Washington for him; he said it was all too much. We had heard that same kind of thing from other hostages, that reentry is extremely difficult when a lot of people are around, except that they had at least wanted to see their wives and children. Frank was cantankerous and just wanted to be left alone.

The hostage families had developed a real sense of community by then, and both Fifi Reed and Ferial Polhill called me from Germany with news of their husbands' condition and of Terry.

Three days after Reed was released, and the night before he was scheduled to arrive back in the United States, No Greater Love held a dinner party to celebrate Robert Polhill's release and Robert and Ferial's tenth wedding anniversary. It was held in Washington at the Four Seasons Hotel, which, at Carmella LaSpada's request, had graciously donated its dining room for the evening. It was the first chance I had to meet and talk with Robert Polhill.

Robert reminded me very much of Ben Weir—he had that same kind of quiet goodness. He said he was shocked to learn about the treatment the other hostages had undergone. After being held for the first two or three weeks, he said, he knew the captors weren't going to do anything to him; he was safe, he would not be killed, and it was simply a question of living through captivity.

Most hostages, with rare exceptions, emerge from their captivity with a kind of aura around them, and Robert Polhill had his. A hostage's life will never be the same. He has been placed in a situation in which he's had to reach down and grab the essence of his strength, the basic bottom line of what he is. Once the hostages have done that, and once they've mastered or overcome their fears, it gives them a sense of supreme confidence and an aura of spirituality. I know this sounds very cosmic, but it's true. I know from all of those I've talked to that it gives them a deeper appreciation of the simpler things in life.

I've tried to learn that too. I am always reminding myself to say, "Thank you, God," if the day has been without disaster, or if it has been particularly beautiful. When your sense of family has been threatened, or in some cases destroyed, you notice little pockets of peace and you give thanks.

Robert didn't know much about the treatment of the other prisoners, and he listened to our stories as much as we did to his.

At the dinner everybody was drinking champagne except Carmella and me, and David Miller of the National Security Council kept apologizing to Robert Polhill for Robert's having been in captivity for so long. He did it over and over again. Finally, after about six or seven apologies, Robert kind of lost what I think of as his mini-temper.

"Look," he said to Miller, "I don't want to hear another apology. I was in Lebanon when I had been told to get out. I stayed at my own risk. I neither asked for nor expected my government to get me out of there. Anything that has been done for me is a bonus, because they didn't have to do it. And I don't want to hear any more apologies."

I was really impressed. The hostage families had taken a lot of flak when the BUC professors were taken and I respected Robert for accepting his share of the responsibility.

By this time our man in the NSC was slurring his words. "I'm glad you're out," Miller said, "but I'd have rather seen you dead than stay there that long."

Miller told us he had been an advocate of a rescue mission that had been proposed during government meetings. Even if some of the hostages had been killed, he said, it would have been more acceptable to him than the years they spent in captivity with everybody standing around wringing their hands and not really doing anything.

Robert said yes, there was a time very early in his captivity when he felt he would not survive it anyway. He was in his fifties, he was a diabetic, he thought he would die, so better a rescue attempt than just to die in that stupid room. But once they started giving him his diabetes medication, and once he began to cope with captivity, he was less willing to be killed or to die.

We all noticed how hoarse Robert's voice was. So several weeks later, when the diagnosis was made that he had throat cancer and would have to have his larynx removed, it was just devastating. You had to wonder where fairness and justice are in this world.

Frank Reed came out angry and shooting from the hip. He blasted British Prime Minister Margaret Thatcher and the U.S. government, and although what he said or did not say was really none of my business, I had to protect Terry as best I could.

On the phone from Wiesbaden Frank was already saying that he wanted to call a press conference. I felt this was the wrong thing to do until he had had a chance to find out and understand what had happened in his absence. He had been in a cell for three and a half years; he didn't know what the government was doing or what needed to be said. He also didn't know what effect one misdirected phrase could have.

Rather than have Frank Reed hold a press conference and be kind of a loose cannon, Carmella LaSpada and I had come up with the idea of having No Greater Love sponsor one for him. Then, at least, he would be speaking in a controlled environment.

The day after the Polhills' anniversary dinner, Reed was scheduled to arrive at Andrews Air Force Base from Wiesbaden. Carmella had made a call to Michael Mahoney at the State Department and was told that we—meaning myself, Carmella, the Polhills, and other hostage family members who had planned to be there—would not be greeting Frank at Andrews, as was the custom with previous released hostages. Senator Ted Kennedy would be greeting him. Kennedy had never been very helpful to our cause, but Frank was from Boston and Kennedy was one of his senators.

I called Mahoney back. "Michael," I told him, "you don't want to do that. I promise you, you don't want to do that." But Mahoney was adamant, so I hung up.

I called the NSC and talked to David Miller. I said, "This is nonsense. This is not going to happen. Every member of that family has gone to Kennedy for help for the past thirty-nine months of Frank's captivity and he has turned them down flat. Now he's going to make this his show? No way."

Miller said, "I'll call you back."

Five minutes later Miller called. "It's okay. You're in."

The plane landed and we all formed a receiving line on the tarmac at the portable steps while Frank's daughters Marilyn and Jackie climbed up to greet him for the first time. They had no sooner gotten to the top of the stairs than Kennedy went barreling up, elbowed them out of the way, and presented their father with a three-pound lobster.

Reed loved it. He just thought it was the most wonderful thing. I doubt he was aware that when Kennedy had picked them up to bring them to the airport that morning it was the first time they had met him.

We organized the press conference for a Sunday. Traditionally, these ceremonies had not been political anyway, but if any political people were going to show up I thought they should be ones who had helped us. I called the offices of Senator Daniel Patrick Moynihan of New York and Senator Robert Dole of Kansas, both strong supporters of our cause. If Kennedy was going to be there, they should be there too.

I started tracking them on Saturday, which under normal Washington, D.C., circumstances would have made them pretty much unreachable. But they both got back to me and I explained that I thought it would send a very strong public message if they were at the press conference the next day.

I had spoken with Senator Moynihan many times before. He had been so loyal to us and had read things into the *Congressional Record* on our behalf for years. I had never met Senator Dole, but I needed his perspective as well. I was pleased and grateful that on such short notice they both set aside other plans and immediately agreed to attend.

As we were milling around before the press conference that Sunday morning, I brought Bill Foley over and introduced him to the senators. Senator Moynihan said to Bill, "What needs to be said?"

Foley told him, "Somebody has to go up there and call a spade a spade. The Israelis are our allies and they need to weigh in in a positive way in this situation, because otherwise we're never going to get it resolved." The captors had let it be known that one of their demands for the hostages' freedom would be an exchange of prisoners.

Dole got up and made a good speech, saying that every country holding hostages needed to release them and that this situation needed to be brought to an end. Then Senator Moynihan went to the podium.

As I remember it he said, "Well, somebody's got to say it: Israel, if you want to be a part of the world community you've got to act in a decent and humane manner. Hostage-taking is hostage-taking, and you can't be part of it. It's not only against the Geneva Convention, it's against the laws of humanity. You need to release Sheik Obeid and those hostages. You need to do it now."

You could almost hear the gasp from the press. Dole was used to doing this kind of thing, but for Moynihan it took on more significance. He was a consistent supporter of Israel and for him this was really a bombshell.

Finally, Frank Reed got up and spoke. We had asked that he write his remarks down because he had just gotten out of captivity and had a tendency to ramble. So he was reading from his notes and he was doing okay, not saying anything really harmful.

But then Frank's eyes left the paper and I knew we were in trouble.

He started drawing this bizarre analogy, the premise being that Senator Dole's daughter gets raped. It made no sense and I think was quite embarrassing for Senator Dole. Eventually Frank ran out of steam and left the podium, and the rest of us gave a great sigh of relief.

Reed damaged his credibility early on. He had come out saying that the hostages were in good condition and good health. Then he gave a press conference and said they were sick and dying. "Terry Anderson is not well," he'd said. The press began commenting on his mental state.

Reed was very unsure about when he'd last seen Terry. The best we could figure out what that it was a year to eighteen months before. They did not get along.

Frank did not like Terry and he spoke extremely disparagingly about Tom Sutherland. Almost the first thing he told me was that for the last four months he spent in a cell with Sutherland, he spoke not a word to him.

"How can you not speak to somebody held with you under those circumstances?" I asked.

"Because I hated him."

I was immediately turned off by what I perceived as the depth of his loathing for these two men. All the other hostages who had been held with Terry and had come out were extremely impressed by my brother's intelligence. They all had the same things to say: that Terry has a photographic memory, that nobody could beat him at hearts. They had told me all the stories about Terry that I had collected. According to Frank, however, any time he and Terry had had a confrontation—be it over cards or politics or statements of fact—Frank came out on top. He could beat Terry at anything, he said; any time they got into an argument, Terry turned out to be wrong.

I found this a little questionable. I'm sure there are people who can beat Terry at many things, but none of the hostages had been able to do it, and Frank Reed did not exactly seem like a brain surgeon to me.

Several weeks later I received a call from a friend of mine in the State Department who told me in confidence that they were running a battery of tests on Frank, as they did on all returning hostages, and that their findings indicated that Frank Reed had toxic levels of arsenic in his system.

Arsenic testing, I was told, is done through hair and fingernail samples. The State Department did not have the facilities to run these tests, and because they wanted independent confirmation of their initial findings they had sent a second set of samples to independent laboratories and were waiting for the results.

I was shocked, but I couldn't really believe it; it didn't seem likely to me that anybody had deliberately administered arsenic. I called around and was told that you could pick up arsenic traces from eating utensils or other such objects. I was anxious to see what the lab results would be.

When the results arrived, the doctors were astounded to find that Reed had twelve times the toxic level of arsenic in his system. My State Department contact said, "There is no way this arsenic poisoning was accidental. Low dosages were administered over a long period of time and an extra jolt was given to Frank Reed in the day or two before his release."

One of the side effects of arsenic poisoning, he told me, was passivity. One can only speculate that Reed and the other hostages were given arsenic as a tranquilizer, a means to subdue them.

I was terrified and furious. They were poisoning Frank Reed. Were they poisoning my brother too?

My State Department confidant told me, "The State Department does not want this information out. They have to release it but they're going to do it in a way that will cause as little publicity as possible. And they're not going to give all the facts. But I thought you should know."

I, in my naive manner, shouted, "But they can't do that! This has to be public because this has to stop!"

"One can only hope for the best."

He was right. The news was released on a Friday night, which is traditionally a slow news night—all the media biggies have gone home and staffers are manning the desks. The State Department diluted the story, did not mention exactly how much arsenic had been found in Reed's system, did not mention their conclusion that the poisoning was long-term and deliberate. And the story caused not a ripple.

The government just did not want to reopen the hostage issue. They didn't want an enraged public, to say nothing of the politicians, demanding that they do something to end this atrocity.

I couldn't make a public scene without divulging my source, whose identity I had promised to keep secret. The best I could do was call a friend of Terry's on the *Washington Post* and a friend I had made at CNN and say, "This is the story. You cannot source me, but the State Department has all of the information. If you question them they're going to have to answer."

But the government is very cagey. Once they had released the medical bulletin they all went home and were unavailable to the press for the weekend. Although the *New York Times* and the *Washington Post* did report the findings, the reporters could not get confirmation of the situation's seriousness. So we were out here knowing what was happening, that at that very moment the captors could very well be poisoning the hostages—and long-term arsenic poisoning can be fatal—and wondering just how long the State Department was going to successfully avoid the issue of the health of the hostages.

When the media did finally pursue the story, the State Department just closed its doors and clogged up the information.

Poisoning the hostages. If it's deliberate, it's an abomination. If it's accidental, it's still a very serious problem.

* * *

I had been convinced after my trip in February and my meeting with President Bush that we were definitely on the road to resolution. My support of Bush's nondeal solution didn't mean I thought what we had done in the past was wrong. Far from it. All it meant was that world and regional events had at last conspired in our favor.

Rumors began surfacing from reliable sources that the hostages were coming home; August was the month, and once again hope was nurtured. David and I and my son Eddie spent the early summer painting and polishing and making sure that every little thing was just right for Terry's return. There was nothing that could happen this time, I was sure, that could possibly derail the initiatives to release the hostages.

On August 2, 1990, President Saddam Hussein's Iraqi army invaded Kuwait, and once again the mess hit the fan.

A few days later I received a visit from our new-for-the-umpteenth-time State Department liaison, Nick Riscutti. He said he'd had a meeting in nearby Lexington, Kentucky, and decided to drop by to meet me. In several telephone conversations we'd seemed to hit it off, and he made the trip in spite of everything else that was going on, which impressed me. We both had social work backgrounds, and it was pleasant to talk to someone who seemed truly interested in a good relationship with the hostage families.

In the course of our conversation, however, Riscutti said that we had Jimmy Carter to blame for the situation in Iraq and Kuwait. I exploded.

"I'll tell you exactly who's to blame here," I said angrily. "The Reagan Administration can take credit for this one. Why wouldn't Saddam Hussein believe he could do this and get away with it? We showed him it was okay by our past behavior. What the hell, two hundred forty-one U.S. Marines were blown away and we did nothing in response. Bill Buckley died, Peter Kilburn was executed, and we watched Colonel Higgins swinging from a rope in twenty-three-inch living color in our living rooms and did nothing. Six Americans live today in dirty rooms somewhere in Lebanon, and does the world get mad? Hell, no. But let the world oil market be threatened and we go to war. What does this say about our values, Nick? What does this say about our priorities?"

Riscutti looked really uncomfortable, and I apologized for making him the target. I explained that I knew he wasn't personally to blame but that he also hadn't lived through the history of this situation with the hostage families. Every government agent who had been involved in this scenario saw only his little piece of it. There was no one who had stood witness to the government's failure to end the captivity of these innocent Americans.

I didn't have much to do with Nick Riscutti after that. He was a nice enough fellow but for five and a half years the State Department had been trying to convince me that a spade was a damned shovel and I didn't have the patience to listen to it anymore.

The only government official with whom I was in contact was Randy Beers of the National Security Council. We had spoken together many times by phone and several times in person. It still gave me little shivers when I sat in Ollie North's old office, now Beers's, at the Old Executive Building. Randy, though very cautious, seemed sympathetic and aware of the day-to-day situation of the hostages. When I would press him for information that he wasn't anxious to give he always spoke very carefully, as if tiptoeing through a mine field. Although he never gave away much, he was only a phone call away, like Ollie had been, and I appreciated that.

Not only did the Iraqi invasion of Kuwait create a world crisis, it had a direct effect on Terry and the other hostages. Imad Mughniyah's brother-in-law and the other prisoners being demanded by the captors in exchange for the Western hostages were in jail in Kuwait, enemies of the invading Iraqi government. For days we agonized over their fate. Would Hussein's army summarily execute them? Would they be used as bargaining chips in interregional prisoner swaps? Had they escaped?

I have a deep faith and belief in God, and as part of our relationship retain the right to carry on running conversations and mentally voice my complaints to Him. I'm always careful to give silent thanks every day for the gifts that I've been given, but I'm not shy in berating Him when I think He hasn't been paying attention.

I know that sometimes you have to take negative situations on faith, believing that a greater good will be served somehow. But this was a tough one. I paced and cursed and mumbled and swore and generally worked myself into a lather as the days passed and the situation only got worse.

Our cause was in the toilet once again as thousands of hostages were taken in Kuwait and the airwaves were filled with their pictures and stories. With thousands of innocent Americans caught up in international terrorist activities, few people wanted to hear about six hostages in Lebanon. It seemed like Iran-contra all over again. The press had other fish to fry and the politicians were occupied. As we did in 1986, we had no choice but to simply wait it out.

On August 24, Irish hostage Brian Keenan was released. I had very mixed feelings about going to Ireland to see him. It had been several years since I had had firsthand reports about Terry's life and conditions, and I wasn't at all sure that I wanted to hear about them now. What if things had deteriorated? What if Terry was sick or had been beaten or, worst of all, had lost all hope of freedom?

I knew that it had been almost a year since Brian had seen my brother, but, given the awful amount of time that had passed since Terry was taken, a year seemed like the recent past. I finally decided to stop being a baby about it and left for Ireland. After all, I had always insisted that if Terry could take it I could.

Carolyn Turolla and I flew to London and spent two days finalizing the meeting with Keenan. His schedule was hectic as he tried to meet the families of the men he had shared captivity with, so we spent our spare moments quietly touring the city. My stepson David Jr. was stationed there, but even a pleasant dinner with him and Ray Barnett, who was also in the area, failed to stop my mind from churning over the past five and a half years.

I tried to control it, but, as composed as I wanted to be, I felt my anger building. As I wandered through the food section of Harrods department store one morning my head began swimming, and I had to sit down on a sales bin as the nausea threatened to erupt. After about ten minutes the spell passed, but I knew I was headed for physical trouble again. I was eating myself alive because there was nowhere to place the fault for what had happened, no doorstep on which to lay the blame.

I spoke to Randy Beers the day I left for Ireland and he expressed his hope that Keenan's release was the harbinger of more releases soon. As the plane took off for Dublin, I felt myself becoming increasingly emotional about our meeting. I had never reacted this way before and had a difficult time sorting out and understanding my feelings.

I began to wonder if maybe my reluctance to see Brian was because I was afraid of what he might say about my efforts to bring Terry home. Was Terry still happy about the publicity I was generating? Was I saying and doing the right things? Was Terry angry because I had failed to press the right buttons, turn the right keys? Was that dreaded mantra of the inactive based in truth—had publicity prolonged his captivity?

By the time Brian and I collided in a bear hug in his hotel room, I was an emotional wreck. As he pulled back to look at me, Brian said laughingly, "Why, you even look like him!"

"All of us Andersons tend to look like one another as we grow older," I said, "which is not too bad for the men of our clan but isn't thrilling for the women."

Odd, but Brian Keenan reminded me of Terry. When he got up as we were talking and paced a little, he walked like Terry. Certain ways he'd turn his head, certain expressions he used, reminded me physically of Terry.

I started talking and couldn't stop. I just flat unloaded on this innocent victim. Poor Brian. He hadn't contended with enough in the past four and a half years, now he had me to deal with.

Words tumbled over one another and I didn't pause long enough between questions to allow him to answer.

"I'm so glad that you're out, and I know your sisters and all that they have done for you, and how difficult it has been and what a wonderful job they have done. How long has it been since you saw Terry?"

"Eleven months," he said. I didn't wait for him to elaborate, I just plowed on ahead.

"What does Terry know? How was he treated? How is his health? How is his mental health?"

Keenan hadn't seen Terry in almost a year but he said that the night before he was released he was taken into what he knew to be Terry and Tom Sutherland's room. He felt they had been taken out of there only temporarily because all of their things were still there. He explored the room and found Terry's Bibles. Terry was doing a historical study of the Bible, he said, and had learned French, apparently from Tom Sutherland. He had a Bible in French as well as a Catholic and a Protestant Bible in English. Brian found a book of Tom's with a letter in it from Tom's wife that had been published in a Beirut paper.

Keenan said what particularly convinced him that it was their room was that Terry and Tom were the only two of the hostages who demanded to be clean-shaven and so had been furnished with shaving gear. There were two sets of shaving gear in the room.

There were two bolts on the wall that the hostages' eighteen-inch chains usually hung from. Pushed up next to the wall, close enough so Terry could ride it and still remain chained, was an exercise bicycle. That bizarre picture stayed in my mind, Terry in his underwear on his exercise bike. I could just kind of hear him clanking and pedaling, pedaling and clanking.

I kept asking Brian questions, and before he could really put the period to each sentence I was on to the next. "How long has it been? Who were you with? When were you moved? How were you treated?" I wanted to make so much noise that there would be no silence and I wouldn't have to ask *the* question, the one I had asked every single hostage, the second question after "Is Terry okay?" "Does Terry know what I'm doing and how does he feel about it?"

I have always been afraid, in the back of my mind, that I was not doing the right thing for Terry. What I was doing was obviously not having results; Terry was not out of there. Did this mean that I had done the wrong thing, that I had made the wrong choices? Would Terry blame me?

By the end I was trembling, shaking, and crying, and I just couldn't stop. I was not in control and I couldn't seem to get in control.

Brian was stunned. We sat almost knee to knee, and as I kept up this outburst he kind of retreated into his chair almost as if I were physically abusing him. Finally, when I was forced to gasp for breath, he interrupted me.

"Hold it! Just hold it! Get a grip on yourself, girl. This surely isn't what Terry needs when he gets out. He doesn't need a weeping, wailing woman to deal with. He needs the sister he left behind, the sister who stood so strong and dealt with the world on his behalf."

I snuffled myself into silence.

Brian assured me that Terry was aware of what I was doing . . . and that he loved it. Terry had the best lines of communication of any of the hostages, he said, because of me: not only was Terry given the letters that we published in the Beirut papers on his birthdays, but every time there was a story about my travels or meetings the jailers showed it to him.

"Why," Brian laughed, "they told him one time they were going to make you an honorary member of the Islamic Jihad. Terry said he didn't think you'd be too thrilled by that but thought they knew a fellow terrorist when they saw one."

There it was, the obvious opening for the dreaded question. There was no avoiding it.

"Brian, if they liked or admired what I was doing, does that mean that I prolonged Terry's captivity? Did they keep him so that I would continue to plead their cause?"

I didn't know that I wanted to hear his answer.

"Hell, no," he said. "Terry said that he knew the day he was taken that it would be at least five years until he saw freedom again. He knew when Ben Weir was released that he'd be the last one out, and he's lived with that reality for the past five and a half years.

"Peggy, in captivity you learn to live with what is; not what you want it to be, but what is. Terry has learned to live with his reality and he has no particular problem with that. What you've done is to provide him with a link to the outside world. Through your efforts he knows that he's not forgotten, that everyone has done their best to free him, and that one day, hopefully soon, he'll see freedom again."

The hostages were determined that the past was indeed the past, he said. They had a life to get on with, and they wanted to put the past behind them. Their priorities had changed. They weren't out for revenge.

In fact, Brian and John McCarthy, the hostage with whom he had shared most of his captivity, seemed to have a really bizarre sense of humor. Brian said they had kept each other in stitches. Now mind you, living in these conditions, they had decided that, when they were released, rather than write a book they would compose an operetta. Gilbert and Sullivan meet the Ayatollah. And at the grand finale the two of them would come dancing down a staircase in black tie and tails, shaking their top hats and singing, "Goodbye, Hezbollah . . ."

Brian Keenan was truly not angry. He saw nothing amiss, and all of Ireland welcomed him as a hero.

This didn't sound like the Terry Anderson I had known, or the Terry in captivity I had heard about. "Is Terry mad at the AP?" I asked. "Is Terry mad at the government? Who's Terry mad at?"

Brian looked puzzled. "He's not mad at anybody, really," he said. "None of the Americans like Reagan. Terry's advice to Reagan would be to leap on his horse and ride off into the sunset." There were several times during their captivity that Reagan's public rhetoric almost cost the hostages their lives, Brian said. And there was the raid on Libya, when they came as close to being executed as they ever would.

For the hostages, the five and a half years had been like they'd been for us, their families: cyclical. It's almost like the stages of grieving: first the denial, then the anger, finally the acceptance of what is. The hostages had passed through all those phases, and in the last year or two they had become very introspective, very moral. They had made a pact with one another, Brian told me: they would do things with their lives on the outside that would have value, that would be moral, that would in their own ways make a better world. And each would see to it that the promises made in captivity were kept. If anybody started straying off the straight and narrow, the others would phone him up and say, "Hey, get back on line here."

Terry wasn't angry? That made me angry.

"Sure," I told Keenan, "you guys have gone all holy and we've become a bunch of hooligans."

I had kept a fantasy close to my heart. I had pictured myself taking Terry around to all the people who had turned their backs on me, everyone who had been callous or mean. I kept thinking, "All you people who hurt me, you just wait till my brother gets home. Are you going to be sorry." I had fed on this fantasy. I was going to make somebody accountable. I was going to make people look at Terry, and he would face down the ones who said they did nothing because publicity was going to prolong his captivity.

It wasn't going to be. I was not going to get my revenge, as little and as unsatisfactory as it might have been. I had to accept that it wasn't going to happen. "Look, Peggy," Brian said, "there's nothing more you can do. Quit."

I was crying, just blubbering and shaking as I said to him, "Brian, I don't know how. I don't know how to stop what I'm doing. I don't know anybody I can go to who can reassure me that 'Yes, you've done everything you can, it's going to be over with. Go home.' "

Brian said, "I'm telling you this, Peggy: you go home, and you'd better get yourself in shape so that you can be there for Terry when he gets out. If he sees what I'm seeing now, he's not going to be able to deal with it."

I had so much churning inside of me that again I reacted physically. A few days after I returned from Ireland to Kentucky I was back in the hospital for my ulcers.

The downside was that I was in the hospital again. The upside was that I was in complete isolation and I was finally able to reach some conclusions about these years.

Facing the fact of Terry's acceptance, his lack of anger, I felt mine starting to dissipate, almost a physical release at the anger leaving me. I had always known it was not a pretty emotion: the desire for revenge, the desire for atonement, the desire to make somebody pay.

And as I began to heal emotionally I began to heal physically.

I realized I can't do any more than my part. I've had a role to play in this, and the very fact that we sustained an unpopular issue for five and a half years—that those who know there are hostages in Lebanon know Terry Anderson, that I've given him a future—has to be enough.

I thought about it for a long time afterward, and finally I realized that my judgment of what I had done no longer depended on Terry's opinion. If Terry were to come to me tomorrow and say, "You did the wrong thing for me, you cost me an extra four and a half years," or if he were to tell me that what I did was not helpful, or that it was harmful, I finally feel secure enough that I could say to him, "Well, Terry, I'm sorry to hear you feel that way but I did what I felt I had to do." I'd feel bad about it, of course, but if I had it to do over again I couldn't do it any other way.

Sure, all of us might have used different strategies, maybe different political initiatives; maybe we would have done some logistical things differently. But the morality of what I did was right. To ignore what was happening would have been obscene. I could never have lived with it. I could never have walked into the future, as I am doing now, feeling whole and secure and right about what I did.

And I know now, finally, that I don't have to look for my worth in my brother's eyes, or anybody else's. I have to look for it in my heart.

I did the only thing that I could do. Whether it was right or wrong, whether it did or did not prolong Terry's captivity, I couldn't not do it.

My fantasy of Terry's release has changed over the years. In the beginning I pictured David and Dad and Rich and me, and we'd be over in Wiesbaden, celebrating. Then it was going to be Rich and David and me, then David and me. Little by little my fantasy has evaporated.

Terry's release is not going to be a time of joyous celebration. It will be wonderful because Terry will have reached freedom, but then I'm going to have to tell him about Dad and Rich, and help him try to deal with the fact that his world, as it existed when he was taken, is no longer there. And that's going to be difficult. But, after all these years, I finally know I'm up to it.

ACKNOWLEDGMENTS

MY DEEPEST GRATITUDE AND LOVE GOES TO WHAT I THINK OF AS THE "BIG 3" in my life: Faith, Family and Friends. My God, my family and my friends have all been by my side during this terrible ordeal, and all have held me up when my knees buckled with pain or despair. My husband, David, has been my friend, my rock and my love. He has helped me to believe in myself and has given me the strength and the freedom to do what I had to do for Terry and the other hostages.

My children, Melody and her husband Randy, Eddie and David, Jr., have provided an island of strength and pride in the midst of the chaos. My grand-sons Randy and Danny have brought me joy and love, and when they put their arms around my neck, my world rights itself. My brother and sister, Judy Walker and Jack Anderson, and their families have helped me to survive. David's family; my church, the Cadiz Baptist; and my friends—*you know who you are*—have all kept me rational in an insane situation.

I have a deep pride in and love for the other hostage families, both former and present. They may not always have agreed with me, but they gave me their support and their encouragement. Like me, they were ill-prepared to deal with a situation of this magnitude, but they all rose to the occasion. I'm so proud to be a part of that elite and special group known collectively as "the hostage families."

A great deal of my strength and determination has been fortified by the advice and knowledge of former hostages. Jerry Levin, Ben Weir, Father Jenco, Jean-Paul Kauffmann, Marcel Fontaine, Frank Regier, Nick Daniloff, and all who know what captivity means, have remained bound by chains of pain to those they left behind. It is these men who told me what I had to do, and their advice was my bottom line when an action was in question. They have been my link to Terry and my proof that hostages *do* come out.

I thank Associated Press for its financial support of my activities and for never censoring or trying to control what I chose to do on Terry's behalf. The greatest gift they gave me was the guidance and friendship of Chuck Lewis (former AP bureau chief in Washington, D.C.) and Carolyn Turolla, my liaison with New York AP. Chuck and Carolyn went far beyond what could reasonably have been expected of them as AP employees. Carolyn has gamely accompanied me on journeys into places that I know prickled the hair on the back of her neck, and Chuck has become a vital part of the extended family I rely on so heavily for support and information. "God never loved me in so sweet a way before, 'til he brought thee to me and said, behold a friend."

To Tony Turolla, and to the Lewis family—Chuck, Sarah, Peter, Patrick and the lovely Barbara—thank you for allowing me to borrow Chuck and Carolyn. You are among the unsung heroes in this scenario.

To Carmella LaSpada and her organization, No Greater Love, I owe a debt of gratitude that can never be repaid. To all of those who have supported and participated in our ceremonies, God surely has a special place for you in His heaven. I'd like to especially acknowledge the financial support that the AFL-CIO executive council—and especially the International Association of Ironworkers, Sheet-Metal Workers, the Brotherhood of Painters and Allied Trades, and the Eastern Paralyzed Veterans Association—have given to help keep No Greater Love operating. Many thanks to Bebe Gribble for singing our praises, to the teachers and children of St. Thomas More Cathedral school in Arlington, Virginia, and St. Francis DeSales school in Philadelphia, and everyone who has participated in the hostage campaigns and ceremonies, bless you all.

The Journalists Committee to Free Terry Anderson deserves special thanks for stepping in when I had run out of energy and ideas—David Aikman, Ed Caldwell, Don Mell, Bonnie Anderson, Carmella LaSpada, and all the rest. Those who were Terry's friends have now become my friends, and those who did not know either of us are to be admired for making our cause theirs. Tom Brokaw, Nick Daniloff, and Dan Rather have lent more than their names to the committee and I appreciate their participation in the ceremonies and meetings.

Bill Foley and his wife Cary Vaughan are among the most dedicated and committed of Terry's friends. I have talked to Bill just about every day for the past several years and I trust his knowledge and judgment of Terry and the climate they shared together in Beirut. We bolster each other's emotions, pretend we can figure out what every obscure move in the Middle East means to the hostage situation, and lie to each other about when this nightmare is going to end. We tell ourselves that surely tomorrow release will come (if not today), freedom is almost always at hand; and we assert with conviction each time a positive rumor emerges, *"This is really it this time!"* We don't let the fact that we have never, ever been right deter us from our rampant speculations. Thank you, Terry, for bringing these people into my life.

I deeply appreciate the loyalty and the courage of Senators Robert Dole and Daniel Patrick Moynihan, who have stood strong on the hostage issue and have worked diligently to resolve it. Senator Moynihan has stood shoulder to shoulder with me throughout the past five and a half years and has both my affection and gratitude. Secretary of State James Baker has my deep respect for trying to pursue a more evenhanded American policy in the Middle East in the face of formidable opposition.

I have a special appreciation also for the personnel at the Washington embassies, who never closed their doors to me. To the officials at the Syrian, Lebanese, Greek, Algerian and other embassies, who offered advice and consolation: Thank you. To Bushra Kanafani, the acting ambassador from Syria, and to the ex-ambassador from Algeria, Mohammed Sahnoun, a special recognition for offering their friendship as well as their good offices.

To special friends Penny, Sylvia, Candee, and my best friend Marsha Barton; Jack LaVriha, and the Free Terry Anderson Committee from Lorain, Ohio; Penne and Bruce Laingen, H. Ross Perot, Jesse Jackson, and all who have worked on the campaign to free the hostages: Thank you for coming into my life.

An extra-special accolade goes to Anne Zickl for her untiring and devoted support of our cause, and many thanks to her husband and family for lending her to us. I suppose that one day soon we'll have to give her back, but until then we'll keep working her butt off. She'll learn to never again utter those damning words, "Is there anything I can do to help?"

To Eileen Donahue, aka Ellen Doohoo, aka Elaine Donahey, and "Al": Although you could be arrested for practicing psychiatry without a license, because of my deep gratitude I'm not going to press charges. This time. Consider the following warning for the future: Being my friend could be hazardous to your mental health.

To Ray Barnett and Lela Gilbert and to all of the dedicated staff of Friends in the West, you have shown me what it truly means to see God work in my life. You are the yardsticks by which all other Christians should measure themselves. "Surely goodness and mercy shall follow you all the days of your lives."

To the many thousands of Americans who responded to our call for help by mailing postcards, writing letters of support, tying yellow ribbons and praying their hearts out; without your support we would have been forced to give up the fight. Because you cared, and sent that message to Washington by the thousands, we had both a cause and a case.

To my lawyer/agent Bob Barnett of Williams & Connolly in Washington, D.C., thank you for believing in my story and asking me to write it. To Peter Knobler, thank you for separating the wheat from the chaff with such a gentle and gifted hand. And to Alice Mayhew of Simon & Schuster, thank you for bringing Peter and me together and for the dignity with which you allowed me to bring this whole project to fulfillment. To Gail Olson, thank you for your rapid transcribing.

Last, but far from least, to Terry Anderson: my love, my pride and my awe for the example that you set for us. To do less than what I have done on your behalf would have shamed me in the face of your faith, your strength and the courage you have shown to the world. I have always been proud of you, but never more so than during the past five-and-a-half years. Like me you never gave up hope, the conviction that someday, some way, this nightmare would end. It is that hope that has sustained and strengthened us both and allowed us to survive the awful pain of these past years. In the words of Samuel Johnson, ''Hope is necessary in every condition. The miseries of poverty, sickness, of captivity, would, without this comfort, be insupportable.''

I love you, little brother, much more than I ever knew.

—Peggy Say

INDEX

ABC News, 13, 126, 194–95
  hostage policy of, 207
  in Paris, 213, 216
Abu Jihad, 118
Abu Nidal, 105, 130–32, 241
Achille Lauro, 161, 195
Adams, Al, 220, 239
Adams, John, 163, 164, 169–70, 182
AFL-CIO, 305
African Children's Choir, 189
Aikman, David, 208–209, 210, 224,
  306
Ain el Hilwewe, 9
Alfeid, General, 125
Allen, Charlie, 101
All Fall Down (Sick), 67–68
Amal militia, 151
American Civil Liberties Union
  (ACLU), 26
American University (Beirut), 11–12,
  105, 148, 155, 171
American Veterans, 252–53
Amin, Idi, 189

AmVet Auxiliary Humanitarian of the
  Year, 252–53
Anderson, Bonnie, 194, 236–37, 255,
  306
Anderson, Bruce, 15, 22, 70
Anderson, Dr., 256–59
Anderson, Gabrielle, 12–13, 21, 251
Anderson, Glenn Richard, Sr., 16, 30,
  37, 69–70, 104, 107, 109, 259,
  260, 303
  alcoholism of, 15, 23
  final illness and death of, 90–98
  media and, 31, 32–33, 69, 93
  State Department and, 34–36
  Terry's messages to, 227
  Terry's relationship with, 21–22, 27–
  28
Anderson, Glenn Richard "Rich," Jr.,
  15, 19, 89, 100, 116, 259, 260,
  303
  alcoholism of, 22–23, 34, 35–36,
  104, 111
  belligerence of, 23, 36, 37, 46–47

Anderson, Glenn Richard "Rich," Jr.
   (*Cont.*)
   in Bush meeting, 76, 78–80
   deathbed video appeal of, 111–12,
      189
   father's death and, 91, 95–96
   final illness and death of, 104–105,
      109–114
   Hodgkin's disease of, 16, 90
   media and, 31, 34, 69–71, 73, 109,
      111–12, 113
Anderson, Jack (columnist), 107–8
Anderson, Jack (Peggy's brother), 15,
   17, 22–23, 31, 304
Anderson, Jeannie, 109, 112–13, 114
Anderson, Judy, *see* Walker, Judy
   Anderson
Anderson, Lily, 15, 18, 19, 22, 94–
   95
Anderson, Mihoko "Mickey," 12–13,
   14, 21
Anderson, Penny (Peggy's sister-in-
   law), 47, 96–98, 171
Anderson, Sulome (Terry's daughter),
   54, 70, 84
Anderson, Terry:
   as ABC News "Person of the
      Week," 207
   as "Alan Lunn," 250
   anniversaries of kidnapping of, 99–
      100, 188, 211–12, 226, 240, 241,
      279
   as AP correspondent, 8, 9–12, 13,
      14, 21
   awards of, 252–54
   details of captivity, 74–75, 145–49,
      194, 214–15, 298–301
   family relationships of, 15, 20, 21–
      25, 27–28
   kidnapping of, 29
   letter from, 84–85
   North's deal for release of, *see* Iran-
      contra
   one-thousandth day of captivity of,
      199–200
   photograph released by captors of,
      181
   Scowcroft on, 243–44
   sensitivity of, 14
      videotaped messages from, 158–
         60, 167, 200–202, 215, 226–28

in Vietnam, 9, 14
   as youth, 7–8, 15
Anderson family:
   alcoholism in, 15, 21, 22–23, 34,
      35–36, 70–71
   cancer and, 90–98, 109–114, 259
   financial status of, 15–17
   media and, 31–33, 69–71
   privacy of, 111
Andrews Air Force Base, 171, 290
Anglican Church, 142, 179, 273
"anniversary journalism," 203
Apple, R. W., 261–62
Arab Democratic Party, 125
Arafat, Yasser, 118, 119
   Peggy's meeting with, 263, 268–73,
      282
   on politics of Iranian hostage crisis,
      229–30
Aridi, Salim, 209
Arlington National Cemetery, 198, 219–
   220
arms-for-hostages deal, *see* Iran-contra
Arnold, Terry:
   attempt to silence Peggy made by,
      115–16, 231
   manipulation of Peggy and media by,
      233–37
Assad, Hafez, 83, 117, 125, 126, 184,
   276, 277, 278, 279
Associated Press (AP), 246, 301
   Athens office of, 121–22
   Beirut office of, 8, 9–12, 21, 76,
      84
   Damascus office of, 124, 126–27,
      141–42
   media blitz arranged by, 38–43
   Peggy's expenses paid by, 83–84,
      118, 213, 238–39, 262–63, 305
   Peggy's relationship with, 45, 53,
      109, 194, 216
   Terry as correspondent for, 8, 9–12,
      13, 14, 21
   and Terry's kidnapping, 29, 34, 54
Associated Press Managing Editors
   (APME) meeting, 165–66

Baddawi, 10–11
Baker, James, 306
Baltimore Sun, 209
Baptist Convention Center, 188

Barnett, Ray, 188, 189–90, 228–29, 297, 307
Barton, Marsha, 91, 306
Bassil, Madeleine (Terry's fiancée), 28, 38, 39, 42–43, 54, 70, 73, 76, 84, 227
Batavia High School, 212
BBC, 11
Beck, Chip, 219
Beers, Randy, 296, 297–98
Beirut, Lebanon:
    American University in, 11–12, 105, 148, 155, 171
    AP office in, 8, 9–12, 21, 76, 84
    camaraderie of press corps in, 12, 13–14, 28
    conflict in, 8–9, 11
    fluidity of situations in, 194
    Glenn Anderson's visit to, 21–22
    hostage families' appeals in, 111–12
    journalists in, 8–12, 13–14, 28, 30, 33–34
    kidnappings in, 29, 30, 36–37, 155, 160, 180, 194–95, 211, 287
    killing of CBS newsmen in, 36
    Peggy's consideration of visit to, 137–38
    TWA hostages in, 58, 61–63
    Waite's disappearance from, 180–81
Beirut University College (BUC), 180, 287
Bekaa Valley (Lebanon), 116
    Israeli shelling of, 68
    Peggy's visit to, 136
    as possible hostage location, 62–63
Belkind, Myron, 273, 274
Berri, Nabih, 151
Boccardi, Louis D., 165–66, 170, 242, 262–63
"bracket creeping," 182
Bradlee, Ben, 261
Bremer, Paul, 197, 220, 235, 241
Brewington, Melody, 18, 19, 90, 94, 143, 304
Brewington, Randy (Peggy's son-in-law), 90, 143, 304
Brokaw, Tom, 209, 211–12, 261, 306
Buckley, William, 146, 158, 198, 215, 219–20, 244, 295
Buffalo Area Metropolitan Ministries, 264, 277

Burns, Robert, 194
Bush, Barbara, 280–85
Bush, George, 59–60, 88, 154, 199, 239, 261, 277
    Iran-contra and, 227
    in meeting with hostage families, 76–80, 87, 144
    Peggy's meeting with, 280–85, 295
    postcard campaign addressed to, 254
    refusal of meetings with, 240, 244, 280
Bush, Margaret, 281
Bush Task Force, 101

Cable News Network (CNN), 58–59, 70, 155, 198, 209, 211, 294
Cadiz Baptist Church, 304
Caldwell, Ed, 116–17, 209, 213, 214, 216, 254–55, 306
Camp David, 159
Candlelight Ceremony of Hope for Peace in Lebanon and the Release of the Hostages (1988), 211–12
candlelight prayer vigil (1986), 99–100
Carter, Jimmy, 63, 68, 101, 295
    Peggy's meeting with, 228–30
Carton, Marcel, 213, 216, 220
Catholic Relief Services, 36–37, 166
CBS, 36, 62, 63–64, 211, 280
    in Paris, 213–14, 216, 219
Centers for Disease Control, 229
Central Intelligence Agency (CIA), 101, 146, 182, 195, 198, 220, 231, 241, 244
    ex-agent of, 247–48
Christmas Without Terry (1985), 88
Cicippio, Joseph, 155, 259–60
Coates, Ken, 267
Collett, Alec, 105, 115–16, 130–31, 231, 242
Collett, Elaine, 105, 130–31, 210
Commodore Hotel (Beirut), 21–22, 225, 227
Communist Party USA, 45
Congressional Record, 199, 208, 267, 291
contras, 103, 173, 177
Crespo, Enrique Baron, 267, 282
Crystal Cathedral, 190
Cuomo, Mario, 110, 113, 157–58
Customs Service, U.S., 246

Damascus Sheraton, 124–25, 136, 141, 239
D'Amato, Alfonse, 198–99
Daniloff, Nicholas, 159–60, 161, 196, 211, 212, 305, 306
Day on the Hill, 66–69
Dayton Beach Community College, 25–26
"Dear World, a Message of Hope (1989)," 257
diplomat's initiative:
North in, 152–55, 160–62, 163–64
outline of, 150–53
State Department bypassed in, 152, 162–64
Do, Chae-Sung, 196
Dole, Robert, 291–92, 306
Donahue, 59, 60–61, 62, 65, 164, 203, 204
Donahue, Eileen, 307
Donahue, Phil, 60–61, 175, 204
Donaldson, Sam, 144, 208, 224
Doonesbury, 225
Dornan, Robert "Bullet Bob," 66–67, 130
Douglas, Leigh, 105
Druze Muslim militia, 124
Dukakis, Michael, 224
Dymally, Mervyn, 67

Eagleton, William, 141–42
East Bethany Baptist Church, 45, 48, 190
Eckert, Fred, 40–41
Elysée Palace, 218–19
Eran, Oded, 184, 187
European Parliament, 267, 282

Face the Nation, 59, 65, 164
Fadlallah, Mohammed Hussein, 84, 119, 189, 245
Farm Workers Union, 26
Fascell, Dante, 68–69
Fatah Revolutionary Council, 130
Fisk, Robert, 33–34
Foley, Bill, 9–11, 14, 194, 209, 225–226, 255, 263, 280, 291, 306
Fontaine, Marcel, 213–16, 217, 305
Foreign Press Association, 24
France:
hostage policies of, 200, 206

media coverage of hostage issues in, 217, 225
Peggy's trip to, 213–19
Free Terry Anderson Committee, 306
Friends in the West, 189, 228, 307
Fuellgraf, Chud, 222
Fuellgraf, Marty, 222

Genesee County Cablevision, 83
Genesee County Mall, 46
Geneva Convention, 292
Georgetown University, 261
Ghorbanifar, Manucher, 173
Gilbert, Lela, 189, 228–29, 307
Glass, Charlie, 194–95, 207
Goldsmith, Mike, 269, 271
Gorbachev, Mikhail, 167, 200
Greece, 58, 117, 121–23
Greenwood, Lee, 252–53
Gribble, Bebe, 305
Gumbel, Bryant, 203–204

Hagey, Steve, 209
Hajj (captor), 74–75
Hall, Fawn, 102–103, 154
Hamilton, Lee, 68
Harris, Ezell, 254–55
Hasenfus, Eugene, 111
Heinzerling, Larry, 245, 262, 266, 267, 270–71, 276, 277
Helms, Jesse, 111
Hezbollah, 57, 151, 184, 186, 187, 189, 245, 260–61, 272, 278
Higgins, William, 211, 223, 244, 249, 260, 295
Holy Trinity Church, 211
hostage families:
Beirut appeals of, 111–12
in Bush meeting, 76–80, 87, 144
camaraderie among, 171
in England, 273–75
Eric Jacobsen as spokesperson for, 67, 101–102, 165, 166–67
Iran-contra and backlash against, 176, 177–79, 182, 199, 212, 244, 246
in Reagan meeting, 85–87, 144
State Department liaisons with, 34–36, 58, 62, 63–64, 99, 105, 107–108, 163, 164, 169–70, 182, 233, 254, 295

House Foreign Affairs Committee, 68–
69
Hussein, Saddam, 295, 296

International Commission of Jurists, 264
Iran, 46, 81, 83, 100–101, 106–7, 161,
260, 267
arms-for-hostages deal of, 170, 172–
173, 175, 177, 244
increased international relations of,
240–41
influence of, on hostage situation,
272
Journalists Committee meeting with
officials from, 210
Peggy's attempted visit to, 132–35
Peggy's meeting with officials from,
184–87
U.S. downing of civilian aircraft
from, 223
see also Khomeini, Ayatollah Ruhollah; Rafsanjani, Hojatolislam Hashemi
Iran-contra:
backlash against hostage families re-
sulting from, 176, 177–79, 182,
199, 212, 244, 246
hostage issue affected by, 181–83,
188, 206, 227, 240, 284, 297
media and, 170, 175–76, 177–78
North's role in, 169, 170, 172–75
Reagan and, 170, 175–77, 182, 244,
284
State Department and, 174–75, 241,
245–46
Iranian hostage crisis, 57, 63, 68, 101,
196
Reagan's manipulation of, 224, 229–
230
Iranian Revolutionary Guards, 151, 249
Islamic Jihad, 34, 57, 153, 155, 181,
231, 285, 300
Israel:
Bekaa Valley bombed by, 68
Iran-contra and, 174
Moynihan's message to, 291–92
negotiations used by, 62
Sheik Obeid kidnapped by, 260–61,
292
Shiite prisoners of, 58, 62, 151–52,
186, 261

Soviet emigrants in, 276
U.S. embassy of, 183–84
Israeli Air Force, 9, 12

Jackson, Jesse, 56, 70–71, 83, 306
Batavia appearance of, 46–50
in State Department meetings, 45–46,
52
at third anniversary of Terry's kidnapping, 211–12
at Vietnam War ceremony, 44–45
Jacobsen, David, 67, 76, 85
details of captivity, 74, 146–47
letter from, 155
in meetings with French hostages,
213–14, 217–18, 219
release of, 169–72
videotaped message from, 140–42,
158–59
Jacobsen, Diana, 100
Jacobsen, Eric, 100
and David Jacobsen's release, 171–72
in meeting with Bush, 78
as spokesperson for hostage families,
67, 101–102, 165, 166–67
Jacobsen, Paul, 85, 86, 100
Jenco, Martin, 194, 201, 213, 266,
276, 280, 305
activism of, 159, 165, 211
captivity of, 36–37, 74–76, 101
hearing loss of, 167–68
on hostage conditions, 144–49, 155–
156
on Jewish hostages, 146
release of, 138, 139–43, 161, 166
Waite and, 142, 180
Jenco family, 36–37, 38, 39, 41, 44,
52, 63, 75, 139, 142, 144
Jennings, Peter, 195, 207, 209
John Paul II, Pope, 263, 264–67, 282
Jones, Mr. (State Department official),
34–35
Jouejati, Rafic, 82–83
Journalists Committee to Free Terry
Anderson, 250, 253, 254, 305–6
formation of, 208–10
goals and work of, 209–10, 211–12
letter to Mitterrand from, 213, 217,
218–19
U.N. meeting of, 224–25
Jumblatt, Walid, 124

Kanafani, Bushra, 306
Kauffmann, Jean-Paul, 213, 217, 219,
    225–26, 305
Kauffmann, Joelle, 217, 219, 225–26
Kennan, Brian, 297–302
Kennedy, Edward M., 290–91
Kennedy, John F., 218
KGB, 160
Khiyam prisoners, 151–52, 186
Khomeini, Ayatollah Ruhollah, 233–34
    death of, 260
    and influence on captors, 100–101,
        205
    Peggy's attempts to meet with, 46,
        106–7
    Peggy's letters to, 106–7, 184–85
    State Department on, 83, 100–101
Khorrasani, Rajai, 210
kidnapping:
    of Beirut University College profes-
        sors, 180, 287
    of Cicippio, 155
    of Glass, 194–95
    of Higgins, 211
    of Reed, 155
    of Sheik Obeid, 260–61, 291
    of Soviet citizens, 277–78
    of Terry, 29
    of Tracy, 160
Kilburn, Peter, 101, 158, 242, 244, 295
    apparent expendability of, 115–16,
        231
    captivity of, 41
    death of, 105–6
    negotiations for release of, 108
    Qaddafi's purchase of, 105, 130, 231
Kirby, Jack, 64
Kissinger, Henry, 204, 206–7
Kodellas, Dionyssis, 129
Koppel, Ted, 184, 204–7
Kuwait, 69, 240–41
    Iraqi invasion of, 295–97
    Shiite prisoners in, 57, 75, 150–51,
        154

Laingen, Bruce, 57, 182, 261, 306
Laingen, Penne, 57, 306
Langendorfer, Edward, 18, 93–94,
    190–91, 236, 295, 304
Langendorfer, Edward, III, 5, 190–92
Lantos, Tom, 68–69

Larry King Show, 59, 60, 61, 65, 208
Larson, Sharon, 45
LaSpada, Carmella, 188–89, 225, 288,
    289, 290, 305, 306
LaVriha, Jack, 306
Lebanon International School (Beirut),
    155
Levin, Jerry, 36, 62, 73, 155–56, 159,
    171, 209, 305
Lewis, Chuck, 261, 305
Libya, 101–102, 231–32, 238
    U.S. bombing of, 105–106, 107,
        108, 115–16, 231, 242, 301
Literacy Council, 281
Livingstone, Neil, 233
Lollipops for Hostages, 188
"Lost Life of Terry Anderson, The,"
    241

McCarthy, John, 217, 219, 259, 273,
    274, 300–301
McCarthy, Pat, 274, 275
McFarlane, Robert "Bud":
    in arms-for-hostages deal, 170, 172–
        173
    at Bush meeting, 77–78
    on Khomeini, 100–101, 105–6, 205
    in meeting with Jackson, 46
    Nightline appearance of, 204, 205–6
    at Reagan meeting, 87–88
MacLeod, Scott, 241–42
Mahoney, Michael, 182, 197, 199, 220,
    240, 254, 290
Marcos, Ferdinand, 246
Marcos, Imelda, 246
Maria (AP reporter), 121–22
Marine Corps, U.S., 74, 103
    bombing of barracks of, 32, 34, 295
    in Middle East, 11
    Terry in, 9, 14, 15
Mass of Hope (1989), 261
May 1986 deal, 151
Mayor, Frederico, 273
Mears, Walter, 165, 166, 196
media, 101–102
    Anderson family and, 31–33, 69–71
    and Bush meeting, 76, 79–80
    candlelight vigil and, 100
    in Damascus, 124, 126, 139–41
    insincerity of, 37–38
    Iran-contra and, 170, 175–76, 177–78

Jacobsen's release and, 169
kidnapping of Glass and, 195
meeting with Carter and, 228–29,
    230
on Peggy's Middle East trip, 119–20,
    123, 138
release of French hostages and, 213–
    214, 216–19
release of Reed and, 288
State Department manipulation of,
    233–37, 241–42
TWA hostages and, 58–65
U.S. bombing of Libya and, 105–6,
    107, 108
U.S. downing of Iranian civilian air-
    craft and, 223
videotapes of Terry and, 201, 202,
    228
Waite and, 274–75
Weir's release and, 72–73
Meet the Press, 59, 65
Mehedi, Mohammad, 186–87
Mell, Don, 29, 209, 225, 262, 268,
    271, 276, 277, 306
Methodist Center, 74
Miller, David, 244–45, 246, 280–81,
    283, 289, 290–91
Mineta, Norman, 67
Mitterrand, François, 213, 219
Mohtashemi, Ali Akbar, 272
Morell, Jill, 217, 219, 274
Mother Teresa, 120
Motter, Eileen, 228–29
Mount Hermon (Lebanon), 136
Moyers, Bill, 209
Moynihan, Daniel Patrick, 199, 291–
    292, 306
Mughniyah, Imad, 57, 167, 241–42,
    243, 244, 278, 296
Murphy, Richard, 162–64, 174–75

Nabulsi, Hala, 135
National Council on Islamic Affairs, 186
National Human Rights Day, 199–200
National Presbyterian Church, 72
National Press Foundation, 252, 253
National Security Council (NSC), 249,
    280, 282, 289, 296
    Arafat meeting and, 263, 272–73
    Bush's relationship with, 282–83
    see also specific individuals

NBC, 13, 32, 72, 112, 201, 209, 212,
    213, 218
negotiations:
    false leads in, 54–55
    Israeli use of, 62
    Jackson's success with, 44
    pressuring for, 38, 40–41
    U.S. refusals of, 57, 59–60, 84–85,
        101, 151, 254, 261
    U.S. use of, 62, 108, 159–60, 195–
        196, 205, 212, 227
    see also Iran-contra
Newsweek, 167, 241
New York Times, 62, 165, 262, 294
Nicaragua, 45, 57, 100, 111, 173
Nightline, 184, 203, 204–07
Nir, Amiram, 154
No Greater Love, 188–89, 196, 198,
    199, 207, 211, 225, 288, 290, 305
Norland, Rod, 167
North, Oliver, 87–88, 101, 168, 181
    arms-for-hostages deal of, 169, 170,
        172–75
    in diplomat's initiative, 152–55, 160–
        162, 163–64
    helpfulness of, 102–4, 110–11
    on Peggy's Middle East trip, 119
Nova, 99

Oakley, Bob, 55–57, 67, 78, 101, 118–
    119, 182, 197
Obeid, Abdel Karim, 260–61, 292
O'Neill, Thomas P. "Tip," 252
Overseas Press Club, 253

Padfield, Philip, 105
Palestine Liberation Organization
    (PLO), 9, 11, 118–19, 126, 229,
    261, 269–73
Papandreou, Andreas, 117
Papandreou, Margaret, 117, 120, 121,
    123, 126, 130
Pauley, Jane, 60, 112, 203
Pepper, Claude, 67
Pérez de Cuéllar, Javier, 70, 224–25,
    263
Perot, H. Ross, 230, 306
Phelan, Dr., 92–94, 95–96
Pierce, Bill, 10–11
PLO, *see* Palestine Liberation Organiza-
    tion

Poindexter, John, 152
Polhill, Ferial, 288
Polhill, Robert, 180, 285
  release of, 287–90
Polowetsky, Nate, 29, 39
postcard campaign, 254–55
presidential campaign (1988), 224, 227
  hostage-release initiatives postponed
    by, 248–49

Qaddafi, Muammar el-, 107, 238–39
  purchase of hostages by, 105, 130,
    231
"quiet diplomacy," 86, 166, 167, 177,
    196, 205, 207, 228

Radio and Television News Directors
    (RTND), 71
Rafsanjani, Hojatolislam Hashemi, 260–
    262, 272, 283
Rather, Dan, 209, 210–11, 306
Rathor, Dr., 92
Ratner, Jackie, 58, 62, 63–64
Reagan, Nancy, 86, 88–89, 172
Reagan, Ronald, 40–41, 185, 239, 282,
    295, 301
  bombing of Libya ordered by, 105,
    108
  Christmas communications from, 88–
    89, 199
  Iran-contra and, 170, 175–77, 182,
    244, 284
  Iranian hostage crisis and, 224, 229–
    230
  letter from, 202–3
  media pressure on, 166–67
  meetings refused by, 67–68, 76–77,
    78
  in meeting with hostage families,
    85–87, 144
  negotiations refused by, 57, 84–85,
    261
  North's relationship with, 152, 163–
    164
  on release of hostages, 72, 107–8
  Peggy's letter to, 175–77
  and TWA hijacking, 63
  on videotapes of Terry, 159–60, 228
Red Cross, 58, 91, 264
Reed, Fifi, 280, 285, 287
Reed, Frank, 155, 218, 219, 280, 285

arsenic poisoning of, 293–94
  release of, 287–88, 290–93
Reed, Jackie, 291
Reed, Marilyn, 291
Reed, Tarek, 288
Regier, Frank, 305
Reporters Building, 13
Reston, James, 209
Reuters, 127–28
Reykjavík summit, 167
Riscutti, Nick, 295–96
Rome airport massacre, 130, 264
Rooney, Andy, 207
Roswell Memorial Park, 90–93, 105,
    109–11
Runcie, Robert, 273

Sahnoun, Mohammed, 41, 306
Said (guard), 149, 156, 218
Said (PLO representative), 118–19
St. Jerome Hospital, 93
Salinger, Pierre, 204, 206, 213, 216,
    218, 219
Savoy Hotel, 273
Say, David, Jr., 114, 297, 304
Say, David, Sr., 21, 23, 26, 27, 29,
    37, 46, 55, 71, 100, 102, 114,
    116–17, 139, 143, 170, 178, 180–
    181, 184, 187, 191, 193, 201,
    229, 234, 236, 250–51, 252, 256–
    257, 259, 295, 303, 304
  Glenn Anderson's death and, 90–91,
    94, 96
  on international tour, 262–63, 268
  and kidnapping of Terry, 30–31, 33
  in meeting with Bush, 280–85
  in move to Kentucky, 221–23
  previous marriage of, 51
Say, Peggy:
  celebrity status of, 156–57, 162, 185,
    222, 224
  criticism of, 170, 176, 177–79, 187–
    188
  employment of, 18–20
  family obligations of, 15–17, 19–20
  and father's death, 90–98
  first marriage of, 17–18
  grandson's death and, 190–92
  as Iran-Israel go-between, 184–87
  media savvy of, 56, 58–61, 87, 88,
    101–2, 156

Middle East tours of, 121–43, 162,
  268–73, 275–78
as organizer, 48–51, 99
premonitions of, 28–29, 71
social work of, 26–27
Syrian television appearance of, 283–
  284
Terry's relationship with, 7–8, 20,
  22–25
ulcers of, 256–59, 262, 302
as youth, 15–18
Schuller, Robert, 190
Schultz, Larry, 48
Scowcroft, Brent, 242–44, 246, 280
Sharaa, Farouk al-, 276–78, 279, 282
Sharif, Bassam Abu, 127–29, 268, 269,
  272
Shiites, 46, 57–58, 62, 75, 78, 84, 260
Shultz, George, 62, 88, 162, 199, 248
Sick, Gary, 67–68
Simpson, Danielle, 264–65
Singh, Mithileshwar, 180
SLA, see South Lebanon Army
Sleit, Mustafa, 13
Sleit Building, 13–14, 74
Socialist Workers Party, 45
Soghanalian, Sarkis, 246–50
South Africa, 14
South Lebanon Army (SLA), 151–52,
  186
Soviet Union, 160, 189, 212, 227, 276,
  277–78
Stahl, Lesley, 60, 167
State Department, U.S.:
  attempt to silence Peggy made by,
    115–16
  Bush's relationship with, 282–83
  Counter-Terrorism office of, 39, 55–
    57, 197, 220, 235, 239–41
  on dealing with Iran, 83, 100–102
  "devaluation" of hostages by, 181,
    182–83, 197
  Iran-contra and, 174–75, 241, 245–
    246
  Jackson's meetings with, 45–46, 52
  Jacobsen's letter and, 155
  Jacobsen's release and, 171
  as left out of diplomat's initiative,
    152, 162–64
  liaisons with hostage families, 34–36,
    58, 62, 63–64, 99, 105, 107–108,

163, 164, 169–70, 182, 233, 254,
  295
  limited Middle East expertise of,
    183, 194
  on media contact, 38, 58–59
  media manipulated by, 233–37, 241–
    242, 293–94
  and meetings with embassies, 39–40,
    41
  on negotiations, 62, 87, 99, 101,
    107–8
  on Peggy's Middle East tours, 117,
    118–19, 263, 282
  release of French hostages and, 213,
    214–15, 220
  release of Reed and, 288, 293–94
  on Soghanalian, 247, 249, 250
  on TWA hostages, 58–59, 62–64, 79
  U.N. initiative of, on Iran, 240–41,
    243
  on videotape of Terry, 202
  Waite and, 179
  withholding of information by, 41,
    107–8, 165, 183, 196–98
  see also specific individuals
Steen, Allann, 180, 280, 285
Steen, Virginia, 280, 285
Stein, John, 99
Stethem, Robert, 57–58
Strait of Hormuz, 241
Sununu, John, 281, 283
Sutherland, Tom, 74, 75, 146, 148,
  159, 180, 186, 194, 218, 231–32,
  238, 292, 298–99
family of, 274
Syria, 12, 44, 58, 82–83, 84, 286
  Iranian relations of, 184, 278
  Peggy's appearance on television in,
    283–84
  Peggy's visits to, 117, 123–43, 239,
    263, 275–78
Syrian Arab Airlines, 123–24

Tabatabai, Hossein, 233–34, 237
Temple, Wick, 39
Terry Anderson Day, 46–50, 157
Terry Anderson Fund, 48, 49–50, 83
Thatcher, Margaret, 290
Time, 10, 13, 208–9, 241
Times (London), 13, 33
Tlass, Mrs. Mustafa, 137

Tlass, Mustafa, 84, 124, 136–37
Today, 32–33, 59–60, 112, 164,
  203–4
Touma, Tony, 126, 136, 140, 142
Tower, John, 244
Tower Commission, 244
Tracy, Edward, 160
Tripoli, Lebanon, 10
Trudeau, Gary, 225
Trumpower, Michael, 230–37
Tunisia, 268–73
Turner, Jesse, 180
Turolla, Carolyn, 39, 194, 213, 217,
  245, 251, 262–63, 270–71, 276,
  297, 305
TWA flight 847, hijacking of:
  Bush on, 59–60
  diplomat's initiative and, 153
  media and, 58–65
  State Department on, 58–59, 62–64,
    79
  Stethem's death in, 57–58
  U.S negotiations and, 58, 62, 63–64,
    195, 227

Uganda, 189
UNESCO, 273
United Nations (U.N.), 70, 123, 194,
  224–25, 231, 240, 243, 257, 263,
  264, 277
United Press International (UPI), 13,
  196, 209
USA Today, 156, 175–76

Vaughan, Cary, 11–12, 13, 209, 225,
  306
Vickers, Tom, 48, 49, 113, 190–91
videotaped communiqués and appeals:
  ABC News policy on, 207
  CIA interest in original copies of,
    241
  on death of Higgins, 223, 260
  of Glass, 195
  of Jacobsen, 140–42, 158–59
  from Rich Anderson, 111–12, 189

of Terry, 158–60, 167, 200–202,
    215, 226–28
  Visions of Hope as, 83
Vietnam War, 9, 14, 44–45
Vincennes, USS, 223
Visions of Hope, 83

Waite, David, 274, 275
Waite, Frances, 274–75
Waite, Terry, 90, 142–43, 160, 203
  disappearance of, 180–81
  family of, 273–75
  May 1986 deal of, 151
  Nobel Peace Prize nomination of, 179
  threats against, 195
  U.S. involvement of, 179–80
Walker, Judy Anderson, 15, 17, 22, 31,
    37–38, 39, 41–43, 45, 69, 84, 91,
    113, 304
Wallace, Mike, 207
Wall Street Journal, 165
Washingtonian, 223, 234, 237
Washington Journalism Review, 253
Washington Post, 165, 212, 261, 281–
    282, 294
Weir, Benjamin, 214, 288, 300, 305
  activism of, 159, 178–79, 211
  captivity of, 37, 146, 148
  on hostage conditions, 72–76, 155–
    156
  in meeting with Bush, 78–80
  press conference of, 72–73
  release of, 71–72, 161
Weir, Carol, 62, 72, 78, 178–79
Weir, John, 61–62, 78
Weir family, 37, 38, 39, 41
Wiesbaden, Germany, 171, 287–88,
    290, 303
World Day of Prayer, 190

Young, Katherine, 129
Young, Robin, 129
Yusef, Walid, 131–32

Zickl, Anne, 50, 188, 194, 254, 307